Y0-AGX-485

Livonia Civic Center Library
32777 Five Mile Road
Livonia, MI 48154
(734) 466-2491

Repairing and Restoring
CLASSIC CAR
COMPONENTS

Repairing and Restoring
CLASSIC CAR
COMPONENTS

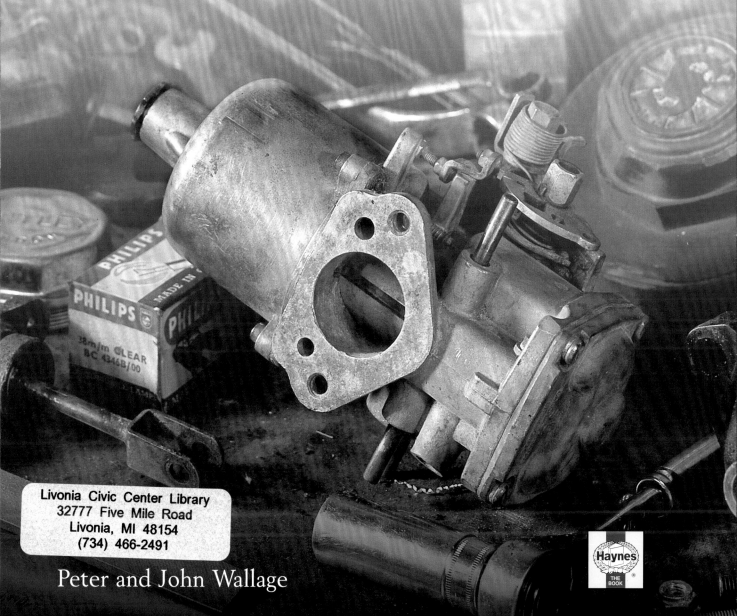

Livonia Civic Center Library
32777 Five Mile Road
Livonia, MI 48154
(734) 466-2491

Peter and John Wallage

JAN 0 9 2002

© Peter and John Wallage 2001

All rights reserved. No part of this publication may be reproduced, stored in a retrieval system or transmitted, in any form or by any means, electronic, mechanical, photocopying, recording or otherwise, without prior permission in writing from Haynes Publishing.

First published in August 2001

A catalogue record for this book is available from the British Library.

ISBN 1 85960 694 6

Library of Congress catalog card no. 2001131386

Published by Haynes Publishing, Sparkford, Nr Yeovil,
Somerset BA22 7JJ, UK
Tel: 01963 442030 Fax: 01963 440001
Int. tel: +44 1963 442030 Fax: +44 1963 440001
E-mail: sales@haynes-manuals.co.uk
Web site: www.haynes.co.uk

Haynes North America Inc., 861 Lawrence Drive, Newbury Park, California 91320, USA

Printed and bound in Britain by J. H. Haynes & Co. Ltd, Sparkford

Illustrations courtesy the authors except where credited.

WARNING
While every attempt has been made throughout this book to emphasise the safety aspects of repairing and restoring components, the publishers, the authors and the distributors accept no liability whatsoever for any damage, injury or loss resulting from the use of this book. If you have any doubts about your ability to safely carry out any of the work described in this book then it is recommended that you seek advice from a professional engineer.

Jurisdictions which have strict emission control laws may consider any modifications to a vehicle to be an infringement of those laws. You are advised to check with the appropriate body or authority whether your proposed modification complies fully with the law. The publishers accept no liability in this regard.

3 9082 08570 7415

Contents

Introduction

Despite predictions from the doom and gloom merchants, and real or imaginary legislative threats from our EU masters, interest in classic cars shows very little sign of abating. Maybe there are not so many from-the-ground-up, last-nut-and-bolt restorations going on as there used to be, but there are thousands of classic cars out there, either restored or original and in the hands of loving enthusiasts but on which, from time to time, things go wrong.

Before we go further, perhaps we ought to define, or try to define, what we mean by a classic car. Forget the dictionary definition of classic, it's got very little to do with the case. Had this book been written ten years ago, it wouldn't have entered our heads to think of models like Mk I and Mk II Escorts, front-wheel drive Austin and Morris 1100s and 1300s, and the much-derided Mk III Cortina – the archetypal Repmobile – as classics. Go back another ten years, and cars like the Mk II Triumph 2000 and the Rover Three Thousand-Five were still under warranty. Our own classic Audi hadn't even been born.

So is age the criterion? Not on its own, though there comes a time when MOT-failed old bangers get carted to the scrapyard in large numbers because their value is too low to warrant repair. Those that are left, the ones in better condition, acquire something of a rarity, nostalgic or 'Classic' value. People like to own and drive them because 'You don't see many of those about nowadays.' It was once said – and there's a grain of truth in it – that if two English people with the same interest meet, they form a club. If a third joins them, they start a club magazine. Cars don't *become* classics, owners *make* them classics.

If this includes you, here is a book you need. Your classic may be running well (perhaps it had an engine overhaul a few thousand miles ago) but every so often you detect a misfire, or it starts using far too much petrol. Maybe it doesn't start as readily as it used to, or one of the bulbs failed and, when you went to replace it, the bulb holder came to pieces in your shocked hands.

When you bought your rebuilt engine, the price quoted was probably 'without auxiliaries'. That means you didn't get a rebuilt starter, dynamo or alternator, carburettor, or distributor. If you had some welding and a spot of respraying done on the body, you didn't get new lights, new door locks, or a new wiper motor – or the few dozen other components that make a car work. Your otherwise reliable classic is suffering from the syndrome known as restored component deficiency.

In this book we show you how to overcome this without, we hope, your having to spend a fortune. Yes, there are new-old-stock, new 'pattern' and rebuilt components out there which you can bolt on, but they can be pricey. For earlier classics, from the 1950s and even 1960s, they are often very pricey. This is not because of a 'milk the enthusiast and get rich quick attitude', at least not with reputable firms. Skilled labour, rents and rates are costly, as is making special machine tools to turn out a few hundred unobtainable components that were once cheap because they were made in the tens of thousands.

The quality of workmanship that goes on in obscure backyard sheds and railway arches we can't vouch for, except to say that we have come across 'restored' and 'rebuilt' components that seemed to result from an attitude of 'Check it and, if it works, clean it and paint it.' If you pay cut prices you can't expect good workmanship and skill. We would advise caution in buying the output from these cut-price cheap-jacks whose wares you sometimes find on market stalls. If a component is beyond home restoration, and we show you how to look for this, then either trade it in to a reputable firm or look for one in better condition that you can restore.

Restoring components in your home garage has two things in its favour. The first is that it's pleasant and not very dirty work – you don't get up to your elbows in oil and grease – and the second is that you don't need a winch to move them about. You've got everything to gain, including saving yourself a lot of money and, if the worst comes to the worst, nothing to lose except your time. Unlike an engine that's been reduced to a mound of pieces, or a body that's had so much rusty metal hacked out that it's in danger of collapse, it doesn't take long to button a component together again and trade it in –

provided you haven't broken anything taking it apart. However, with some components – like a lamp cluster with rusted-out contacts and bulb holders, a handbrake where the ratchet won't hold, or switches that don't and locks that won't – you can't trade them in because no-one offers an exchange scheme.

Maybe you've got a heater motor that doesn't work. Quite often, all that's needed is to clean the commutator, relubricate and fit new carbon brushes, but often these motors were classed as 'sealed for life and maintenance free', and they were held together with rivets. Sealed for life sounds fine, till you come to the end of the projected life, usually ten to fifteen years, sometimes less. Because they were never intended to be repaired, separate parts never were available for these motors, and the average garage won't even entertain a repair. Don't worry, we show you how to take them apart and, if possible, repair them.

We also cover horns, wiper motors, semaphore traffic indicators, dynamos, cut-outs, regulators, alternators, starters, distributors, fuel pumps, carburettors – all the components which, if they're not working properly, turn your car into a beautiful, but rather useless, static exhibit. There are few things less useful than a car which doesn't work. We haven't covered *every* single component on a car, there just wasn't room, but if you follow our principles, you can apply them to almost any part.

Some component restoration calls for a little skill in working with metal. Things like filing, grinding, hacksawing, riveting, soldering different metals and so on. There are right and wrong ways to go about these jobs, and the average amateur approach is often the wrong way. Don't worry if you're unskilled in workshop practice. We show you how to use hand tools properly to tackle these workshop restoration jobs effectively. We don't tell you to use them to make useless objects from anonymous lumps of metal, which is the thorough but somewhat boring way they teach at many engineering colleges, but to make parts and repair actual components. We also drop in a few tips about staying safe in your workshop. Restoring components should be a pleasure, not a chore. Enjoy it.

Peter and John Wallage

Acknowledgements

The authors would like to thank the following people and companies who have assisted them in the preparation of this book:

Thomas Ackermann for giving us the benefit of his many years' experience as an engineer and restorer. John Angliss for the use of some of his workshop equipment. Burlen Fuel Systems Ltd for help and advice on SU and Stromberg carburettors. Cox Auto Electrical for advice on obsolete components. Lucas Aftermarket Services for service sheets on old Lucas equipment. Webcon Ltd for help with information on Weber carburettors and the loan of carburettors for photographing. Motor Trader for permission to use several diagrams from its service data sheets. The old Smiths Instrument Company for passing on to us information and service booklets when the company closed down. Sykes Pickavant and Dremel UK for help with the use of their tools. Breakers yards Tanner and Woodgate in East Kent for letting us root round their yards finding components. And, finally, numerous autojumble stall holders who helped us to find suitable components for photographing.

Chapter 1

Workshop practice

Many people skip this sort of chapter in a book because they know how to use hand tools. At least, they think they do, but the very fact that in the old days of five-year engineering apprenticeships, the first year was spent on learning how to file, saw, drill and tap holes in metal using hand tools, indicates that it isn't a knowledge and skill that we're all born with. In this chapter we want to show you how to use the basic hand tools properly, because their proper use can make all the difference between a successful and pleasant restoration of a classic car component and a job that becomes a chore.

It can also give you a great deal of satisfaction because the proper use of hand tools is rarely taught these days as part of a vehicle technician's skill. The cost of labour is so high that it is cheaper from the customer's point of view to replace a component rather than restore it. Today's vehicle technicians in most garages are very skilled and knowledgeable. They have to be because of the complexity of modern cars which depend almost as much on electronics as mechanical working for their successful running. Even so, these technicians are not fitters in the older sense of the word, they are what used to be called mechanics.

The difference between a fitter and a mechanic was summed up many years ago by the foreman in a tool room in which Peter trained. A mechanic is a man who is skilled in finding out what's wrong with something, replacing the worn parts with new ones and getting it to work again. A fitter can repair things and, when necessary, make or adapt a part to be a perfect fit when a new part isn't available. In restoration, you need both types of skill. So, as well as covering things like undoing seized parts, cleaning, polishing and other things that a restorer often needs to do, this chapter is basically about fitting. Please don't skip it, even if you do know how.

Files and filing

We'll start with the most basic of all engineering hand tools, the file. Please remember that a file is a cutting tool, not a rubbing-down tool. Yet you see so many people using a file with one hand only, without bothering to fit a handle to its tang, and rubbing it back and forth at high speed across the metal like a demented fiddle player, using the middle part of the file only. When they've finished with it, they drop it on the bench or throw it in a toolbox along with all the other tools so that it loses its sharpness in no time at all. That's not the way to use it.

Files come in various lengths and are classed according to their cut and their shape. The cuts, starting with the coarsest, are 'coarse' (sometimes called 'rough cut'), 'bastard', 'second-cut', 'smooth' and 'dead-smooth'. You'll probably find the 'second-cut' is the one you use most, with the 'smooth' for finishing off. Six or eight inches is a useful length for work on most components, though a 12in file can be very useful for some jobs. Sometimes, you'll find

a selection of needle files essential for fine work.

The main shapes are classed as 'flat hand', 'hand', 'square', 'round', 'half-round', 'triangular' and 'pillar'. The most popular shapes in the average tool shop are 'hand' and 'half-round', but the 'hand' isn't the most useful for general use. It's rectangular in section, but in a plan view it's got a tapered curve each side, so you start off with a narrow cut which gets wider along the stroke. Better, is the 'flat hand' which has parallel sides. It also has a safe edge, an edge with no teeth on it so you can work into square corners. Very few tool catalogues these days list a parallel-sided half-round file. They all taper, which is a pity because one with parallel sides, if you can find it, can be very useful. The shape of the square, round and triangular (sometimes called by its ancient name of 'three-square') are self-evident, and another useful shape is a 'pillar' file, which is like a 'flat hand' but much narrower. It often has two safe edges. There are other specialist shape files like 'knife', more usually found in a pack of needle files, and 'warding' files made for locksmiths to cut the intricate patterns and shapes in lock wards or levers, but they haven't got much application in component restoration.

Before you start, fit a handle to the file. You can buy file handles in any tool shop worthy of the name, and they come in various sizes to suit various sizes of file. File handles always used to be made of wood, but most are nowadays made of plastic. There isn't a lot to choose between wood and plastic, and either will do the job. Needle files aren't usually fitted into handles. Instead of a tang they have a plain metal part for the handle. This is fine for some work, but we usually prefer to fit them in a pin chuck which is easier to hold and gives better control.

Most filing is done, or should be done, with the work held in a vice, preferably level, with the face being filed at the top. Ideally, the work should be at, or very slightly above, elbow height. This isn't always easy to achieve, particularly if you're filing something still on the car, but you should aim for it in your workshop.

Hold the file in both hands, one at the handle and the other at the tip, and file with slow, straight strokes, using the full length of the file, or almost the full length. Don't hurry it; you won't get the metal off any quicker. A speed of two strokes a second is quite fast enough. Take a little time to practise filing a flat surface till you can make the full stroke with the file held level, not tilting up and down. A file doesn't cut backwards, so ease the pressure or even lift it slightly off the work on the back stroke. With a sharp file and steady pressure you'll see the swarf coming off the work, and you'll be surprised at how quickly it comes off.

When you're filing a thin edge, it's difficult to hold the file parallel to the edge, but resist the temptation to file at right angles to the work. Hold the file at an angle to the edge, but still make your strokes parallel to the edge. That way you get a straight edge, not one with bumps and hollows. Some people finish off the last few strokes of an edge with draw-filing, holding the file at right angles to the edge and drawing it back along the work. It leaves a nice straight grain on the edge, but it's frowned on by old-time craftsman fitters because the teeth of a file are made to cut in a forward direction, not sideways, and with draw filing it's only too easy to end up with a

wavy edge instead of a straight one. We prefer to finish an edge with the file as near parallel to the edge as possible. When you're almost down to the finish line, change to a file with finer teeth to finish off, and give just a couple of light strokes along the corners of the edge to take off the burrs without producing a chamfer.

There's a technique to using round files or the curved part of half-round files. Because they're tapered, the cut gets wider as you move along the stroke. Start the stroke at the tip with a light pressure, and increase the pressure the nearer you get to the handle to allow for the greater resistance of the wider part of the blade.

If you're enlarging a round hole, with the work held vertically in the vice, ease off the pressure when you get to the bottom part of the hole because the weight of the file adds to it. If you keep the same pressure all the way round it's easy to finish up with a hole that's pear-shaped at the bottom.

An awkward shape to file accurately is an internal angle. A right angle, or an angle larger than a right angle, is the easiest because you can use the safe edge of a 'flat hand' or 'pillar' file to avoid biting into the adjacent edge. The more difficult one is an angle less than a right angle. You have to use a 'half-round' or triangular file to get into the corner, and there's a danger that the back, curved part of the 'half-round' will bite into the adjacent edge. Use slow, deliberate strokes, and turn the work round in the vice frequently so you take a little off each edge at a time. If the extreme corner of the angle isn't too critical, it makes filing easier, and gives a neat job, if you drill a very small hole right at the intersection of the lines.

Generally, the harder the material, the finer-toothed the file you should use. A 'second cut' or 'bastard' file which might be fine for roughing down mild steel will just bounce along the top of hard steel. With a really fine-toothed file

it's even possible to take down hardened and tempered steel, but dead-hard steel surfaces need a grinding stone.

Brass is pretty easy to file, and shouldn't give you any problems, but with softer metals like aluminium alloy and Mazak die-castings it isn't easy to get a perfectly smooth surface. The soft metal swarf picks up in the teeth of the file and leaves scores across the surface. It's better not to use a brand-new file on steel, it clogs too easily. On the other hand, a worn file won't cut into soft metals easily, it slides off. So the general rule is to use new files on brass or aluminium until they have become 'worked in', before you use them on steel. Always use a lubricant on aluminium. Some people like to rub chalk on the file for this, but we've found a liquid lubricant, paraffin or even ordinary cheap washing-up liquid, is best to stop the swarf sticking in the file teeth. Even so, frequently wipe the loose swarf off the surface of the work, and regularly clean the file teeth with a wire brush.

When you've finished using a file, clean its teeth with a wire brush and store it somewhere, like in a rack over the bench, where it won't lose its sharpness by banging up against other tools.

If you must file soft solder, keep a couple of old files just for the purpose. Solder clogs hard into the teeth of a file after a few strokes, and it can be extremely difficult to get out with a wire brush. A file with its teeth clogged with solder is useless. It's possible to reclaim a solder-clogged file by using a blowlamp to melt the solder before brushing it out. It will still be OK for use on solder, but by heating it you will have reduced the temper of the file, which makes it useless for filing harder metals.

Hacksaws and sawing

Similar techniques apply to using the much-misused hacksaw. Pick up a hacksaw in the average person's garage, and you're likely to find the teeth worn down in the middle of the blade and unused at each end. Quite apart from the fact that you're getting only half the life from each blade, a saw blade like this is a sure recipe for it binding in the cut when you do use the full length.

If you're buying a new hacksaw frame, pay a little extra to get a good one. There are some very cheap frames on the market which look very attractive, but often,

when you take the blade out, the part of the frame that adjusts to take different length blades wobbles and flaps about. The result is that when you put tension on the blade, the frame bends and twists, and so does the blade. You'll never get a straight, accurate cut with a twisted blade. Put tension on the blade, then hold the saw up and sight along it. Both the blade and the frame should be straight and parallel to each other. If they aren't, don't waste your money.

At one time, all hacksaw frames had round wooden handles like file handles, but the later pistol-grip type of handle is far better and easier to use. On most 'junior' hacksaws (a useful tool based on the original Eclipse Junior) the frame is just a length of bent sprung rod, but you can get rigid-frame pistol-grip junior hacksaws, and we prefer them because they are easier to hold properly. With a saw, and with a file, you'll find it much easier to guide the tool and make accurate cuts if you hold your index finger along the handle. Because of the rubber finger guard at the end of the handle on a bent-rod junior hacksaw frame, most people use it with all their fingers curled round the handle with the back of their index finger against the rubber guard. You don't get the best control like that. It's more difficult than with a rigid frame to use your index finger along the handle, but it can be done, and you'll get a more accurate cut.

With junior hacksaw blades you don't usually get a choice in tooth pitch (the number of teeth per inch or centimetre), they all come with 32 teeth per inch (or per 25mm), but you do get a choice with larger hacksaw blades, even though some general tool shops don't stock them. You should have blades with at least two, preferably four, different tooth pitches. The standard pitches available are 14, 18, 24 and 32 teeth per inch (tpi).

When you buy a hacksaw complete with its blade, you almost always get a 24tpi blade which the shopkeeper will probably tell you is a good, all-purpose general blade. It isn't. It's fine for brass, copper, aluminium and cast iron, but it's too fine a pitch for the best cutting of mild steel or tool steel such as a high tensile bolt. There isn't enough space between the teeth for the swarf to clear properly. Mild steel cuts best with a coarser, 14tpi blade, and tool steel with an 18tpi blade. The big exception to all this is when you're cutting thin sheet

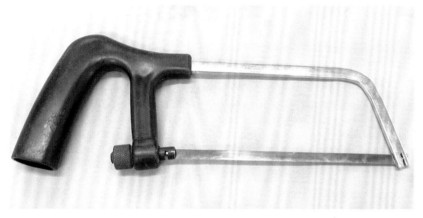

Fig. 1.1. A junior hacksaw is often more convenient to use on components than a full frame one. We prefer the rigid frame type to the 'bent wire' type.

Fig. 1.2. Always hold a hacksaw, large or small, with your index finger along the frame. It gives you better direction and control.

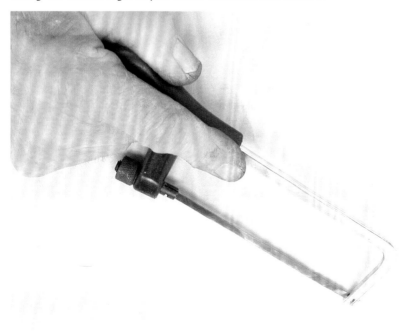

metal or thin-walled tube. For these, you need a 32tpi blade, whatever the material. With sheet metal you should cut with the blade at an angle to the work to get at least two teeth, preferably more, against the metal all the time. With thin-walled tube you can't do this all the time because when you get to a diameter, the blade teeth are at right angles to the wall. The danger is that two adjacent teeth will straddle the metal and the blade will bind or jump, possibly even break its teeth. For this reason, ease off the pressure and make slower strokes as you get near the diameter of a thin tube. For plastics, such as an insulating block or sheet Paxolin, use a fine 32tpi blade, and saw slowly. If you saw too fast, the heat can melt the swarf behind your blade and you find the blade stuck solid.

Except for round bar or tube, where it doesn't make any difference, don't start a cut with the saw horizontal or with the handle tipped down towards you. You're likely to catch a tooth on the edge and snap it off. Start the cut on the corner furthest away from you with the handle of the saw held higher than the tip. Bring the saw back horizontal as the cut progresses.

Please pay a little extra to get good quality blades. There are some blades, often sold on market stalls, that seem ridiculously cheap. They are, they're cheap and nasty. They're made from inferior steel, badly tempered, and you find that either the teeth are so soft that they wear down by the time you've cut through a quarter-inch bolt, or they're so hard that they break off. Blades like this are an absolute waste of money. They're frustrating to use, and you can't do accurate work with them.

Use a hacksaw in a very similar way to a file. Hold it at both ends, even a junior hacksaw, and cut with slow, deliberate strokes using the full length of the blade. Again, two strokes a second is quite fast

enough. Move the saw in a straight line and try to avoid 'see-sawing' as your arms move back and forth.

Like a file, a saw blade doesn't cut backwards, so ease off the pressure to nothing on the back stroke. In most cases, use a lubricant. It helps to keep the blade cool as well as clearing the swarf and giving you a smoother cut. On steel, a squirt from the oil can is fine, but we prefer to use paraffin on aluminium alloys. With brass and copper, some fitters like to use paraffin and some prefer to cut brass and copper dry. We leave it up to you. Cast iron is a self-lubricating material because of its high carbon content, and can be cut dry.

Drill bits and drilling

You'll probably find yourself using drill bits a lot in component restoration, for drilling off heads of rivets as well as drilling holes. As with all tools, it pays to get good drill bits. Cheap ones aren't hardened and tempered properly, and though it might say HSS (High Speed Steel) on the box, all HSS steels aren't the same. The cheap ones just don't keep their edge. Even good drill bits can be ruined if you don't use them properly. The usual reasons are drilling at far too high a speed and letting the drill bit get too hot. The following table gives the recommended rpm speed for the sizes of drill and materials you're most likely to use in component restoration.

These speeds apply to drill presses and other drilling machinery where the speed can be altered to fine limits, and with the appropriate lubricant, but the principle applies equally to hand-held electric drills. You seldom find the rpm marked on a hand electric drill, and even on a variable speed one it usually says something like A, B, C and so on. However, the top speed, which most people use without thinking, is often 3,000rpm or more, far too fast for the work we're doing. You can see that drilling in steel needs only half the speed of drilling in brass or aluminium, and the larger the drill, the slower should be the speed. There's a speed reduction of a half, for example, between a 1/4in (6mm) drill and a 1/2in (13mm) drill in the same material. In general, a wise rule is: if in doubt, drop the speed.

A faster speed doesn't drill any faster, it just overheats the drill bit and draws out the temper so it goes blunt quickly. We also like to cut the speed down when using drills smaller than 1/4in (6mm), especially very fine drills, because they break so easily. Keep your drills sharp. We know a very experienced fitter who can use a bench grinder to sharpen a drill bit by hand, but we freely admit that we can't. A drill bit must be sharpened not just to the correct angle and relief angle, but also with its point truly central or it will wobble and drill an oversize hole. If you've got a bench grinder, you can get a reasonably inexpensive attachment for sharpening drill bits. Provided you buy good

drill diameter in & mm	RPM in		
	steel	cast iron	brass & aluminium
1/4in (6mm)	1050	1300	2100
5/16in (8mm)	850	1060	1700
3/8in (10mm)	700	875	1400
7/16in (11mm)	600	750	1200
1/2in (13mm)	525	650	1050

quality drill bits in the first place, an attachment like this will pay for itself over again. Don't let a drill bit get too hot when you're sharpening it. If you're rescuing a very blunt drill bit, which may take a fair time to sharpen, quench it frequently in oil or water.

If you've got a pillar drill, a very useful tool, by all means use it whenever you can. If not, you can get bench attachments, often called drill presses, for most popular makes of hand electric drill. When you're using a bench-mounted drill, always hold the work in a drilling vice. If you hold it by hand, and the drill bit binds and spins the work, it can do horrible damage to your fingers.

There are times when it's not practicable to use a pillar drill. Drilling the heads off awkwardly-placed rivets on a component, or drilling a hole in a component that hasn't got a flat surface to clamp it level in a drill vice, are examples. In these cases where you have to use a hand-held drill, always clamp the work somehow, either by a G-cramp to the bench or in the vice. Don't hold it in one hand and the drill in the other, it's far too dangerous.

With practise, it's possible, even easy, to drill a hole square and straight using a hand-held drill. If you're not sure about your ability to do this, practise on some odd pieces of metal, or old components that are beyond recall, till you are. Time spent practising saves frustration on a component you want to restore.

For drilling small holes, say 1/8in (3mm) diameter and smaller, the ordinary hand-held electric drill can be rather clumsy. For this sort of fine drilling we find a Dremel tool ideal. Even with a small drill like a Dremel, always clamp the work firmly. Small drills like this pack a powerful torque, and if the work spins in your fingers it can cripple your hand for life.

Whichever drill you use, always centre punch the place where you want to drill the hole. If you don't,

the drill bit will wander, and you'll never drill the hole in the right place. For any hole larger than 1/8in (3mm) diameter, always put through a smaller pilot drill first. A twist-drill bit hasn't got a point, it's got a chisel shape at the sharp end, and a centre punch dot isn't large enough to position a large diameter drill bit. Apart from that, by using a pilot drill you're drilling out less metal each time which makes the job easier. For larger holes, we often use two pilots, so for a 1/2in (13mm) hole we might start with a 1/8in (3mm) drill bit, then 5/16in (8mm) and finally the 1/2in (13mm). It sounds long-winded, and you've got the trouble of changing drill bits, but you get a better result.

Except for brass, copper and cast iron, which can be drilled dry, always use a lubricant, as much to keep the drill bit cool as to help clear the swarf. For steel, a squirt of oil is fine, but for aluminium alloy we prefer paraffin.

As most classic cars were built before the UK became involved in metrication, all the drilled holes are in imperial sizes, and the nuts and bolts are either imperial or unified sizes (which also use imperial measurements). It's becoming increasingly difficult in the average tool shop to buy drills in anything but metric sizes. It's also becoming more difficult to buy BSF and BA nuts and bolts. You often have to send to a specialist tool supplier for them. One such supplier is Tracy Tools Ltd in Dartmouth, and it's well worth sending for their catalogue. Even so, for convenience, many restorers have now switched to metric sizes and use metric nuts and bolts. So, for example, if they come across a stripped 1/4in BSF or 2BA thread in a component, they will drill and tap to the next metric size up.

However, imperial size drill bits are still available from Tracy Tools, and come in three ranges: number sizes, letter sizes and inch sizes. Number sizes run from No. 80 (0.0135in diameter) up to No.1

(0.228in diameter). Letter sizes run from A (0.234in diameter) up to Z (0.413in diameter). Inch sizes start at 1/64in diameter (though the 1/64in and 1/32in are quite hard to find) and go up to 1/2in diameter in 1/64in steps. After that they usually go up in 1/32in steps. Most well-stocked engineering tool shops keep metric drill bits in 0.5mm steps from 1mm up to 10mm, and in 1mm steps after that. If you ever need a drill bit smaller then 1mm – as you might, perhaps, for drilling a hole in an instrument printed circuit board – try a model shop. Your normal electric drill probably won't hold very small drill bits, so you'll need a Dremel or similar miniature drill.

Taps and dies

You can buy taps and dies separately or in sets complete with a tap wrench or die wrench (often listed in catalogues as a die holder), or you can buy combined sets of taps and dies. Of the two, you'll find that you'll use taps more often, either for cleaning out a corroded thread or when a thread is stripped and you have to open up to the next size and tap a new thread. In the latter case, whether you stay with the original type of thread or change to a metric thread for which it is easier to get screws and bolts, is up to you. In either case, you have to drill out to the core diameter of the new thread, using what is usually called the tapping size drill.

You may want to use letter and number size drill bits, as well as imperial and metric, for tapping, so we have included tables giving the sizes of these drill bits in decimal inches. However, you may find yourself wanting to tap a thread for which you haven't got the nominally correct size drill bit. In that case, you want to find the nearest drill you have to the root diameter of the thread (the diameter at the bottom of the threads). The easiest way to do this is by trial and error. Choose a tapped hole of the same thread or, if you can't find one, the die for that size thread, and try the shanks of your available drill bits till you find one that fits snugly. Use this as your tapping drill.

LETTER DRILL SIZES

letter	size (in)	letter	size (in)
A	0.234	N	0.302
B	0.238	O	0.316
C	0.242	P	0.323
D	0.246	Q	0.332
E	0.250	R	0.339
F	0.257	S	0.348
G	0.261	T	0.358
H	0.266	U	0.368
I	0.272	V	0.377
J	0.277	W	0.386
K	0.281	X	0.397
L	0.290	Y	0.404
M	0.295	Z	0.413

NUMBERED DRILL SIZES

No.	size (in)	No.	size (in)
1	0.228	16	0.177
2	0.221	17	0.173
3	0.213	18	0.169
4	0.209	19	0.166
5	0.205	20	0.161
6	0.204	21	0.159
7	0.201	22	0.157
8	0.199	23	0.154
9	0.196	24	0.152
10	0.193	25	0.149
11	0.191	26	0.147
12	0.189	27	0.144
13	0.185	28	0.140
14	0.182	29	0.136
15	0.180	30	0.128

Many electrical components and quite a few fuel pumps and carburettors from the classic era used BA (British Association) threads. The most usual sizes are the even-numbered BA sizes: 2BA, 4BA, 6BA and, less frequently, 8BA.

BA (British Association) THREAD TAPPING SIZES

BA No.	tapping drill
0	5.0mm (³/₁₆in)
1	No. 15
2	No. 22
3	3.4mm (⁹/₆₄in)
4	3.0mm (⁷/₆₄in)
5	No. 37
6	2.3mm (³/₃₂in)
7	No. 46
8	1.7mm (¹/₁₆in)

Other tapping drill sizes you might need to know are for the old imperial sizes BSF (British Standard Fine) and BSW (British Standard Whitworth), UNF (Unified Fine), UNC (Unified Coarse) and metric. You may never want to work on American car components, but for a short time after the 1939–45 war, some British component makers used UNF and UNC threads. These were introduced during the war to make interchangeability between English and American components easier. The shape of the unified threads was very similar to BSF and BSW and, as you can see from the tables, the BSF number of threads per inch was quite close to that of UNF, particularly in the smaller sizes. It's quite easy to make a mistake between them unless you use a thread gauge, so be careful. If you force a BSF thread and a UNF thread together, thinking you've got just a tight or dirty thread, you'll strip one or the other of them.

BSF (British Standard Fine) TAPPING SIZES

size (in)	threads per inch	tapping drill
¼	26	No. 7
⁵/₁₆	22	G
⅜	20	O
⁷/₁₆	18	U
½	16	²⁷/₆₄in
⁹/₁₆	16	³¹/₆₄in
⅝	14	³⁵/₆₄in
¹¹/₁₆	14	¹⁹/₃₂in
¾	12	²¹/₃₂in

BSW (British Standard Whitworth) TAPPING SIZES

size (in)	threads per inch	tapping drill
¼	20	No. 7
⁵/₁₆	18	D
⅜	16	O
⁷/₁₆	14	⅜in
½	12	X
⁹/₁₆	12	¹⁵/₃₂in
¹¹/₁₆	11	³⁷/₆₄in
¾	10	⅝in

UNF (Unified National Fine) TAPPING SIZES

size (in)	threads per inch	tapping drill
¼	28	No. 3
⁵/₁₆	24	H
⅜	24	Q
⁷/₁₆	20	V
½	20	²⁹/₆₄in
⁹/₁₆	18	½in
⅝	18	⁹/₁₆in
¾	16	¹¹/₁₆in

UNC (Unified National Coarse) TAPPING SIZES

size (in)	threads per inch	tapping drill
¼	20	³/₁₆in
⁵/₁₆	18	D
⅜	16	N
⁷/₁₆	14	S
½	13	¹³/₃₂in
⁹/₁₆	12	¹⁵/₃₂in
⅝	11	¹⁷/₃₂in
¾	10	⅝in

On cars and car components, BSF and UNF are usually used in steel and cast iron, BSW and UNC in aluminium and Mazak die castings, and BA in brass. Except, as mentioned, many makers of electrical components and a few other odds and ends used BA threads in steel, brass and Mazak die-castings, and it isn't unknown to find the odd BSF or even BSW

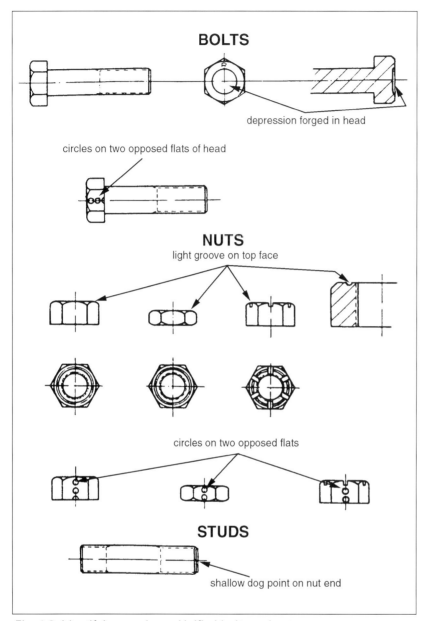

BOLTS

depression forged in head

circles on two opposed flats of head

NUTS

light groove on top face

circles on two opposed flats

STUDS

shallow dog point on nut end

Fig. 1.3. Identifying marks on Unified bolts and nuts.

blind hole slightly deeper than the thread of the screw you want to use so there's no danger of the screw bottoming before it goes tight. Start the thread with the first tap, then send through the second tap and, if it's a blind hole, finish with the plug tap. In many cheaper tap sets you get only two taps for each size, one which is halfway between a first and second tap, and a plug tap.

Use the same lubricant for tapping as you would for drilling, and don't just screw the tap straight down the hole. Take it half a turn at a time, then back off a quarter of a turn to clear the swarf. If you don't, the swarf is likely to clog the tap threads and give you a very ragged thread in the work.

If you're tapping out a stripped thread to a larger size, you'll have to open out the clearance hole in the mating part. Various engineering handbooks give clearance hole sizes for different diameter threads, but we must admit that we don't always consult them. If we don't happen to know the clearance size off by heart, we usually hold the screw or bolt we want to use against the shank of a drill and pick a drill that's just a shade larger. An exception to this is when using a fitted bolt. These bolts have accurately ground plain portions above the thread, and the clearance hole is reamed, or should be, so that the bolt acts as a positioning dowel. We've come across these in engines and gearboxes, but not on components.

Dies

There might be occasions when you want to make a new stud, or thread the end of a rod, or clean up a damaged external thread. This is where you use a die. Unlike taps, you use only one die for cutting an external thread.

Older style dies, particularly large sizes, were often square and in two parts which fitted in a special die holder, but most dies these days, at least in the sizes we use for car components, are one-

thread somewhere in the same component. On later components, you might even come across the odd metric thread. All very confusing if you're not prepared for it, so if you find a thread that feels too sloppy, or which goes tight after a few turns, check it before something strips.

A thread gauge, mentioned above, is a very useful little tool for identifying threads. If you haven't come across one, it looks like a stubby penknife with a series of little saw blades. You hold various

blades against the thread till you find one that fits exactly.

Taps

Good quality taps come in sets of three for each size, 'first tap' (sometimes called taper tap), 'second tap' and 'plug tap'. The first and second taps have tapers ground on them to help to start the thread square to the hole. The plug tap doesn't have a taper. It is used for the final cut on blind holes where you can't send the tap right through the work. Always drill a

piece and circular. On good quality sets, the die is cut through on a radius at one side to allow it to be expanded for the first cut. There are two countersinks, one each side of the cut, for closing it up to the final thread diameter. The thread of the die is tapered on one side to give a lead-in.

The die holder has three pointed-end screws at the side, a central one which pushes into the cut to expand the die, and two others which fit into the countersinks to close the die. Remember always to slacken off the closing screws before you tighten the expanding screw, and loosen the expanding screw before you tighten the closing screws.

It's very difficult to cut a true square thread on a rod with the end cut square, so put a small taper on the rod either with a file or on a fine grindstone to give the taper in the die somewhere to sit to start the thread. Fit the die in the holder, tighten the expanding screw and screw in the closing screws just enough to stop the die rotating in the holder. Start cutting the thread using plenty of lubricant, making three quarters of a turn and then backing off, just the same as cutting a thread with a tap.

When you've made the first cut, close the die slightly by loosening the expanding screw and tightening the closing screws, and go down the thread again. Clean off the swarf and try the thread in a nut or in a tapped hole, and continue cutting the thread a little deeper till you get the fit you want.

Cheaper circular dies are not slotted. They just have one screw holding them in the die wrench, and they usually have slightly more taper at the start of the thread to help you start square. They are not so accurate as split dies because you can't adjust the thread; you just cut it. However, used with care and plenty of lubricant they will cut a reasonable enough thread for most purposes.

There's one type of thread that can give you problems when you try to clean it up with a die. You find it on the ends of wheel spokes, and just occasionally on the ends of connecting rods for carburettors. It's known as a rolled thread, and it isn't cut into the rod, it's formed in a rolling machine which actually pushes the thread up so that it's a slightly larger diameter than the rest of the rod and stands proud. It's used partly as a cheap method of automated production and partly because it doesn't weaken the rod by cutting down into it.

Damaged rolled threads can be very difficult to clean up successfully. Have a go by all means, but usually the answer is to make a new rod from a bar the outside diameter of the thread, and cut a new thread on it.

Dealing with damaged studs

Studs with damaged threads are a pain. Studs usually come in pairs or in a row or circle, and there isn't enough room between them to turn a die wrench. One alternative is to use a die nut, which is a fixed-size die with a hexagon on the outside. You screw it down on the damaged thread as far as you can with your fingers and then use a spanner. You may be successful in cleaning up the thread, but we wouldn't bank on it, and usually the only course is to take the old stud out and fit a new one. It's easy to say that, but often not so easy to do.

Old studs can be very tight, especially in die-castings where corrosion between the steel stud and the aluminium die-casting has almost welded them together. There are three methods of getting a stud out.

You can try locking two nuts together on the exposed thread, and then unscrewing the bottom nut. It's the classic method, but very often it won't deal with very tight studs. The second method is to use a universal-size stud extractor. These usually work on larger size studs, 5/16in and above, but can be a bit brutal on very small sizes so that the stud often snaps off. It helps a lot with die-castings if you warm the die-casting first to try to break the corroded bond. Either put the die-casting in a medium heat oven and cook it for half an hour or so, or heat it with a flame against a heat-reflective block if you've got one (an old fire brick is ideal), or against a steel plate. Use a gentle flame, and play it evenly all over the casting, as there's a danger you'll get differential expansion and crack it if you don't. Also, don't get it too hot. You won't melt it, but you may well distort it so that other parts don't fit properly.

If the stud breaks off, or you just can't shift it, the last method is to drill it out. If you're very careful and accurate you can get the old stud out without damaging the threads in the component, but in many cases you'll have to drill oversize and tap a larger size thread. In this case, you have to enlarge the clearance hole in the mating part of the component to take the larger size stud. If this can't be done, because there's not enough metal round the hole, you can either have a Helicoil insert put in the stripped thread so that you can use an original size stud, or if you know someone with a lathe, get them to make up a stepped stud with the larger thread at the bottom to screw into your enlarged hole, and the rest of the stud turned down to the original size and threaded with the original size thread.

If you're lucky, the stud will have broken with part of it still proud of the surface. File it down flush with the surface before you start to drill, and make a centre-punch mark as accurately as you can in the centre of the stud to guide the first drill. We say first drill because you shouldn't try to drill out a broken stud in one go. Use a small drill first so that you can check that you got the hole central in the old stud. Then use gradually larger drills till, with luck, the old threads will pick out like wire, leaving the internal thread intact so that you can clean it up with a tap.

In tool shops you'll find a type of stud extractor that looks like a tapered tap but which has a very coarse left-hand thread. The idea is that you drill a hole in the broken stud, and screw in the extractor. As it's got a left-hand thread, the theory is that the taper will bite into the broken stud and unscrew it.

It might, and we're prepared for people to say that they've had lots of successes with these tools, but we don't like them. When you screw them in the hole, they expand the stud which makes it even tighter. Also, being very hard, they're quite brittle, and we've seen more than enough broken off inside the stud they're supposed to extract. If this happens, you've got a real problem because the extractor is far too hard to drill out. We've heard of people in this predicament going to a specialist firm to have the broken extractor removed by spark erosion, but they've had to pay a lot of money, usually far more than the worth of the component they're restoring.

The method of dealing with broken studs also applies if you have to cut the head off a screw or bolt because someone has used the wrong size spanner or screwdriver on it and either rounded the hexagon or chewed up the slot on the screw head.

Spanners

Spanners usually have their size marked on them. On imperial size spanners you usually find both BSF and BSW marked (sometimes abbreviated to BS and W), the size referring to the diameter of the screw thread. A BSF spanner fits the hexagon of a smaller size BSW bolt or nut. BA spanners have the appropriate BA size marked on them. With unified threads, however, the spanners are marked with the distance across the flats of the bolt or nut hexagon – sometimes, but by no means

always, with the letters A/F stamped next to the size. Metric spanners are marked with the size of the bolt diameter in mm. One peculiarity of unified bolts and nuts is that with 7/16in and 9/16in diameter bolts, the distance across the flats of the bolt head hexagon isn't the same as the distance across the flats of the hexagon on the matching nut – the A/F size for the bolt being 1/16in smaller than for the nut – don't ask us why, we didn't design them.

You might hear people talk about 'equivalent' size spanners, implying that some spanners for one thread system will fit the hexagons of a different thread system. Some of them seem to fit, more or less, but if we had a pound for every hexagon that's been rounded by someone using an 'almost fits' spanner, we could retire in luxury. On the subject of rounded hexagons, there are some spanners on the market (Sykes-Pickavant is one firm that makes them) which are very useful for dealing with rounded hexagons when an ordinary spanner slips. Instead of the spanner jaws being parallel, they have small bumps on them. These bumps lock against the flat sides of the hexagon without having to rely on the corners. We find that they will usually deal with all but the worst rounded nut and bolt hexagons.

Soldering

Soldering is something you'll meet with frequently in restoring electrical components. It's one of the easiest skills to master, yet so many people make a mess of it and finish up with a high resistance joint, often called a dry joint.

The steps for successful soldering are quite simple. Use a soldering iron the correct size for the job. Use a solder with built-in non-corrosive flux, not killed spirits, baker's fluid, or any other type of external flux. They do the job well, but they leave behind a

corrosive residue that will turn the components green and horrible in a few weeks. Clean and tin the bit, a dirty bit with blobs of old solder on it won't solder properly. Clean and tin both components you want to join. Bring the components together and heat them with the soldering iron till the solder flows.

Note that you always heat the wire or the connector tag first, then touch it with the end of the solder wire till the solder flows. Never put solder directly on to the bit of the iron except when you're tinning it. Sometimes it's quite useful to use a small flame gun, sometimes called a pencil flame gun, for soldering small jobs, but don't use it on electrical components or wiring, as it's difficult to control the spread of the heat and you'll melt the nearby insulation. For soldering most electric cables you need only a fairly small iron, but sometimes when you're dealing with a heavy cable, the small iron doesn't give enough heat. We find a soldering gun very useful for this sort of work. It also has the advantage that it heats very quickly and cools very quickly.

In many cases when you're soldering wires to a terminal, you need to use a heat sink – something that will carry the excess heat and stop it running up the wire and melting the insulation. A pair of fine pointed-nose pliers is good for this job. If you need to join wires, say where the old wire moulded into a component has broken off short, always use heat-shrink tubing to insulate the join. Don't use wrap-on insulating tape, it doesn't last. To bind bunches of wires together into a loom you can use self-amalgamating tape. If you can't find this in a tool shop, try a plumber's supplies shop. Making looms comes within the realm of car restoring rather than component restoring, but you may need to make a short junction loom, for example where you solder new wires on to something like an alternator multi-plug.

Cleaning and polishing

Before we get on to specific components, a few words about cleaning and polishing and about getting seized things apart – often a frustrating business.

There are quite a few proprietary degreasing and cleaning fluids on the market, most of which do a very good job, but they can be rather expensive if you've got a lot of components to clean. We usually use two tubs of cheap white spirit which is very cheap if you buy it in large plastic containers from a builder's merchant. A couple of plastic bins or even washing up bowls make ideal washing tubs. With components that are completely mechanical we usually dump them complete into one tub and leave them there for a few hours, then scrub them with a brush to get the worst of the muck off before transferring them to the second, cleaner, tub for a rinse. When the white spirit in the first tub gets too dirty to use, we swap the tubs around, using the second tub for the first soaking, and put clean white spirit in what is now the second tub.

It's surprising how a long soak, 24 hours if necessary, in white spirit will free old caked-on muck

Fig. 1.4. A bead blast cabinet is a very useful thing in a restoration workshop.

and even the white corrosion that grows on aluminium die-castings that have been long neglected.

Don't soak electrical components in a tub because the white spirit may attack the insulation. Instead, put them on a rack over the tub and use a brush dipped in the white spirit sparingly to wash off the outside.

After you've dried most of the white spirit off with a rag, the rest will dry quite quickly so you can start dismantling and put the

separate pieces into white spirit again for individual cleaning. A cheap kitchen sieve makes an ideal container for washing off small parts and screws. Just put them in the sieve, shake it about in the white spirit and leave them to drain. Aluminium parts which had a white crystalline corrosion on them will still have black or dark patches left after washing, and the easiest way to get rid of them is with a brass wire brush. After that, if you want to, you can polish them.

Fig. 1.5. When you're bead blasting, hold the component up so that the blast doesn't create a fog of dust from the floor of the cabinet.

Fig. 1.6. It took about 10 seconds to blast the rust and paint off this horn casing.

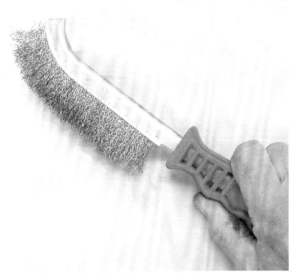

Fig. 1.7. We prefer this thin type of wire brush to the wider wooden-handled ones. You can get these with steel or brass wires.

Fig. 1.8. A buffing wheel, or a buffing mop in a drill, soon puts the shine back on bead-blasted aluminium components.

Quite a few of the bits you restore will have rust on them. If they are going to be painted, get rid of as much as you can with a steel wire brush and then use a rust killer. There are various types of rust killer on the market, most of which convert the rust to an inert substance, often iron phosphate, which has a dark grey or black look. This is OK if you want to paint them, but it's a nuisance if you want to leave them steel colour as, for example, on carburettor linkages. We have, however, found that the type of rust remover which you dilute with water, and then soak the parts in it, leaves a very light grey residue which can be brushed off before finally cleaning with a wire brush and emery paper. This type of rust remover tends not to be stocked by accessory shops and places like Halfords. We've usually found it sold on stalls at autojumbles and classic car rallies. so when we see it we often buy enough to last till the next rally. The brand we're currently using is Corro Dip, which is imported from Australia.

You might want to polish some of the aluminium components you restore, such as SU carburettor dashpots, or some of the brass bits

if your engine bay has any. A special high-speed polishing motor with a 6in or 8in wheel does the job quickly, but it isn't worth buying one just for two or three components. Get a buffing wheel, 4in or so diameter, and a mandrel for it, to fit in your electric drill. Your drill is unlikely to be powerful enough to take a buffing wheel of a diameter much larger than this.

It's not easy, indeed it's very difficult, to polish something with a hand-held electric drill fitted with a buffing wheel. It's much better to mount the drill with its buffing wheel in a vice and offer the component up to it. Almost all hand electric drills made in the last 15 or so years have the E neck, or European neck, for taking a clamp to mount the drill. Don't just clamp the body of the drill in the vice, use the proper attachment.

Buffing soap, as it's called, comes in cakes which vary in coarseness. Usually, the coarsest is grey, moving through white, yellow, pink and red as they get finer. The coarsest ones can bite quite deeply into aluminium, so we'd advise starting with the yellow and going coarser only if the yellow won't remove the marks. Keep a separate buffing

wheel for each colour soap, and finish off with the dark red one. If you want a really high final polish, use a separate buffing wheel charged with metal polish such as Brasso.

Two things about polishing. The first is to wear a pair of really heavy gloves. Leather welding gloves are ideal. If you slip, and catch your fingers on the revolving buffing wheel it can take the skin off in a split second. The second is that polishing like this is often a very messy job. If you work with the wheel revolving towards you, the muck gets thrown downwards, and you find your trousers or overalls get smothered in it. It's less messy to mount the drill or buffing motor, if you can, so that you are able to stand end-on to it, then most of the muck gets thrown clear of you.

Unseizing

Lastly in this chapter we come to the often frustrating job of taking apart things which have seized together because of corrosion. The first attack is to squirt the parts liberally with a penetrating freeing agent such as WD-40 or Castrol Easing Fluid. If, after a quarter of an hour or so, gentle tapping doesn't free them, squirt them again and leave them for 24 hours before trying again. If this fails, then for mechanical components, try prolonged soaking in a mixture of diesel fluid and paraffin, but don't do this with electrical components. With these, all you can do is keep persevering with freeing agent and gentle tapping.

If this doesn't work, you have to resort to heat, but (again) not on electrical components because the heat will undoubtedly ruin the insulation. Remember that your previous soaking in freeing agent or paraffin and diesel will have left a flammable residue, so apply heat well away from the bench. Out in the open is best, where a sudden burst of flame won't do any damage. Lay the component on a firebrick or a sheet of steel, and play a blow lamp flame over it. Keep the flame moving so you heat the component evenly all over, otherwise you might distort it.

When it's too hot to touch, squirt the parts which are seized with freeing agent. It will smoke and fizz as the cold freeing agent hits the hot metal, and this treatment very often does the trick, and gentle tapping will get things apart. Remember that the component will still be very hot, so use heavy leather gloves to handle it while you're tapping it. If it doesn't start to move, try heating again and more freeing agent, but be

Fig. 1.9. A ratchet screwdriver with multiple bits is very handy, but don't get the cheapest of the cheap.

prepared for a burst of flame when you heat the freeing agent. Remember we said gentle tapping. A large number of gentle taps round the seized parts is much more effective than a few heavy blows, and much less likely to damage things. Once the part starts to move, don't force it. Keep applying more freeing agent, more heat if necessary, and keep tapping or working the parts back and forth until they come apart.

Neither *all* the tools you're likely to need, nor *every* workshop process and practice you might

Fig. 1.10. Always use the correct size screwdriver bit for the screw. You see the chewed-up results of not doing this on plenty of components.

Fig. 1.11. These 'star' sockets from Sykes-Pickavant are excellent for gripping the sides of rounded-off nuts.

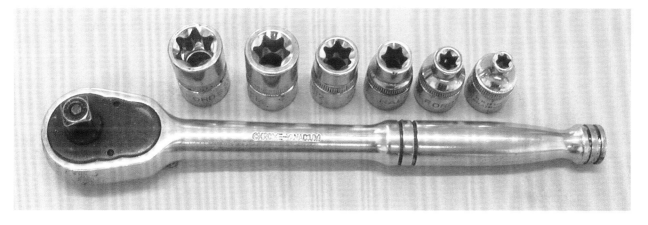

Fig. 1.12. A set of thin-wall nut spinners is a useful addition to a ratchet screwdriver with detachable bits.

have to apply, are included here, but if you follow what we've given you, you'll have a good grounding. Any special tools needed for specific jobs are described in the relevant chapters. You probably already have a lot of the tools, anyway, but if you're renewing them, buy the best quality you can afford. Some inexpensive tools, like the popular boxes of a ratchet screwdriver with a set of different bits, are fine for non-professional use, provided you don't buy the cheapest of the cheap, but renew the bits when they show signs of wear. We also use cheap brass wire brushes, and throw them away when they wear, but cheap steel wire brushes usually have too few bunches of coarse wires spaced too far apart. They bounce on the surface of a component rather than getting down into the pores of rusty steel to get the rust out. With cutting tools, files, hacksaws, taps and dies, the ones you find on an 'any tool a pound' type of market stall can make a job hard work. Too often, the quality of the steel is poor, and either the teeth are too soft so they wear out in next to no time, or they're too hard and chip off. Buy the best quality cutting tools you can afford, and look after them. Clean them when you've finished using them, and keep them in a rack over the bench, or wrap them up, so that they don't lose their edge banging up against other tools in your tool box.

With practice, using hand tools properly becomes second nature. You'll find that repairing a part that can't be obtained, or making one good component from two damaged ones, becomes a pleasure rather than a chore.

Except for the Weber DGAV and DCOE carburettors, where Weber was kind enough to lend us new ones, all the components we have used in this book have been bought from breakers or autojumbles. Some of them were in very poor condition, and time constraints have stopped us from restoring them fully, but we chose them to show that a component has to be very bad indeed to be past restoring. We wouldn't advocate that you choose the worst examples you can find, the better they are before you start, the easier the restoration, but if you're really stuck, even the poor ones can be brought back to life.

Now let's get down to restoring some components.

Chapter 2

Ignition distributors

Before we start stripping down a distributor, we'd like to clear up a point about coil polarity with negative and positive earth systems. Until about the mid-1950s, almost all cars had negative earth systems. We say almost because, though we've never come across an older positive earth system, they might have existed somewhere. Then there was a short time when makers changed over to a positive earth system. Various reasons were put forward, all no doubt valid in theory. One was that a positive earth system gave less corrosion in radiators and aluminium heads.

Be that as it may, the change didn't last all that long, and makers went back to a negative earth system. This didn't matter at all so far as things like bulbs and many other parts were concerned, but it caused a lot of confusion with things like radios and alternators which are sensitive to polarity. With dynamos it didn't matter, because a dynamo can be polarised for either system, and most people thought it didn't matter with coils and distributors.

However, Lucas said that they were wrong; it did matter, because if a coil were wound so that the centre electrode of a plug was 'negative' in relation to the body of the plug, it gave a better spark. The reason for this is that back in the 19th century when electricity was in its infancy, scientists got the flow of electricity wrong. They called the terminal *from* which they thought it flowed the 'positive' terminal, and the one *to* which they thought it flowed the 'negative'

terminal. Later, it was discovered that the electron flow is actually the other way round, from 'negative' to 'positive'. Changing over the names of the terminals would have caused too much confusion, so they were left as they were. We put 'negative' and 'positive' in quotes to get that sorted out, but from now on we'll drop the quotes to avoid more confusion. When we say positive and negative we mean the terminals which are marked positive and negative (or red and blue) on the battery.

The other thing that was discovered is that electrons jump much more readily across a gap if the negative electrode is hotter than the positive electrode.

On a plug, the centre electrode gets a lot hotter than the body, so if the centre electrode is made negative in relation to the body, you can get the same spark intensity with anything from 10 per cent to 40 per cent less HT voltage or, put the other way round, you get a much better spark for the same HT voltage. So Lucas, and most other coil makers, wound their coils to give what's called a 'negative spark', irrespective of whether the vehicle had a positive or negative earth system. The low tension terminals on older coils, when a negative earth system was universal, were usually marked SW for Switch and CB for contact breaker, but this was dropped, and the terminals were marked + and –. This meant that the same coil could be used for positive and negative earth systems. On a positive earth system the + terminal is connected to the contact breaker,

and on a negative earth system the – terminal is connected to the contact breaker.

All very straightforward, except for one snag. Some car makers who changed from negative to positive earth insisted that the low tension terminals on the coil were still marked SW and CB. This means that if you pick up a coil marked SW and CB at an autojumble, either second-hand or new-old-stock, you need to know what car it came from and whether the car had a positive or negative earth system. Unfortunately, you can't tell by looking at a coil which way round it was wound, but if you know for certain that coil you've picked up was intended for a car with a different polarity system from yours, you can still use it, and get a good spark, provided you reverse the low tension terminals at the coil.

You might come across, or might have, what Lucas called an inhibited coil. On these, one low tension terminal has a male Lucar push-on terminal and the other has a female Lucar terminal, and the wiring loom has the appropriate mating terminals on the coil leads. Usually, the male terminal on the coil is the + one and the female terminal is the – one. Once again we say usually because, though we've always found that to be the case, it doesn't mean that there aren't exceptions, so you still need to know the make and polarity of the car for which it was made.

We hope we haven't made confusion even more confused. A coil will still work if you connect it the wrong way round, but you won't get so good a spark at the plugs. If a car's been running for a long time with the coil connected the wrong way round, you can often get an indication of this by looking at the rotor arm and the electrodes inside the distributor cap. If the coil is connected the wrong way round, to give a positive spark at the plugs, metal is transferred from the rotor arm to the cap studs so the rotor arm wears away and gets a hollow in it. The studs get bumps or pips. If the coil is connected the proper way round, metal is transferred from the studs to the rotor arm so the studs wear away and get hollows, and rotor arm gets a bump. You might think this is a disadvantage because distributor caps are more expensive than rotor arms, until you remember that, on a four-cylinder engine, the distributor cap studs get a quarter of the wear that the rotor arm gets. On a six-cylinder engine they get only a sixth.

There's one last point to watch out for if you're buying a second-hand or new-old-stock coil. Some cars, many Fords in particular, had a ballasted ignition circuit. On this circuit, the coil is designed to run at lower than battery voltage, usually at around 9 volts to 10 volts. A ballast resistor is connected between the ignition switch and the low tension terminal of the coil to reduce the voltage. Sometimes this is a separate resistor wound on a porcelain block, and sometimes it is a resistive lead. When you operate the starter, the ballast resistor is by-passed so that you get full battery voltage at the coil. This means that in cold conditions, when the battery isn't feeling at its best, and the heavy drain of a starter cranking a cold engine drops the battery voltage, the coil still gets its proper voltage to give a good spark. When the engine's hot, the coil is over-run, but as this is only for a few seconds, it doesn't hurt it. However, if you use a coil from a ballasted system on a car that gives full battery voltage to the

coil all the time, the coil will overheat and its life will be shortened. So, if you find your coil's getting too hot to touch, it may be that you're using a coil from a ballasted system on one that hasn't got a ballast resistor in the circuit.

There's nothing you can do to restore a coil that's dead or on its way out, and to check whether or not a coil is in perfect condition requires a test bench with an adjustable spark gap under pressure. You can, however, get a very good idea of a coil's condition by measuring the resistance of its windings. Set your meter to ohms, and measure the resistance of the primary circuit, between the two low tension terminals. It should be quite low, about 0.7 ohms to 0.9 ohms. If you get a reading much higher than this, the coil might still work but its recuperation time will be longer and it will probably cut out at high revs. If the primary windings check out OK, check the resistance of the secondary circuit between the HT terminal in the centre tower and one of the low tension terminals, it doesn't matter which. Here, you should get a reading between 4,500 ohms and 7,000 ohms. That's a pretty wide tolerance, and with readings outside these figures the coil might still work, but it's on its way out.

Now we get to the distributor itself. We've chosen two for illustration, Lucas and Motorcraft, because these are the most numerous on British classic cars, but other makes are very similar to overhaul.

Start with the distributor cap, too often neglected. It's a tribute to the insulating properties of the plastic used for the cap that most of them put up with 30 or more years of having 30,000 volts pushed through them. However, there comes a time when, usually from lack of cleaning, they develop tracking, a path of carbon from one electrode to another which causes shorting out and cross firing. When this happens, it isn't long before

the carbon track becomes a burnt path, then a crack, and the cap's reached the end of its life.

There used to be compounds on the market back in the 1950s and 1960s that claimed that you could repair a badly tracking cap by making a Vee groove along the tracking path and applying the compound. Magic compounds such as this are trotted out as new from time to time, often claiming to be developed from space-age technology. Forget them. Along with H_2O bombs, gefarators (extra air valves in the inlet manifold), spark 'intensifiers' to fit into HT leads, economy devices to fit between the carburettor and the manifold, and the rest of these gadgets from which optimistic inventors hoped to make a fortune, they died away and the survivors belong, in our opinion, in a motoring museum. They all had an element of sound theory, often distorted or exaggerated, but if they were any good they would have been taken up by car or component manufacturers and built-in.

If you catch the tracking inside a cap early enough it's sometimes possible to get rid of it by polishing it out with something like Duraglit wadding, but don't build your hopes too high. The best cure is to look for a cap in better condition.

Other ailments, apart from physical damage, with which distributor caps become afflicted are corrosion inside the towers and burning of the electrode studs inside. Corrosion inside the towers can usually be cleaned out with fine emery cloth and patience, and the electrode studs can also be cleaned with emery, but if they have developed really deep pitting it's best to look for a cap in better condition.

Similarly, the brass part of rotor arms can be cleaned up, but many people forget that rotor arms too can develop tracking or, something much more difficult to spot, leakage when part of the HT spark leaks down from the brass part through the plastic to the distributor cam. The result is a very weak spark and poor running, or no spark at all. You can't see anything wrong with a leaky rotor arm, and it needs a very high voltage test bench to check it properly, but you can check if it's leaking badly. Put the rotor arm on the distributor, take the HT lead out of the distributor cap central tower, the lead from the coil, switch the ignition on and keep flicking the points open as you bring the HT lead down to the brass part of the rotor arm. It's best to hold the lead in an insulated pair of pliers for this test to avoid getting a jolt up your arm. If the rotor arm is leaking, you'll get a spark from the end of the HT lead across to the brass part of the rotor arm. If you can bring the lead right down to touching without getting a spark, the arm's probably OK.

There are two bushes for the drive shaft on most distributors, one at the drive end and one at the cam end, and there's also a thrust washer, usually at the drive end, to control the end play of the shaft. On the type of distributor which has an offset dog drive, it's unusual to find any serious wear in the bush at the drive shaft end because there's no side thrust on the shaft. You sometimes do find wear on the drive end bush on the type of distributor which is driven directly off the camshaft by a skew gear because of the separating force of the gears. When two gears are running in mesh, because of the shape of the gear teeth there is a force, known as the separating force, trying to push the gears apart, and this causes a side thrust on the drive end bush. However, the wear in the bush has to be pretty serious before it affects the running of the engine. You probably wouldn't notice much wrong till you got to a worst-case scenario where the wear would allow the gears to come so far out of mesh that they would wear rapidly to the point where one or more teeth were too worn to mesh,

but we've never come across a bush as badly worn as this.

Even so, you wouldn't want to put a distributor with a badly worn drive end bush, and probably a worn skew gear as well, into a rebuilt engine with a new camshaft.

Wear in the bush at the cam end of the drive shaft can directly affect the running of the engine because, as the shaft wobbles, the points gap changes, so you can't set it accurately, and the ignition timing will vary as the shaft wobbles. As a test, set the points gap accurately to any convenient setting, say 0.010in. Then try the gap on all the

lobes of the cam, pushing the cam sideways to see if the gap varies. If it varies by less than 0.001in, or even 0.002in, overall, you haven't got a lot to worry about. If the points gap varies much more than that, you won't get the best out of your engine.

End-float on the shaft? You measure this at the drive end, and it should be about 0.002in on a new distributor. It won't be less than this, and in practice it isn't all that critical. The distributor will be quite happy with up to 0.005in or even 0.008in end-float.

Many older manuals gave instructions on how to renew worn

Fig. 2.1. The internals of a Lucas distributor.

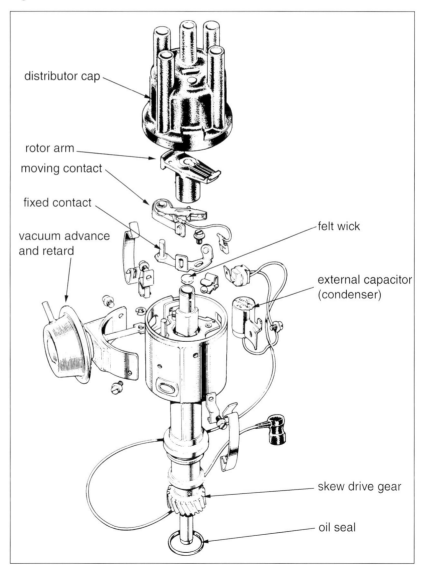

Fig. 2.2. A very popular distributor from the classic era is the Lucas 25D.

Fig. 2.3. Check inside the distributor cap for tracking, burnt studs and a worn carbon brush.

drive shaft bushes, which would still be valid if you could get new bushes. Unfortunately, they just aren't available. We've tried all the specialists we could think of, and they all gave the same answer.

It's possible, if you know someone with an accurate small lathe, to have new bronze bushes made to a light press fit, and ream them out afterwards, but you can't machine and ream oil impregnated bushes without closing up the pores of the metal so they would no longer be self-lubricating and would have a relatively shorter life. Good second-hand, new-old-stock and, in some cases, newly-made 'pattern' distributors for classic cars aren't all that hard to find, at least not at the moment, so if the bushes on your distributor are worn we'd advise getting one on which they're less worn. Assuming that you're happy with the bushes, it's time to get on with overhaul.

Lucas distributors

On a Lucas distributor body you should find an identification code. The ones most often found on classic cars are the 25, 23 and 22 series. Possibly the most numerous are the 25D models, 25D4 for four-cylinder engines and 25D6 for six cylinders. They all have centrifugal advance and retard, and may have horizontal or top outlet caps.

Fig. 2.4. Check also inside the towers for corrosion. This cap would be rejected because of its chipped centre tower.

Fig. 2.5. Check the rotor arm for burning and for tracking and leakage.

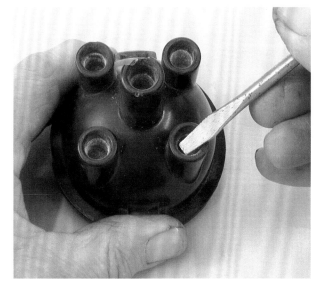

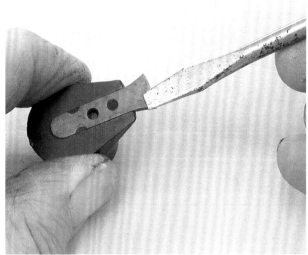

The 25D models also have built-in vacuum advance and retard units with what Lucas called micrometer adjustment. As you turn the knurled knob you feel a series of clicks, and there is an engraved scale on the unit just behind the diaphragm. It gives very fine adjustment, but we haven't found the divisions of the scale to correspond very closely with degrees of advance measured at the crankshaft. Vacuum advance and retard is connected to the baseplate on which the contact breaker points are mounted, and achieves advance or retard by turning this baseplate relative to the distributor cam.

The 22D bodies are basically the same as the 25D but are longer and both four- and six-cylinder models have sintered iron drive shaft bushes. They were available with or without a vacuum advance and retard unit.

23D distributors are again very similar but were not fitted with vacuum advance and retard, only centrifugal advance. All the ones we've come across have sintered bronze shaft bushes.

If you're replacing a vacuum advance and retard unit you need to check the characteristics. These are given by a series of numbers engraved on the nose of the unit where the vacuum pipe fits. There will be three numbers, such as 4 14 8, sometimes spaced out and sometimes separated by slashes, followed by a six or seven figure part number engraved in smaller numbers. The ones you're interested in are the larger three. The first gives the vacuum, in inches of mercury, at which the unit starts to work. The second gives the vacuum again in inches of mercury at which full advance occurs. The third number gives the maximum advance the unit will give in degrees. These are degrees of crankshaft rotation, not distributor shaft rotation.

These figures were specified by the engine maker, and though an engine will run very well with slightly different vacuum advance and retard characteristics, it won't run quite as the maker intended. You won't notice any difference at anything much over half throttle because the vacuum in the inlet manifold drops, and the advance and retard unit does very little work. It's designed to give you extra advance at high engine revs when you're cruising with the throttle only partly open. The right amount of extra advance here can give you more power and better fuel economy. There's not much to go wrong with a vacuum advance and retard unit except, possibly, a punctured diaphragm, though we've found only a couple in many years. It's easy enough to check. When you've got the unit off, try sucking or blowing on the end where the pipe fits. If you can suck air through the diaphragm, it's punctured. If you can't, it isn't.

Always renew the contact breaker points on an overhaul, if you can find a new set which fit. In most cases you will be able to because of a fortunate state of affairs which came about during what we now call the classic era. Before the 1939–45 war, and for some years after it, all distributors had two separate points – a fixed point and a moving point. Then Lucas, and other makers of distributors, introduced points sets, with both points mounted on a baseplate all ready to drop into the distributor. To save carrying on making the old separate points as spares, the new points sets were made interchangeable with the old separate points.

To save making a vast range of points sets, they were cleverly designed so that a relatively small range suited a wide range of distributors. Makers of pattern-parts soon followed suit, and things stayed like that, with literally millions of these points sets being made till the widespread use of electronic ignition killed off contact breaker points on new cars. Even then, the market for contact breaker points for older cars was vast, and still is pretty large, so the chances are that your local parts factor or accessory shop will either have a set in stock to suit or can get them for you. The assistant might look a bit blank when you ask for points for a 1966 Ausfordmobile, but he, or the shop's supplying wholesaler, should be able to look in an 'equivalents' book to find the part number of a set of points that will suit.

If you draw a blank locally, try one of the classic car electrical specialists such as Cox Auto Electrical (01827 712097) or T&J Enterprises (0121 777 3386). In the unlikely event that you still draw a blank, try the one-make car club for your car. If even they don't know of a source of supply, you're running a pretty rare animal, but just in case it does happen and you're stuck with a burnt pair of separate points, we'll run through restoring them.

Distributor contact breaker points burn with a 'pip and crater' action, a pip on one point and a crater on the other. This is because of the normal transference of metal from one point to the other during working. Normally, the pip is on the positive point and the crater is on the negative point. This is accelerated if the capacitor (or condenser, if you like to use the old term) is open-circuit or near the end of its life, but we'll come to that in a moment.

The best, and easiest, way to clean and dress a pair of points is on a carpenter's oil stone. Use plenty of thin oil, and rub the face of the point back and forth, quite slowly, along the full length of the stone. Use the side of the stone so you don't wear a groove in the face and make it useless for sharpening chisels and plane blades, and try to keep the face of the point absolutely square on the stone. On the point with a pip, carry on till the pip has disappeared and you're left with just a small circular dirty mark where it was. There's no need to carry on stoning till the surface is absolutely clean all over or it won't take many cleanings to wear through the hard point facing. If you look at the side of a point you'll see that there's a thin hard facing fused to the main, softer, body of the point.

This applies even more to the point which has the crater. All you need to do is stone until the face of the point is clean except for the crater. There's no need to stone the crater right out, and it's not advisable because they can go quite deep. So long as you've got each point with a good, flat clean area to make and break contact, the points will work well.

Be careful not to bend or kink the long leaf spring on the moving point, and check that the arm is free to swivel on the post on the baseplate. On modern points sets, the hole in the insulated plastic arm has a thin metal bush in it, but on older separate points the hole was bored straight in the insulated arm, which was made of fibre rather than modern plastic. You're unlikely to find the hole worn, but you might find that the post on which it swivels is caked with old dried grease which stops the point swivelling easily. Also, the fibre may have swollen and become tight on the post. If so, ease it out very gently with a fine round file till it's a nice easy fit without wobbling.

There are two wires connected to the end of the points leaf spring, one going to the capacitor, and one going to the connection which takes the low-tension lead from the coil. The capacitor is held to the baseplate by a single screw, and as there's no easy way to check its condition, we advise replacing it on an overhaul. Like points, you shouldn't have much difficulty finding one to fit. Don't worry too much if you can't find a capacitor exactly like the old one. The capacitance isn't all that critical, and almost any distributor capacitor will be OK so long as it fits on the baseplate without rubbing the side of the body or the cam. Make sure the insulation on

the wire that goes to the low-tension terminal isn't chafed. If this shorts to earth you won't get a spark.

On some very old Lucas distributors you may find that the capacitor is soldered to the base plate via a strap which comes halfway over the capacitor. Lucas used to recommend that, if you needed to replace the capacitor, you took the baseplate off, unsoldered the old one using a very small flame, and soldered the new one in position. The service notes warned that you should use only just sufficient heat to melt the solder on the new capacitor so as not to damage it. You can try doing this if you like, but as almost all replacement capacitors have a lug with a hole to take a screw, we prefer to cut the old strap off the baseplate, drill and tap a hole and fix the new capacitor with a screw, just like the later ones. Alternatively, if you don't fancy drilling and tapping the baseplate, you can mount the new capacitor externally with the flying lead going to the low tension supply terminal and the body of the capacitor earthed to the body of the distributor.

Now you can unhook the vacuum advance connection, if one's fitted, undo two screws and lift off the baseplate. If you've got vacuum advance and retard, the baseplate will be in two parts and there will be an earthing wire riveted to the top part and running to one of the baseplate screws. The top part of the baseplate swivels on the bottom part, and quite often it doesn't swivel easily because of dried-out grease between the two parts. They need to come apart for cleaning. If you turn the thing over, you'll see that there's a curved slot with a larger hole at one end. Turn the top part till the peg is level with the hole, then the top part of the plate will lift upwards and can be pushed off the small leaf spring which holds it at the other side.

To take the vacuum advance capsule off, take off the tiny circlip

by the end of the thumb wheel and unscrew the thumb wheel right off. Then the capsule pulls out of the body.

Inside the body of the distributor you'll see the centrifugal weights which are controlled by a pair of short coil springs. The two springs might be identical, giving what's usually known as equal spring advance, or one may be stronger than the other, giving what's known as differential spring advance. If so, one spring will have an elongated loop at one end which is loose on its post. With equal spring advance you get an even advance curve, but with differential spring advance, the initial advance is faster because only one spring is restraining the weights. As the speed rises and the weights move outwards, the second spring also comes into operation to control the advance at higher revs. The elongated hook on the second spring mustn't be tight on its post or this will lead to sluggish initial acceleration because the weight can't start to move soon enough.

If you find that one of the springs is broken you'll probably also find a mark round the inside of the distributor body where the uncontrolled weight has been flying out and hitting it. If so, that's the cause of the high-pitched chattering noise you heard when you revved the engine up.

The weights are carried on the cam assembly which should be free to turn on the drive shaft. If you hold the drive end of the shaft, and put the rotor arm on to get a better grip for your fingers, you should be able to turn the cam assembly anti-clockwise against the springs. When you let it go, it should fly back smartly as the springs pull the weights in. Sometimes, if the distributor's been idle for years, the cam assembly can get quite sticky on the drive shaft. We've even found them seized up solid. Even if it seems free, it does no harm to take things apart for cleaning and lubricating. It also makes it easier to unhook and replace the springs if the cam assembly is out of the distributor body.

Undo the screw in the centre where the rotor arm fits and pull the cam assembly off the drive shaft. There should be a small felt pad over the top of the screw head which should have received a couple of drops of oil every 6,000 or so miles. In many cases, this pad is missing, or it hasn't received any oil for years, which is why the cam assembly sticks or seizes on the drive shaft. If you have to make up a new felt pad, don't make it too thick or the rotor arm won't seat properly.

You'll find a number and a degree sign stamped on the cam assembly, something like 14°. This indicates the maximum advance that the weights will give. If you're looking for a second-hand distributor, or making one up from several, then for an engine in standard tune, make sure this number, as well as the ones on the vacuum advance capsule, are the same as the original ones on your car.

If you've tuned the engine for more power, with things like a ported head, a better flowing exhaust manifold and pipe, and a free-flow air filter, you might like to experiment with cam assemblies and vacuum advance capsules giving a greater amount of advance, springs of different strengths to control the rate of advance at higher revs, or even dispense with the vacuum advance altogether and fit a one-piece baseplate (if you do, remember to blank off the vacuum pipe take-off on the inlet manifold). Most Lucas competition distributors didn't have vacuum advance, they relied on mechanical advance with differential springs governing quite a high amount of total advance.

There shouldn't be any need to take the drive shaft out of the distributor body. If the bushes are so badly worn that it wobbles, look for another distributor. If, however, you want to take it out for some reason, it's held by a taper pin through the drive dog or drive gear. This pin is usually very tight. If you've got an offset drive dog, then before you knock out the pin, check the relationship between the drive shaft and the drive dog. Sometimes you'll find a scribed line across the body and the dog but, if not, put the rotor arm on and look at the distributor from the drive end. In most cases you'll find that the larger 'D' of the offset drive is to the right when the tip of the rotor arm is pointing upwards. Make sure you put things back in the same relationship.

You aren't likely to find either of the spring clips that hold the cap broken but, if you should, they're easy enough to replace. They're held between two lugs on the body by a small rivet. The old clip will spring off the rivet with the help of a screwdriver, and you can just clip the new clip in place.

With all the mechanical parts of the distributor checked and overhauled, remember to check the O-ring where the body fits into the engine block. If it's worn or chewed you'll get an oil leak.

Normally, older classic Lucas distributors should have the points set at 0.012in gap, but in the 1950s Lucas introduced a high-lift cam for which the gap should be set to between 0.014in and 0.016in. You can recognise the cam because it's got sharper corners than a standard cam. You can also check by the number of the distributor. From number 40333A onwards and 40251E onwards, Lucas distributors all had high-lift cams.

Fig. 2.6. If the advance and retard weights are not seized, you should be able to turn the rotor arm anti-clockwise against the springs. Check also for sideways play in the top bearing.

Fig. 2.7. The end-float on the shaft should be between 0.002in and 0.008in, but it isn't all that critical.

Fig. 2.8. You should find the model type number moulded in the top face of the body.

Fig. 2.9. The vacuum advance and retard characteristics are engraved on the collar where the vacuum pipe fits.

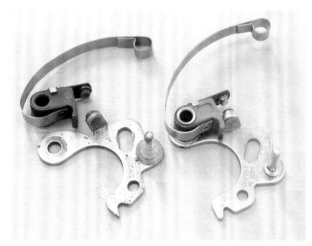

Fig. 2.10. Two types of Lucas points, the early two-piece type (left), and the later one-piece quick-fit type.

Fig. 2.12. With the two-piece type points, check that the fibre cam is free to turn easily on its pivot peg.

Fig. 2.11. Check the points for craters and pips. You can stone them out, but it's usually easier to fit a new set of the later quick-fit type.

Fig. 2.13. Before you can take the vacuum advance and retard unit off, you have to unhook its spring from a peg on the baseplate.

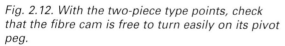

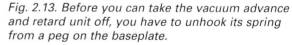

Fig. 2.14. This distributor was giving intermittent misfiring because the earthing strap had broken off.

Fig. 2.15. The two-piece baseplate separated.

Fig. 2.16. The separate components of the vacuum advance and retard unit.

Fig. 2.18. If you are building a distributor from parts, make sure you get the correct advance characteristics by noting the number engraved on the centre piece of the advance and retard mechanism.

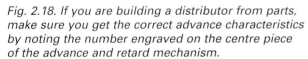

Fig. 2.17. Note the unequal strength springs on the mechanical advance and retard unit.

Fig. 2.19. Don't forget to check the condition of the O-ring oil seal.

Ford Motorcraft distributors

Ford's Motorcraft distributor works on the same principle as Lucas distributors but differs in most details – partly, we assume, to overcome patents and partly to make it cheaper to produce; not that it seems any the worse for that. The spring clips which hold the cap, for example, are held to the body by split pins instead of rivets.

The quick-fit points set is simplicity itself to replace. Two leads, one to the capacitor and one to the low-tension connection come off after you loosen a screw, and two more screws hold the points set to the baseplate.

With the points and capacitor off, you'll see two circlips, one large and one small, on pegs through the top part of the two-piece baseplate. You can leave the

larger one in place for the moment, but you have to remove the small one because it holds the link to the vacuum advance unit. With this disconnected, the baseplate lifts off after you take out two more screws. You shouldn't be able to put it back 180° out because of the cut-out in the body to take the low-tension connector. The vacuum advance unit comes off after you undo two screws. It will have a number stamped on the arm which goes inside the distributor body, and if you are replacing it, get one with the same number.

The top part of the baseplate assembly pivots on the peg with the large circlip, and has an elongated central hole which allows the vacuum advance to pull it round relative to the cam. When you take the circlip off, watch out for the two washers underneath, one plain and one like a curved

spring. If you turn the assembly over, you'll see that there's a headed peg in the movable plate which runs in an elongated slot in the fixed plate. The slot ends in a round hole so that when you turn the movable plate far enough, the head will pass through the hole and the two plates can be separated.

Watch out for the very light gauge coil spring over the pivot peg between the two plates. Also watch out for three small plastic bearing buttons on the underside of the movable plate, as they're easily lost if they pop out either now or when you're cleaning the plates.

Looking down into the body of the distributor, you'll see that the two springs for the advance and retard weights are different strengths, a lighter one with spaces between the coils and a stronger one with the coils close-wound. If you hold the skew gear at the drive end and turn the cam clockwise, the first part of the movement to overcome the lighter spring is quite easy, but the last part when the stronger spring comes into operation is much stiffer. This is Ford's version of differential advance. The springs hook on to pegs in the cam plate and on to turned-up lugs at their other ends.

These lugs are quite soft steel and can be bent slightly in or out to alter the rate at which the springs govern the advance. They can be reached through holes in the baseplate with a stout screwdriver to do this, and they are a prime target for saloon-bar pundits whose book knowledge is far greater than their practical knowledge and experience. They are often altered by professional tuners when an engine has been uprated, but don't experiment with bending them unless you have test equipment connected to the engine to tell you the rate of advance against rpm, and the knowledge to know what you're trying to do.

You'll also see that the cam plate has two slots in it These are marked to identify them, usually markings such as 10R and 15R.

Fig. 2.20. Ford's Motorcraft distributor is similar to the Lucas, but with differences aimed at easier mass-production assembly.

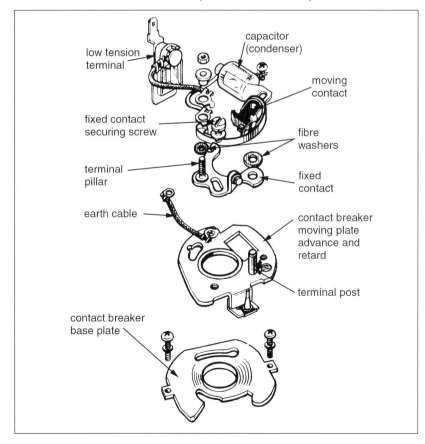

low tension terminal

capacitor (condenser)

moving contact

fixed contact securing screw

fibre washers

terminal pillar

fixed contact

earth cable

contact breaker moving plate advance and retard

terminal post

contact breaker base plate

Fig. 2.21. This long-shaft Motorcraft distributor is from a Ford Pinto engine. Others are similar but with shorter shafts.

Fig. 2.22. Before you can remove the points baseplate you have to take off the smaller of the two circlips, the one which holds the vacuum advance and retard.

One of these slots will engage over a peg which has a nylon guide on it. This peg limits the travel. If you need to strip the distributor further, make a note of which slot engages with the peg, and whether the lighter or stronger spring is fitted to that side of the cam plate. On the distributor we stripped to photograph, the slot marked 15R engaged with the peg, and the stronger spring was on this side.

If you need to take the cam plate out because it's sticky or seized on the drive shaft, first unhook the springs and take off the circlip and nylon guide over the slot in the cam plate. Unlike Lucas distributors, which have a screw through the top of the cam plate where the rotor fits, Ford uses a wire circlip with the ends turned vertically. There's a special Ford tool, like a pair of reverse-action pliers with vertical slots in the sides, which makes taking this off and putting it back very simple, but it can be done with ordinary reverse-action circlip pliers, though it isn't quite so easy.

You shouldn't need to take the main drive shaft out, but if for any reason you do, the skew gear is held by a roll pin, not a taper peg as on Lucas distributors. As with Lucas distributors, check the oil seal O-ring where the body fits into the engine block. Lubrication is the same as with Lucas distributors.

Fig. 2.23. The Ford version of quick-fit points.

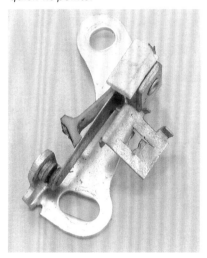

Fig. 2.24. The Motorcraft advance and retard unit has its characteristics stamped on the operating arm.

Fig. 2.25. The Motorcraft distributor has unequal strength springs, and each advance weight is stamped to match the strength of its spring.

Chapter 3

Dynamos

Back in the early to mid-1930s, the output of many dynamos was controlled by a movable third brush inside the dynamo and a so-called 'full-charge' and 'half-charge' resistor usually incorporated in the dashboard lighting switch. At best this was a crude form of control, and in the later 1930s gave way to the two-brush dynamo which we deal with here. Two-brush dynamos have a regulator control and we cover this in the next chapter.

As with most of the electrical equipment in this book, we deal in detail with Lucas products since these were fitted to the vast majority of British classics. Other makes are very similar in principle and their overhaul is much the same.

Before you start stripping down a dynamo to cure a low or non-existent charge it's as well to make sure that the fault is actually with the dynamo. Quite a few cases of 'faulty' dynamos turn out to be a loose or slipping drive belt, corroded or loose connections at the battery or a battery earthing strap that isn't making good earth contact, or a fault in the regulator control box.

If you still suspect the dynamo there are a few simple checks you can make with your meter. Remove the two cables from the dynamo and tuck them well out of the way. They're likely to be labelled D and F and should have different size connectors, but make sure you know which cable goes where, just in case. Now bridge together the two terminals on the dynamo with a short length of bare wire and two small crocodile clips. Set your meter to DC volts and connect it between this wire bridge and chassis earth, and start the engine.

Rev it gently but keep the revs down because the dynamo is running almost without load. Don't let the reading go above 20 volts. At 20 volts or just under, the needle of the meter, or the figures if it's a digital meter, should remain steady or almost steady. If you get no voltage reading at all, a very low voltage reading or one that fluctuates wildly, the dynamo needs looking at.

If this test looks OK, it will show that the dynamo is charging but, because you bridged the D and F terminals, it won't tell you if there is an internal short between the armature and field circuits. The insulated brush in a two-brush dynamo is connected to the D terminal, and the other brush is connected to the body of the dynamo, and through that to chassis earth. If you remove your wire bridge, the field coils aren't in

Fig. 3.1. A typical Lucas dynamo from the classic era.

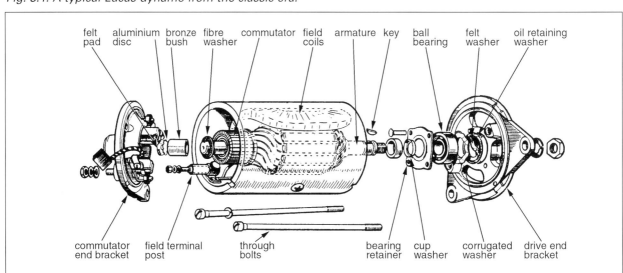

felt pad   aluminium disc   bronze bush   fibre washer   commutator   field coils   armature   key   ball bearing   felt washer   oil retaining washer

commutator end bracket   field terminal post   through bolts   bearing retainer   cup washer   corrugated washer   drive end bracket

circuit. Keep the voltmeter connected between the D terminal and earth, and restart the engine. If when you gently increase engine speed the voltmeter rises to between 1.5 volts and 2 volts, and remains steady, it shows that the armature windings are probably OK and that the brushes are making reasonable contact with the commutator. If the reading flickers about, but doesn't increase with engine speed, it indicates poor contact between the brushes and the commutator. If, however, the voltage increases with engine speed, as it did in the first test, then there's probably an internal short between the D and F terminals.

For a final check you need to borrow a separate ammeter. Keep the voltmeter connected between the D terminal and earth, and connect an ammeter between the D and F terminals. Start the engine again and increase its speed till the voltmeter reads close to 12 volts, nominal battery voltage. The ammeter shouldn't read more than about 2 amps. If it reads much higher, or if its reading jumps and flickers, it indicates an internal short. A steady high amp reading indicates a permanent short somewhere, but a flickering

reading up and down may be caused by intermittent shorting through accumulated carbon dust.

These tests presuppose that the dynamo is on the car and that the engine will run. If you're offered a second-hand dynamo, or you're restoring a non-running car, you can still do a rough and ready check on the dynamo off the car. Two-brush DC generators, or dynamos, will also function as an electric motor, albeit a rather inefficient one from a power point of view. If you connect a battery directly across the D and F terminals, the armature should spin over. If the dynamo's on the ground, keep your foot on it to stop it walking across the floor, and keep your fingers well out of the way of the pulley. If the armature spins quite happily, there's an excellent chance that with cleaning and overhaul it will give good service. If it refuses to spin, it may be just poor contact between the brushes and the armature, but if it smokes and smells, there's a serious internal short.

These tests will show whether the dynamo is basically sound, but it's still wise to take it apart to clean the inside and check the brushes and commutator. Dynamos come apart quite easily. The only part of

the job that usually proves awkward is holding the pulley while you undo its nut. The easiest and simplest way to do this is to run an old fan belt round the pulley and clamp this in the vice so it acts as a strap spanner. This will grip the pulley tight enough to undo even the most stubborn nut.

With the nut off, the pulley will sometimes tap off the shaft, though in some tight cases you may need to use a puller. The pulley is located on the shaft by a half-moon Woodruff key which has to come out before the shaft will pass through the end bearing. Some people make such a meal of taking out a Woodruff key, but nothing could be simpler. Hold an old screwdriver or a blunt cold chisel against one end and give it a tap. Most times it will just pop up to an upright position but sometimes it jumps clean out of its slot, so a rag over it to stop it flying across the garage or into your face is a good precaution.

The rest of the dynamo comes apart after you take the nuts and washers off the field terminal, the smaller of the two, and undo the long through-bolts. If your dynamo has inspection holes in it, slide the cover off and lift the carbon

Fig. 3.2. Use an old fan belt in the vice as a strap spanner to hold the belt pulley while you undo the nut.

Fig. 3.3. You may have a Lucar push-on terminal for the field connection, as here, or you may have a threaded post and nut.

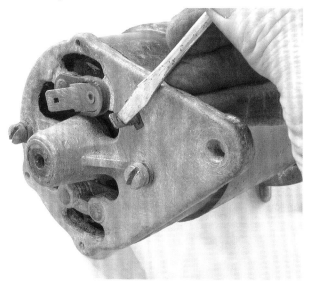

Fig. 3.4. The long through-bolts which hold the dynamo together will probably be very tight.

Fig. 3.5. This dynamo had been standing a long time, and the end-plate and brushes looked a mess. However, they all came free, and there was very little wear.

brushes out of the way before you pull the dynamo apart. Use a piece of stiff wire with a hook on the end to lift the springs, pull the brush up till it stands proud of the holder and wedge it there by putting the spring alongside it. If your dynamo hasn't got windows in it, lifting the brushes clear of the commutator by working through the holes in the end plate is very fiddly. It's easier to let them drop inwards as you pull the end plate off. Take care of any shim washers or spacers when you pull the plates apart, and make a note of where they fit. Most dynamos have a ball bearing at the

drive end to cope with the side pull of the fan belt, and a plain bronze bearing at the commutator end. If these are in good condition there's no need to disturb them, but if the ball bearing feels gritty or sloppy when you turn the end plate, or if the bronze bush wobbles on the shaft, they need replacing.

Some drive-end ball races just press out of the end plate, but with most you have a cover plate which is held either by rivets or by a circlip. The circlip doesn't have ears that you can grip with a pair of circlip pliers, it's just a plain spring ring and you have to ease it round

until one end is level with a recess in the housing and then lever it out with a screwdriver. Be careful when you do this, keep your face out of the way and preferably wear eye protectors. Quite often the circlip will come free with a rush and jump upwards. Under the plate will be a number of washers, usually a corrugated washer, a felt washer and an oil retaining washer. Take note of the order in which they fit.

Some short pieces of tubing and a heavy vice are very useful for

Fig. 3.6. The resistance check on the field windings was within recommended limits.

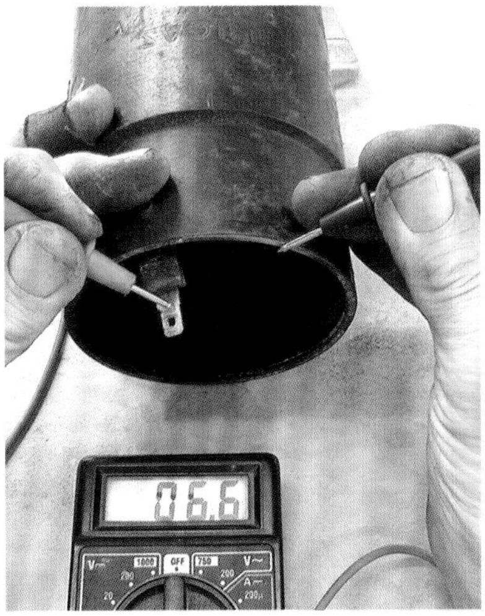

Fig. 3.7. Wedge the spring alongside the brush to hold it out when you replace the end-plate. Then free the spring with a wire hook.

Fig. 3.8. The commutator cleaned up reasonably well, but could do with just a light skim in the lathe.

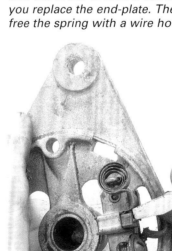

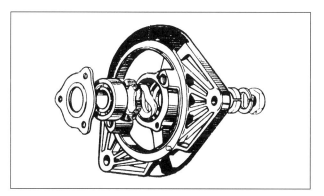

Fig. 3.9. Sometimes the drive-end bearing retainer is held by rivets.

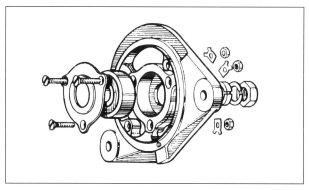

Fig. 3.10. Sometimes the retainer is held by bolts and nuts. Use this method if you have to drill out rivets to renew a bearing.

pressing out the old ball race and pressing in the new one. A few old sockets come in handy for this sort of job. The old worn ball bearing can be pressed out by its centre race, but pressing the new one in like this could damage it, so use a piece of tube or a socket that fits the outer race. Pack the new bearing with high-melting-point grease before you press it in, and use new rivets, steel not aluminium, or bolts and nuts, when you replace the cover plate.

If the bronze bush at the commutator end needs renewing, there are special tools which will pull it out of its blind housing but it isn't worth buying one for overhauling just one or two dynamos. The cheaper way is to find a tap which will screw into the bush (usually 5/8in on Lucas dynamos), screw this in and use it to pull the old bush out.

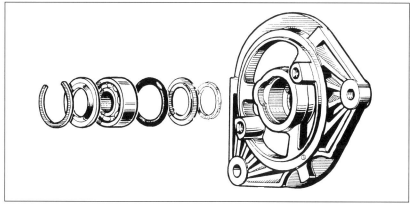

Fig. 3.11. A third variation is where the retainer is held by a circlip.

The new bush should be soaked in engine oil for 24 hours, but if you've forgotten to do this, and you're in a hurry, stand it in a tin of oil in a bath of boiling water for a couple of hours. If you press it in dry it will wear within six months or so. Under the old bush there will be a washer or washers and a felt lubricating pad. You should get a new pad when you buy a new bush. Put enough oil on it to make it wet, but not so much that it runs out all over the armature.

Short circuits on the turns of the armature can't be checked adequately without an instrument known as a 'growler', which you seldom see outside electrical repair workshops, but it's a comparatively rare fault and you need suspect it only if the armature windings look black and burnt. If two adjacent segments of the commutator are burnt, often with a flattened look, it's a sign of an open circuit, or break, somewhere in the windings. In either case, there's nothing you can do at home about it and you need another armature or dynamo.

The commutator will probably be black, or at least badly discoloured. Wipe it over first with a rag dipped in petrol and then clean it with a strip of fine glasspaper. Use glasspaper rather than emery or wet and dry rubbing paper because these two have carborundum in the grit. Carborundum is a conductor, and the grit can bed into the separators between the segments and short them out. You might have a dynamo which has seen long service and the brushes have worn grooves in the commutator. Provided they're not too deep, and you know someone with a lathe, the commutator can be refaced with a light skim using a sharp lathe tool, but don't take it down too far. If you do, then when the carbon brushes wear the coil springs will bind on the housings and won't press the brushes down properly against the commutator.

The insulating separators between the copper segments should be undercut about 1/16in with a hacksaw blade. Snap the blade off and wind a few turns of insulating tape round it to make a handle. If necessary, grind down the sides of the blade slightly to the width of the insulators. Try to make the undercuts square, not vee-shaped, and take off any burrs afterwards with fine glasspaper.

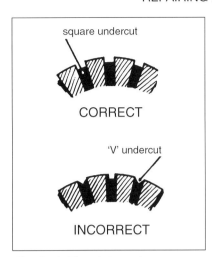

Fig. 3.12. The right and wrong ways to undercut a dynamo commutator.

The inside of the dynamo body, or yoke as it should be called, will no doubt be smothered in black dust from the old carbon brushes. This is a conductor, so clean it out with a brush – an old toothbrush is quite good for this. You'll also find a sheet of fairly thick insulating paper which stops the junction between the field coils shorting out on the inside of the yoke. Check that this is in good condition. If it isn't, get some from your nearest Lucas agent or specialist auto-electrical repairer to replace or supplement it. Don't be tempted to use ordinary card or plastic sheet. Ordinary card won't insulate properly and plastic sheet will probably melt when the dynamo gets warm.

You can test the field coils for shorting, or a break in the windings, with your meter set to ohms. Take a reading between the field terminal and a clean part of the yoke. You should get a reading between 6 ohms and 6.8 ohms. If you get an infinity reading, or no reading at all, there's a break somewhere in the field windings. If the meter gives a reading of 5 ohms or lower it means the field insulation is breaking down.

In either case, find another yoke or another dynamo. Replacing or re-insulating field coils isn't a job we would recommend you do at home. The pole pieces which hold the field windings are held to the yoke by countersunk screws which are done up to a very high torque using a power driver or a wheel screwdriver. We've seen it suggested that you can get the screws undone using an impact driver. You might, but that's only part of the problem. Even if you succeeded in re-insulating the windings with tape and shellac, they have to be held tight inside the yoke with a pole-piece expander while the screws are tightened. If they aren't tightened dead true, there's a danger of the armature rubbing on the windings, and they won't last long if this happens.

Lucas recommends that the carbon brushes are replaced if they have worn down to 9/32in long, but we think that's too short for a reasonable further life, particularly with a commutator that's been refaced. We would renew brushes that have worn down much below half an inch.

The brushes are held by screws and are easy to replace but, before you screw new ones in position, check that they're free to slide in their holders. We've found some 'pattern' brushes to be a little on the tight side. If you find this, rub the brush down slightly by sliding it along a fine flat file or a piece of emery cloth. Some books say you should bed new brushes in by wrapping glasspaper round the commutator, but this is an awkward and fiddling business and we've never had any problems letting new brushes bed in by themselves.

The inner race of the ball bearing at the drive end of the dynamo is a tight fit on the armature shaft. Don't try supporting the end plate and tapping the armature through the bearing or there's a likelihood that you'll crack the end plate. Support the armature or get someone to hold it upright for you and use a piece of tubing against the inner race of the bearing to drive the end plate down.

Before you start the rest of the assembly, wedge the carbon brushes in their holders by putting the springs alongside them. When the yoke and end plates are assembled you can release the brushes either through the inspection windows in the yoke or, with a windowless yoke, by using a small screwdriver through the holes in the end plate. Put the Woodruff key and the pulley back, and use an old fan belt in the vice to hold the pulley while you tighten the nut.

Chapter 4
Dynamo control boxes

One of the problems with a dynamo is that the output increases with speed. If nothing were done about this, all the bulbs, and probably the dynamo as well, would burn out pretty rapidly. Back in the 1930s the output was controlled by a movable third brush inside the dynamo and a so-called 'full charge' and 'half-charge' resistor usually incorporated in the dashboard lighting switch. At best this was a crude form of control, and all post-war classics fitted with dynamos have a regulator control box.

We deal here with Lucas control boxes used with a two-brush dynamo as they are by far the most prolific on British classics, and can be conveniently sorted into three types. Most of the illustrations are line drawings as these, we feel, are easier to follow than photographs. If you understand the working, your chances of a successful restoration are much better than if you just work by rule of thumb.

Many early classics were fitted with the RF95 control box, easily recognisable because it has nine terminals usually labelled, from left to right, A1, A, A2, F, D, two terminals labelled A4, E and A3. It also carries two fuses. The RF95 is a compensated voltage control box and uses the Lucas LRT9 regulator, first introduced in the late 1930s, but none the worse for that, and still capable of giving good results. You may possibly have another RF series control box, the RF96. This

Fig. 4.1. The basic regulator winding is connected to terminals F and D on the dynamo.

Fig. 4.2. The cut-out winding connects to the D terminal on the dynamo and to chassis earth.

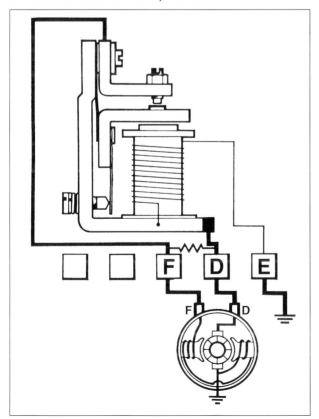

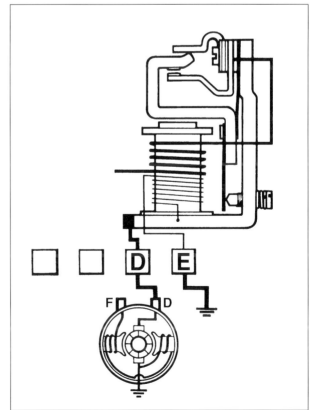

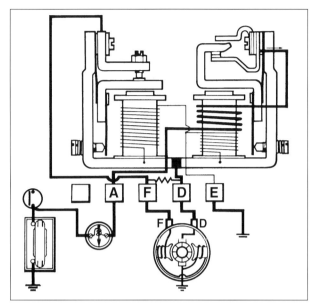

Fig. 4.3. If we put the regulator and cut-out circuits together with a battery and ammeter, we have a charging system, but it is a constant voltage control, and suffers from some drawbacks.

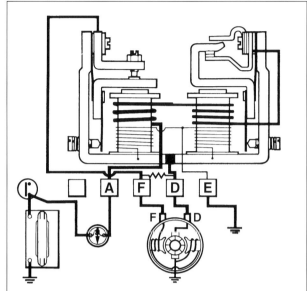

Fig. 4.4. If the heavy winding on the cut-out is given one or two turns round the regulator bobbin before going to the ammeter, the system is compensated for different states of charge of the battery.

has only five terminals, A1, A, F, D and E and is designed to be used with a separate fuse box. It can be used in place of the RF95 and vice-versa, but the change means a lot of rewiring, and you should make sure that the dynamo is suitable for the control box. You may have to change that as well. You may also, at an autojumble, come across an RF97 box. Don't waste your money

on it, whatever the stallholder tells you. It is designed for use on tractors and is totally unsuitable for the dynamos used on higher-revving car engines. Swapping around different output dynamos and control boxes is sometimes advocated by enthusiasts with a bent for electrics, but it can be a very tricky business. It's safer to stick with the model dynamo and

control box originally fitted to your car.

The RF series of control boxes were superseded by the RB series, still compensated voltage control, the most popular being the RB106/2 fitted to a wide range of classics. As with the RF series, there are variations, the RB107 and RB108. Leave them alone, they were designed for tractors,

Fig. 4.5. The RF95 control box was popular on early classics. It has nine terminals usually labelled, from left to right, A1, A, A2, F, D, two labelled A4, E and A3. It carries spare fuses.

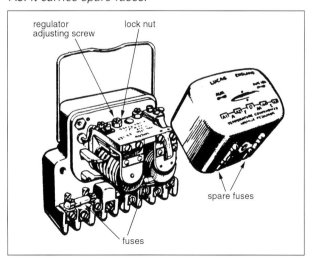

Fig. 4.6. The settings for the regulator part of the RF95 control box.

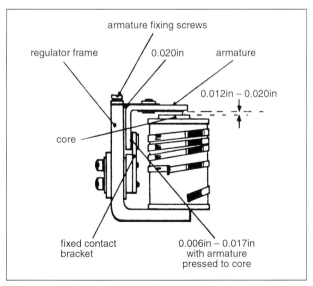

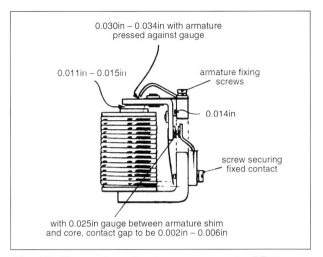

Fig. 4.7. The settings for the cut-out on the RF95.

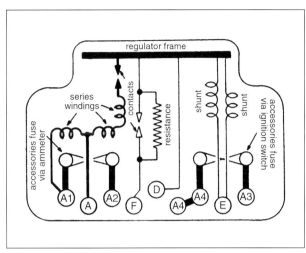

Fig. 4.8. A schematic diagram of the internal connections on the RF95 control box.

stationary engines and some motorcycles.

People had got used to calling the compensated voltage control systems 'CVC' systems, when Lucas caused confusion by introducing a current voltage control system which also became known as a 'CVC' system. The popular control boxes used with this system are the RB310 and the RB311. They are easily recognisable because they have three bobbins under the cover instead of two. The wiring is

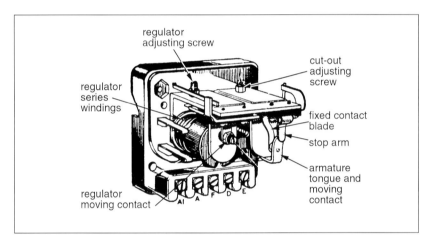

Above: Fig. 4.9. The RB106, and its companion the RB106/2, are updated versions of the RF95, without fuses. The five terminals are labelled A1, A, F, D and E. The method of adjustment and setting was also altered.

Left: Fig. 4.10. Regulator settings for the RB106/2.

Below : Fig. 4.11. Cut-out settings for the RB106/2.

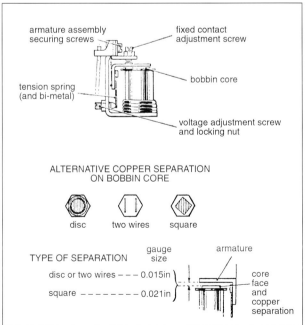

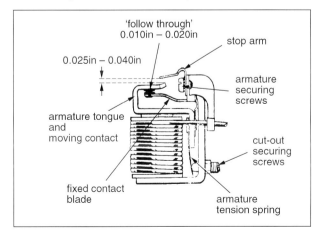

39

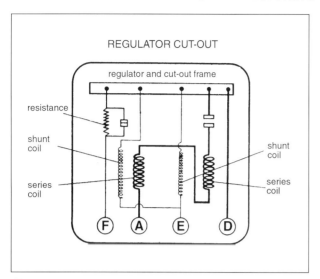

Fig. 4.12. A schematic diagram of the internal connections on an RB106/2 control box.

Fig. 4.14. The settings for the voltage regulator on the RB310 box.

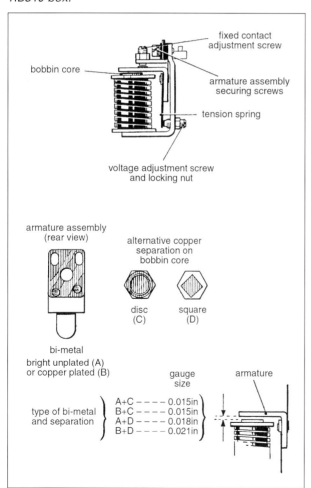

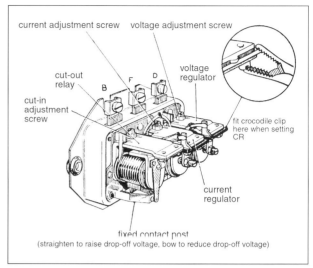

Fig. 4.13. The later RB310 control boxes are also known as CVC boxes, but in this case CVC stands for Current Voltage Control, not compensated voltage control. They have three bobbins, current regulator, voltage regulator and cut-out. There are only three terminals labelled B, F and D, and the frame must be earthed through the fixing screws.

Fig. 4.15. The settings for the current regulator on the RB310 box.

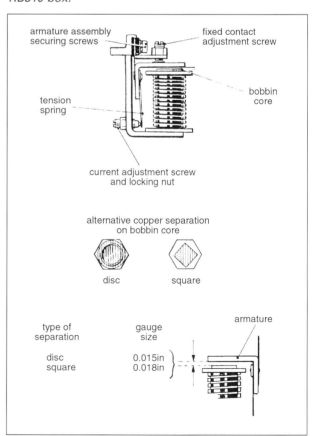

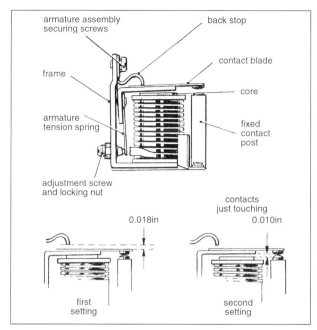

Fig. 4.16. The settings for the cut-out on the RB310 box.

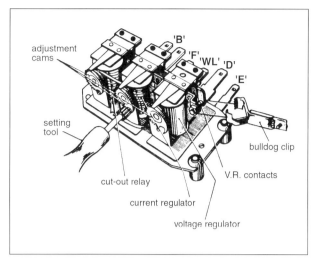

Fig. 4.17. Last in line of the popular Lucas R series control boxes was the RB340. This is electrically similar to the RB310, but the settings are different. It also has segment plates for setting, and the segments are turned by a small tool rather like a gearwheel on a stick. All you have to set on the current and voltage regulators are the air gaps.

simplified with just three terminals, a double one labelled B, one labelled F and one D. Earth for the box is by the metal frame via the fixing screws.

Adjusting control boxes, with a regulator and cut-out, or two regulators in the case of a current voltage control box, is often looked on as something of a black art. Despite this, or maybe because of it, they are a favourite target for amateur adjusting and fiddling, without the fiddler really knowing what tune he's playing. It's much

easier to restore, set and adjust them if you know how they work, what you're doing and why; so forget the idea that theory is boring, it isn't. Stay with us while we run through some diagrams to build up a complete charging circuit and show how a compensated voltage control box works.

In the control box, you have an iron frame with two bobbins mounted on it. Looking at it from the front, the left one is the regulator bobbin and the right one the cut-out bobbin. They are

both, basically, electrically-operated make and break switches.

The regulator bobbin has an L-shaped plate, or armature, attached to the frame by a spring blade which allows it to rock. The top part of the L sits over the bobbin core, and when the core is magnetised it pulls the plate down. There's a copper separator on top of the bobbin to prevent an undesirable iron-to-iron contact. On the top part of the armature is a contact point. This lines up with an adjustable contact point carried on

Fig. 4.18. The air gap settings for the current and voltage regulators on the RB340 control box.

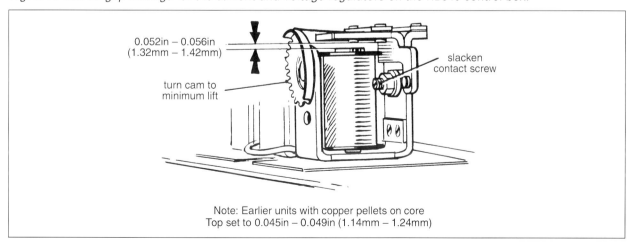

Note: Earlier units with copper pellets on core
Top set to 0.045in – 0.049in (1.14mm – 1.24mm)

41

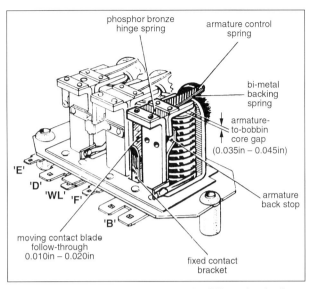

Fig. 4.19. The cut-out setting on the RB340 is similar, but to a different dimension.

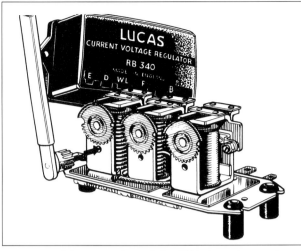

Fig. 4.20. A later version of the RB340 setting tool had a crank handle instead of a screwdriver-type handle. This made it easier to use in confined spaces under the bonnet.

a bracket which is insulated from the frame. The contacts are normally closed. On the vertical part of the armature there's another spring blade which comes down to an adjusting screw. Screwing the adjusting screw in increases the spring tension, and screwing it out decreases the tension.

The cut-out arrangement is basically similar except that the contact points are normally open and, instead of one of the points having an adjusting screw, there's an arm over the top of the points which can be bent up or down to adjust the gap.

As we said in the chapter on dynamos, the dynamo gives its output when the F and D terminals are connected. If we connect the D terminal on the dynamo to the regulator frame, and the F terminal to the adjustable contact, the dynamo will give its output when the contacts are closed. When the contacts open, the output falls off.

The contact points are opened by a winding round the bobbin connected in parallel with the dynamo armature between terminal D on the control box and chassis earth. Because it's in parallel it's often called a shunt winding. As the dynamo voltage rises, the shunt winding magnetises the bobbin core until the magnetic pull is strong enough to overcome the spring tension on the regulator armature plate. When this happens, the points open, breaking the shunt winding circuit. The dynamo voltage falls off and the magnetic pull drops so that the points close again. When the dynamo is running, the cycle is repeated between 40 and 60 times a second depending on the spring tension of the regulator armature plate. By adjusting this spring tension, the output voltage of the dynamo can be controlled to within quite fine limits.

There's a fairly heavy current flowing through the points and, unless something were done to suppress it, there would be heavy arcing across the points when they open and they would soon burn out. The something is a resistor connected across the points between the F and D terminals on the box. When the points are closed, the resistor has no effect because it's short-circuited. When they open, the resistor gives an alternative path for the current to stop it arcing across the points.

To charge the battery, its live terminal has to be connected to terminal D on the dynamo, but if this were a direct connection then as the dynamo output voltage dropped below battery voltage, the battery would try to drive the dynamo, so there has to be a switch in the circuit. This switch is the cut-out.

As with the regulator bobbin, there's a shunt winding round the bobbin between terminal D and chassis earth. As the dynamo voltage rises, the shunt winding gives a magnetic pull which closes the cut-out points and puts the battery in circuit through terminal A on the box. When the dynamo voltage drops, the points open so the battery is disconnected from the dynamo.

Instead of going straight to terminal A, the charging current runs through a second very heavy gauge winding on the cut-out bobbin, often called the series winding because it's in series with the battery. This winding does two things. First, it magnetises the bobbin core to help the shunt winding hold the points firmly closed and stop them chattering. Second, when the dynamo voltage drops below battery voltage there's a momentary reverse current from the battery through this winding which cancels the magnetic pull of the shunt winding and lets the points snap open quickly. There's usually an ammeter between terminal A and the battery to let the driver know the battery is being charged.

So far, we've built up a charging circuit, but it's not yet practical because it's got constant voltage control, and this gives it a serious drawback. If the battery isn't fully charged, the voltage at its terminals will be low. If you also put a load on the battery, headlamps, wipers and so on, its terminal voltage drops still further. The dynamo tries to build this up to the controlled voltage by putting a very heavy current through the charging circuit. With a low-charged battery, this current could easily be enough to burn out the dynamo windings.

This is where the compensating part of a compensated voltage control unit comes in. Instead of going straight from the cut-out bobbin to terminal A, the heavy series winding is taken across and given two or three windings round the regulator bobbin. As this winding carries all the charging current from the dynamo to the battery and, as it's wound round the regulator bobbin, it adds to the magnetic pull produced by the regulator shunt winding to open the regulator points sooner. That way, the regulated output voltage from the dynamo is varied depending on the current flowing which, in turn depends on voltage at the battery terminals, so the system is compensated for different states of charge of the battery.

Even so, we still need some extra compensation when a heavy load, such as the headlights, sidelights, wiper motor and maybe heater motor is put on it. To give this compensation, an extra turn is added to the end of the series winding round the regulator bobbin. Usually only one turn is needed, and it affects the magnetic pull of the bobbin only when a load is put on the battery.

There is one more form of compensation, for temperature. In freezing cold conditions, even a fully charged battery won't give the same voltage as it does when warm, and the dynamo needs to give a higher regulated voltage than it does at normal temperatures. To compensate for this, the tension spring of the regulator armature has a bi-metallic strip behind it which bends with temperature and either stiffens or weakens the action of the spring. The windings inside the regulator box generate a certain amount of heat so, as things warm up, the regulated voltage goes back to its normal setting by which time the battery will have warmed up because it's being charged. On a typical RB106/2 regulator bobbin there will usually be two or two-and-a-quarter turns of the main compensating winding and one turn of the load compensating winding, but these can vary depending on the size and type of the dynamo on the car to which it was originally fitted and the sort of load expected on the battery. Although a small 8hp classic and a large 25hp one from the same period may both have RB106/2 control boxes, the compensating windings may not be the same. Bear this in mind if you're looking for a second-hand box at a breaker's or autojumble.

Now we know how it works, we can get down to the practical side of restoring and setting a compensated voltage control regulator box. If you've just bought a classic that's been neglected, or maybe standing idle for some years, you may find when you get it running that the charging isn't all it should be. The same could apply even when you buy a running classic. Sometimes the control box isn't working properly because of rust or other corrosion inside, or dirty points, but quite often it isn't working properly because someone has been trying to adjust it without knowing quite what they're doing. Very often, people

will try fiddling with a perfectly good control box when the charging problem is outside it so, before you start, make sure that the dynamo, the drive belt condition and tension and the wiring connections are all they should be.

The same applies to the battery. Before you start adjusting the control box, take the battery off the car and charge it up fully, then check it again after it's been standing for 24 hours, preferably 48 hours, to make sure it's holding the charge. If you've got a modern fully-sealed battery you'll have to rely on a voltmeter reading across its terminals, but if you've got the older type where you can top up individual cells, use a hydrometer to check the specific gravity. A battery on which the voltage falls off slightly with standing, or shows a smallish drop in specific gravity on only one cell may well have some useful life left for normal motoring, but try to borrow a fully charged battery in good condition for setting the control box or you may get some confusing readings.

As extreme examples of what you might come across, we picked up two RB106/2 control boxes at an autojumble. One looked very clean inside but had obviously been left on a car in the open for some time because the connectors were badly corroded to the point where one had broken off when someone tried to pull the cables off. The other looked very clean outside, and the stallholder assured us it was in 'perfect order'. Never take assurances like this at their face value. The stallholder might be right but, in this case, he was very wrong.

Inside, the box was a mess. There was quite a lot of corrosion on the cut-out, the regulator points were burnt, the main voltage compensation winding was badly distorted and the load winding was also badly distorted to the point where it wasn't doing much good at all. Underneath, one end of the points resistor had become

Fig. 4.21. Two identical model control boxes from an autojumble. One with amateur wiring repairs, and one with corroded terminals. They could be combined to make a serviceable box.

Fig. 4.22. On the box with the amateur wiring, the resistor underneath had come away from its contact plate. We wonder if this was why someone attempted to 'repair' a perfectly good bobbin winding.

detached from its connection to the F terminal (which probably caused the burnt points) and, as a final bodge, both the earth wires from the bobbin shunt windings had been poorly soldered to the underside of the E terminal. Someone had been attempting to 'repair' it, but we don't think they even got it to a working stage because the red 'guarantee' sealing paint on the adjusting screws hadn't been disturbed. These are two somewhat extreme examples which normally we would throw out or possibly keep for parts, but it would be quite feasible to make good one out of the pair.

Chapter 5

Alternators

Most classic cars from the late 1960s onwards were fitted with alternators in place of a dynamo. The first alternators on British classics were the Lucas 10AC, which had an output of 35 amps, and the 11 AC which gave 45 amps. There was also an uprated version of the 11AC which gave 60 amps. They were quite an advance on the older dynamo, particularly in their ability to give a good output at low revs, and they could be used on either positive or negative earth systems. But they weren't as reliable as they might have been and they had the big disadvantage, compared with later alternators, of needing various other bits and pieces connected to them – a relay, a regulator control unit and a control for the ignition warning light, an aluminium can which looked like an older indicator flasher unit and often gave trouble.

It's possible to overhaul them, but home overhaul isn't recommended because obtaining parts for the basic alternator is very difficult and replacement regulators and warning light controls even more so. Unless you're an absolute stickler for originality for concours showing, and you're having charging problems which can't be cured by checking all the electrical connections, we would advise changing over to the later ACR series of alternators (R standing for internal regulator). The wiring for changing over is quite simple, the only snag being that ACR alternators are NOT suitable for positive earth systems. If you really must stay with the older AC models we would suggest trying one of the classic electrical equipment specialists.

ACR alternators are much simpler to wire in and to overhaul. The regulator is built-in, and there's no need for a separate relay or ignition warning lamp control. They came in five output classes, the 15ACR giving 28 amps, 16ACR 34 amps, 17ACR 36 amps, 18ACR 43 amps and 20ACR 66 amps. The electrical equipment of classic cars is usually quite a lot less than that of current cars, and the 17ACR was possibly the most popular model.

If you've fitted extra electrical equipment and you're doubtful about whether or not to uprate by going to a larger alternator there's a simple way to calculate it. Add together the wattage of all the equipment you're ever likely to have working at the same time. Probably this would be headlamps, side and rear lamps, dash lamps, windscreen wiper, heater blower, radio, two indicator lamps and possibly a repeater lamp and maybe fog or spot lamps. According to Ohm's law, amps are equal to watts divided by volts, so divide the total wattage by 12 and you get the maximum amperage drain on the battery. Say it comes to, perhaps, 370 watts. Divide by 12 and the maximum current drain is 30.8 amps. A 17ACR in good order would cope with balancing this with no problem. If, however, the total wattage came to just over 400, plus a few connections that were perhaps not quite without resistance, you'd be on the borderline with a 17ACR so you might fancy changing up to an 18ACR. The only drawback might be that the 17ACR cuts in at 950rpm (that's alternator rpm not engine rpm) whereas the 18ACR doesn't cut in till 1,250rpm, so you might find the flashers slowing down or the warning light flickering with a full electrical load at tickover. In theory you could fit a smaller pulley to the alternator, but you might have problems with pulley slip. Also, the maximum permissible pulley speed on these alternators, after which there's a danger of burning them out, is 12,500rpm. If you've got a classic sports car that will rev to 6,000rpm plus, measure the sizes of the crankshaft pulley and the alternator pulley and work out the ratio to get the rpm at the alternator.

ACR alternators can be divided into two types, the early battery-sensing models and the later machine-sensing models (see *Fig. 5.9* for wiring circuit). There was a later modification to the machine-sensing models to use what's usually termed the European Termination system which simplifies the wiring and, if you are looking for a second-hand alternator to overhaul, this is the one to go for. You can recognise them quite easily from the terminal grouping on the back, and these are shown in the three diagrams. On the European Termination circuit you'll notice that there's an extra chain-dotted connection from the alternator to the starter solenoid. This is for the 20ACR where the much higher output needs a twin cable to avoid voltage drop without the need for a very heavy and unwieldy thick cable.

Overhaul of all the ACR models is very similar, but before you start stripping things there are a couple of meter checks you can make which will give you an indication of where the problem lies. To do a full output check with the alternator on the car, you need an ammeter with a much higher capacity than you get on an ordinary multimeter which will usually cope with a maximum of 10 amps to 12 amps. However, you can still carry out some useful voltage checks with a multimeter.

Before you carry out any meter checks, make sure the battery is fully charged otherwise you can get misleading readings. As an example, people have been known to change a perfectly good alternator because it won't charge up a badly flat and sulphated battery after the engine's been started with jump leads. Incidentally, one of the few advantages of a dynamo is that it's better than an alternator at coping with very flat batteries.

Don't rely on just a voltmeter check across the battery terminals; take a hydrometer reading of each cell if you can. A fully charged cell should have a specific gravity of 1.270 to 1.290. If any of them show a specific gravity of 1.250 or below, or if your hydrometer reads in coloured bands and shows 'half charged', get the battery charged up off the car. If you've got a 'sealed for life' battery where you can't take hydrometer readings, try to borrow one that you know is fully charged just for the meter checks. Also, make sure the battery terminals are clean and tight, the battery earthing strap and the engine earthing strap, if fitted, are clean and tight and the alternator terminals are clean. If your alternator has a separate earthing strap to the engine, make sure that's also clean and tight, and check the drive belt tension.

Your first check is for cable continuity. Take the leads off the alternator, switch on the ignition and check the voltage between the alternator end of each lead and chassis earth. You should get the same reading as a voltage check across the battery. If you get a zero reading there's a break in one of the connecting leads or, if the zero reading is on the 'IND' lead, possibly a blown warning light bulb.

Assuming all is OK so far, reconnect the alternator leads and use your voltmeter to check for a high resistance in the charging circuit by measuring the voltage drop. Connect the voltmeter between the battery positive terminal and the main output terminal on the alternator. Switch the headlamps on main beam to supply a load, start the engine and run it at about 3,000rpm. The reading on the voltmeter should not be more than 0.5 volts. Still with the engine at 3,000rpm, connect the voltmeter between the battery earth terminal and the body of the alternator. In this case the voltmeter reading should not be more than 0.25 volts.

If you get higher readings, there's a high resistance some-where in the circuit. It could be at the battery terminals, the battery earth lead where it connects to the car body or chassis, the earthing strap between the engine and the car chassis or possibly between the body of the alternator and the engine. This last point is often overlooked, and on many cars from the late classic era onwards manufacturers put a separate earthing strap from the alternator body to the engine instead of relying on the mounting bolts.

As we said, there are further checks that can be made with the alternator on the car, but they need a heavy duty ammeter capable of reading up to about 100 amps. These are seldom found outside a professional electrical workshop and are too expensive to warrant buying for home use. There is one further check you can make with your voltmeter, though it's not a conclusive one without a heavy-duty ammeter. Connect your voltmeter across the battery terminals, start the engine and again run it at about 3,000rpm, holding it there for about 15 seconds to let the voltage stabilise. The voltmeter reading should be between 13.6 volts and 14.4 volts. If the reading is outside these limits, suspect the regulator in the alternator. If the checks so far don't reveal an obvious fault, and you still suspect it of giving trouble, it's time to strip down the alternator and have a look inside.

We will deal here with a Lucas ACR alternator as it's the most popular on British classics. Before you start dismantling, spin the pulley and listen for any roughness in the bearings. If you find any, be prepared to renew at least the front one (which is more likely to be worn). Start dismantling by taking off the black plastic cover at the back. It's held by 1/4in AF bolts which are shrouded quite deep in the cover so you'll need a small socket or a box spanner. Under the cover you'll find the diode rectifier pack on to which the connector plugs, a fairly large white nylon brush housing and, attached to this, a square aluminium box which is the regulator.

On ACR alternators built before 1980 or thereabouts you might also find a separate diode looking a bit like a small capacitor out of a distributor. It sits alongside the rectifier unit, usually on its right when you hold the alternator with the connectors at the top. This is the surge protection diode, put there to protect the regulator should someone be so careless as to remove a battery terminal, or shut off a battery master switch, with the engine running. A short-circuited surge protection diode is quite likely to be the culprit if the ignition warning light stays on when you rev up the engine. A faulty regulator could also cause this fault, though in this case the warning light often gets brighter when you rev up.

Later ACR alternators, as the regulators were improved, didn't

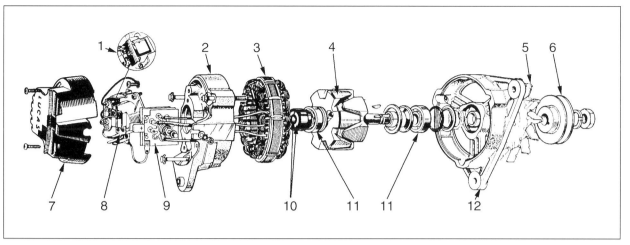

Fig. 5.1. Lucas ACR alternators are all basicaly similar. 1. Output regulator in heat sink; 2. Slip ring end bracket; 3. Stator; 4. 12-pole rotor and field winding; 5. Fan; 6. Pulley; 7. Cover; 8. Brush gear and regulator; 9. Rectifier pack; 10. Slip rings; 11. Ball races; 12. Drive end-bracket.

need a protection diode. If you fit one of the later regulators you can dispense with the surge protection diode or, if it's in good order, leave it on as extra protection. You can assess it by unsoldering one end and checking for continuity across it with your multimeter. A diode can be regarded as an electrical one-way valve, so it should pass current one way but not the other.

All ACR alternators made from the early 1980s onwards are fitted with the improved 14TR-type regulator. Sometimes you'll find 14TR marked on it and, when Lucas first introduced it, they either painted it gold or painted a gold band on it to indicate that it didn't need a surge protection diode. However, as the older models handed in for exchange got fewer and fewer, Lucas didn't bother about the gold paint. If a plain unpainted regulator isn't marked with a type number, the only certain way to identify it is by the Lucas part number, and your local Lucas service centre should be able to do this. If you buy a new one it will be the improved type.

You might want to cannibalise another alternator for a regulator, but watch the colour of the connecting leads. Some earlier ACR regulators were made for temperature sensing and the main lead to the starter solenoid went

via a heat sensor mounted very close to the battery, usually touching it. This lowered the voltage when the battery was hot and raised it when the battery was cold. These temperature sensing regulators aren't suitable for later alternators and you can identify them by the colour of the connecting leads. They are black, yellow, red and orange. On the non-temperature-sensing regulators, the leads are black, yellow, red and white. Make sure you replace like with like.

You can, if you want, check and change the brushes without taking

Fig. 5.2. If no-one has pulled it off, you should find the size of the alternator marked on an aluminium tag.

anything else off. Each brush is attached to a small metal strip held to the top of the brush housing by two tiny hexagon headed screws. However, it's easier, and better, to take the brush housing off as well, because then you can clean the inside of it which will probably be coated with carbon dust, which can short things out. You can also clean and check the slip ring. The regulator is attached to the top of the brush housing so you have to take this off first. Make a careful note of where the connections go because memory is very fallible and if you reconnect it the wrong way round you can ruin it.

Lucas say that if the brushes are less than 3/16in long they should be renewed. The brushes run against a flat slip ring and the outer brush wears more quickly than the central one but, for some reason, the central brush often wears the slip ring faster. On a well-worn alternator you sometimes find it's almost drilled a hole in the centre connection on the slip ring. If the slip ring is in good condition apart from being glazed and dirty you can clean it up with fine sandpaper. A sandpaper nail file board is ideal. Don't use emery paper, please, nor wet and dry rubbing down paper, because these contain carborundum which is a conductor and again can short things out. A

Fig. 5.3. Just one screw holds the regulator to the brush housing.

Fig. 5.4. The brushes are very easy to get at and replace if they're worn.

Fig. 5.5. After checking the brushes, take off the brush housing.

Fig. 5.6. This reveals the slip ring, the equivalent of a commutator on a dynamo.

Fig. 5.7. The slip ring on the alternator is clean and will see further service, though the centre has started to wear.

Fig. 5.8. Before you finish, check that this sliding bush is free to slide. This is particularly important if you are fitting a different alternator to the bracket on your engine.

badly worn slip ring can be replaced by a new one, but you can't get them from Lucas agents, and most electrical specialists prefer to sell you an exchange alternator.

Provided the slip rings clean up well, your next step is to check the rotor winding. Set your multimeter to ohms and check the resistance between the inner and outer slip rings. With a 15ACR and 16ACR the specified nominal resistance is 4.33 ohms, but anything between 4.05 ohms and 4.6 ohms is acceptable. With a 17ACR the resistance should be lower, nominally 4.165 ohms, but anything between 3.90 ohms and 4.4 ohms is acceptable.

An alternator won't work

properly if any of the nine diodes in the rectifier pack have blown. They can blow if someone has tried to connect the battery terminals the wrong way round, or jump leads the wrong way round or, just occasionally, if you carry out any electrical welding on the car body without unplugging the alternator. Poor connection between the brushes and the slip ring, particularly an intermittent connection, can also sometimes blow diodes. One warning of this is an ignition warning light that flickers on and off when you rev the engine, and we've included a chart of other symptoms. If these happen to you, check the brushes and slip ring before the diodes blow.

There are nine diodes in the rectifier pack and you can't replace them individually. You have to change the whole pack, but the same thing as with slip rings applies about supply.

However, if you want to use a second-hand diode pack, it's worth testing them before you solder the pack in place. Before you can test them you have to take the rectifier pack out of the donor alternator, and this means unsoldering three wires. They're all in yellow sleeving, so make a careful note of where each wire connects before you unsolder it. Heat is also an enemy of diodes, so use a heat sink while you're soldering or unsoldering to divert the heat from

ACR ALTERNATOR DIODE FAILURE SYMPTOMS

WARNING LIGHT	ALTERNATOR		OUTPUT	POSSIBLE FAULT
	Temperature	Noise		
Normal at standstill, goes out at cut-in speed but then glows progressively brighter as speed increases.	High	Normal	Higher than normal at 6,000rpm 15ACR 35 amp approx. 16ACR 40 amp approx. 17ACR 38 amp approx.	Live side output diode open-circuit. (May damage rotor winding and regulator output stage, overheat brush boxes and blow warning light.)
Light out under all conditions.	High	Excessive	Very low at 6,000rpm 10 amp approx.	Live side output diode short-circuit. May cause failure of associated field diode.
Normal at standstill, dims appreciably at cut-in and gets pro-gressively dimmer or may even go out at high speeds.	Normal	Excessive	Poor at low speed, slightly below normal at 6,000rpm 15ACR 26 amp approx. 16ACR 32 amp approx. 17ACR 30 amp approx.	Earth side output diode open-circuit.
Normal at standstill, dims at cut-in remains dim or may go out at (much) higher speeds.	Normal	Excessive	Very low at all speeds above cut-in 7 amp approx.	Earth side output diode short-circuit. (The same symptoms would be present if one phase winding were shorted to earth.)
Normal at standstill, dims appreciably at cut-in and gets pro-gressively dimmer or may even go out at high speeds.	Normal	Normal	Lower than normal at 6,000rpm 15ACR 23 amp approx. 16ACR 29 amp approx 17ACR 29 amp approx.	Field diode open-circuit.
Normal at standstill, dims appreciably at cut-in and gets pro-gressively dimmer or may even go out at high speeds.	Normal	Excessive	Very low at 6,000rpm 7 amp approx.	Field diode short-circuit.

Table. 5.1. The symptoms will help you decide whether or not you need a new diode pack.

the diodes. A pair of pointed-nose pliers held on the wire near where you're soldering makes a good heat sink. After unsoldering, the rectifier pack comes off after you undo one nut.

Some people may tell you that you can check for a dud diode by feeling them. They say that if the diode is loose in its housing it's dud, but this is a very unreliable guide. The only way to check them properly is with a meter. As we said earlier, diodes are electrical one-way valves. They should pass current one way and not the other. If any of the nine diodes passes current both ways, or doesn't pass current at all, the whole pack must be replaced. There's no reason why, if you've got a spare alternator that's got good diodes but is otherwise useless, you shouldn't swap the packs over.

The same applies to a badly worn slip ring. It's much easier to replace a slip ring if you take the alternator apart by undoing the two long through bolts and tap the rear part of the body off its bearing.

To take the slip ring off you have to unsolder two wires, one going to the outer track and one to the centre. Like the wires on a rectifier pack, these are not colour-coded, they're both in yellow plastic sleeving, so make a careful note of where each one goes. After you unsolder the wires, the slip ring pulls off the end of the rotor shaft.

Though the rear bearing on an alternator seldom gives any trouble, the front one, which has to take the side pull of the fan belt, sometimes does. To get at it, you take the pulley off and knock the Woodruff key out of the shaft. We showed you the easy way to do this in the chapter on dynamos. The bearing is usually very tight on the rotor shaft, and you have to knock it through. Put the nut back on before you start hammering on the end of the shaft or you'll damage the threads. Often, even the last part, when the nut won't pass through the bearing, is tight, so use a drift with care.

The bearing is held in its housing by a circlip but there aren't any ears to get a pair of circlip pliers on. Instead, you have to lever it out of its groove with a small screwdriver. It's a good idea to heat the housing before you try to drive the old bearing out, and again before you press the new one in. You don't need much heat, immersing the housing in boiling water for a few minutes is usually sufficient. Use something to support the centre part of the housing before you drive or press the old bearing out. A handy way to start the bearing moving is to use a large vice with a block of wood behind the housing and a large nut,

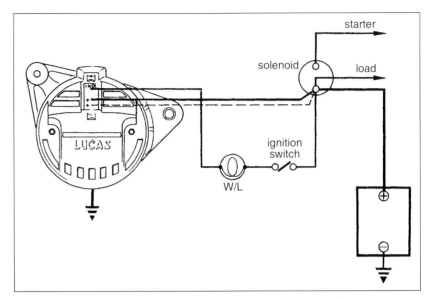

Fig. 5.9. The wiring circuit for a machine-sensing Lucas ACR alternator.

or something similar, against the bearing. If you haven't got a large enough vice you can resort to the time-honoured method of a nut and bolt and spacer washers. Use the same method to press in the new bearing.

Reassembly is, to use the well-worn phrase, the reverse of taking things apart but, before you bolt on the back cover remember to clean the main connector terminals with a sandpaper file. It also pays to check the inside of the connector which fits on them and fit a new one if the contacts are corroded. You'll notice that the two large terminals on the rectifier pack are joined together. You use one of them on the 15ACR, 16ACR and 17ACR, but both of them with twin leads on the higher output 18ACR.

Chapter 6
SU electric fuel pumps

Many classics (among them Rover, Jaguar and Morris) which have their roots in the old Nuffield Group, are fitted with SU electric fuel pumps. Generally speaking they are reliable pumps, their only weak spot being the contact breaker, and the time-honoured method of getting them ticking again, should they stop working, is to give them a thump with the handle of a screwdriver. This might be all right as a temporary get you home method, but it's a sure sign that the pump needs overhauling.

There are three basic models of older SU pumps – L, HP and LCS. Many older classics fitted with SU pumps use either the L or the HP, the familiar ones with a round body. The LCS has a rectangular block body and a higher rate of flow, but most car makers who needed a higher rate of flow than the single L or HP used the double models, in effect two pump units one each side of a common body which doubled the rate of flow. The double versions also took larger diameter petrol pipes, 3/8in outside diameter compared with 5/16in outside diameter on the single pumps. The LCS pumps also took 3/8in pipes. If you have one, overhaul is almost identical to the HP-type, except that the filter is under a flat plate at the bottom of the pump, and the valve assembly is under a flat plate at the top.

The L was the basic design, produced in huge numbers for small cars. Its maximum output was eight gallons per hour, it had a maximum suction lift of about 48in (1.2m) and was intended to be fitted in the engine compartment.

Its maximum output lift was about 24in (600mm), but SU always recommended that it was fitted at approximately carburettor level.

The HP was very similar to the L but with a longer solenoid body, a stronger pump spring and a modified armature assembly. It was made for fitting either under the car or, more usually, in the boot over the petrol tank. It had a higher rate of flow, about ten gallons per hour, maximum suction lift was about 33in (840mm) and maximum output lift about 48in (1.2m) but, again, SU recommended that it was fitted at approximately carburettor level.

Some people don't bother to distinguish between the L and HP, but it's wisest to stick to the recommendations or you might get fuel starvation going up a long steep hill with an L pump in the boot, or down a long steep hill with an HP in the engine compartment.

On later classics, the L and HP pumps were superseded by the AUF range, also listed as the AZX range, with a figure 1 in front of the AUF number. These are all high-pressure pumps with a suction lift of 18in (450mm), designed to be mounted at the back of the car, and will feed a carburettor mounted from 48in (1.2m) above pump level to 6in (150mm) below pump level.

The smallest one, the AUF 200/AZX 1200, is easily distinguished because the inlet and outlet unions are black plastic domes with moulded-on pipes, and are held at the back of the pump by a single clamp washer and two screws. It will deliver seven gallons per hour.

The next one up, the AUF 300/AZX 1300, has a much higher capacity and will deliver 15 gallons per hour. It has conventional screw-in inlet and outlet unions, and a flow-smoothing unit, basically an air chamber and a diaphragm, under a large dome.

There are two dual versions of the AZX 1300 – the AZX 1400 and AZX 1500 – which are essentially two pump units one each side of the body. On the AZX 1400, the two pump units work simultaneously to give a single output of 30 gallons per hour. The AZX 1500 is designed for cars with two fuel tanks, often one each side in the boot, and the two pump units normally work independently with two inlets and a single outlet. Each pump unit will deliver 12.5 gallons per hour, and on some classics they are wired and switched so that you can have either or both working. They also have flow-smoothing chambers.

When SU made minor changes to the pumps, such as a different material for the diaphragm, they increased the AUF or AZX number by 1, so you get AUF201, AUF 202 and so on. In almost all cases, parts from these later pumps are interchangeable with parts from the earlier numbers.

You may also come across L and HP pumps which were reconditioned by SU and fitted with later AUF parts. On these, SU gave them a new designation such as AUA, AUB and so on. This identification is on a small aluminium plate under one of the body-fixing screws.

The action of an SU pump is often thought difficult to

understand, but reduced to its simple basics it's quite easy. You have a fuel chamber, which is the body, closed on one side by a rubber diaphragm. The body has two one-way valves, inlet and outlet. The diaphragm is attached to the armature rod of a solenoid, the long nose of the pump, and the other end of the armature rod is attached to a contact breaker. When the electrical supply is switched off and there is no fuel in the pump, the contact breaker points are closed. When you switch on, the solenoid is energised and pulls the diaphragm away from the body. This gives a suction to pull petrol in through the inlet valve. When it reaches the end of its stroke, the armature rod opens the points so the solenoid is no longer pulling the diaphragm, and a compression spring pushes the diaphragm back towards the body to push petrol out through the outlet valve. If there is a back pressure at the outlet because the carburettor is full, the spring isn't able to push the diaphragm back so the pump stops with the points open. As soon as the back pressure drops, the spring pushes the diaphragm back, the points close and the cycle starts again.

The toggle mechanism of the contact breaker, a capacitor to reduce arcing at the points and cut out radio interference, the rollers or nylon ring to centralise the diaphragm and the chambers to smooth the petrol flow, all of which we'll come to, are just refinements to make the basic idea reliable.

When an SU pump is working properly you can hear it ticking until the carburettor float chamber is full. The float needle valve shuts off the flow and the back pressure stops the pump. If the pump keeps ticking very fast without delivering any fuel to the carburettor, either the petrol tank is empty or there's an air leak on the suction side. If it ticks more slowly but still doesn't deliver any petrol, it probably means the valves inside the pump are dirty. If the pump ticks very

slowly or intermittently after the float chamber is full, you may have a leak in the output pipe or the carburettor needle valve isn't shutting off properly.

If the pump doesn't tick at all when you switch on, check first that you are getting voltage at the feed terminal. If you are, there might be a blockage in either the suction pipe or the output pipe. If the pump labours and overheats, there's probably a partial blockage in the suction pipe or a clogged filter in the pump. If the pump still doesn't work properly after those checks, it's time to take it off and overhaul it.

Before we get on to stripping down the pump, a word about cleaning. If a pump's been standing idle for a long time, or sometimes even if it hasn't, you find sticky deposits of old dried petrol varnish in the body. In some old books and manuals you may read that the way to clean this out is to boil the body in a caustic soda solution followed by a dip in strong nitric acid and a rinse in boiling water.

Don't do it. It will get rid of the old varnish all right, and probably quite a lot of body as well. The method is a hangover from the days when the bodies of SU pumps were made from brass castings, not aluminium alloy. In any case, boiling caustic soda solution and strong nitric acid are very nasty things to have around the garage, so ignore this ancient advice.

If the deposit of varnish and gum is relatively light, a soak in methylated spirit followed by a scrub will shift most of it, and for getting inside the valve ports you can use a gum and varnish removing compound usually sold as carburettor cleaner. You can also use this as an alternative to white spirit for scrubbing off the outside of the body before you start dismantling. It won't hurt the body casting, but watch your eyes and your throat. Wear goggles when you use it, and don't breathe the fumes. Generally, we prefer cleaning the outside of components with white spirit.

It's tempting to start dismantling at the points end of the pump, but it's the wrong place to start because you have to unscrew the diaphragm rod before you can take off the rocking points. Start by undoing the six screws which hold the solenoid to the aluminium body, and mark the solenoid and body so that you can put them together again in the same relative positions. On most pumps there will be six cheese-headed screws and a separate earthing screw, but on early pumps one of the fixing screws was a special earth terminal.

Be careful when you take the solenoid and body apart as early pumps had a series of spherical-edged brass rollers under the diaphragm to centralise it. These fall out when you unscrew it and roll all over the floor. Later pumps have a shaped nylon guide under the diaphragm. All reconditioned pumps have the nylon guide.

On the L and HP pumps there is a sandwich plate between the solenoid and the body, with a gasket each side. On the smaller capacity AUF models – the 200, 300 and 400 – there is usually just one gasket, between the diaphragm and the body, but on the 500 there are usually two gaskets, one each side of the diaphragm. Make a note when you're taking things apart. We say *usually* because SU was quite fond of changing the specifications.

Put the solenoid to one side for the moment while you deal with the body. We'll deal first with the older L and HP pumps. Take out the filter under a plug at the base of the body, and the inlet union at the side, and then unscrew the outlet union at the top of the body. Under this union are the inlet and outlet valves, which are plain brass discs. The inlet valve, right at the bottom of the outlet aperture, will fall out when you tip the body upside down, but the outlet valve is held by a small circlip in a valve cage. There is a thin fibre washer on top of the inlet valve, and a thicker one

Fig. 6.1. All later pumps are fitted with these Melinex valves.

Fig. 6.2. Each valve has it's own cover, all identical, but the inlet and outlet valves are fitted opposite ways up.

on top of the outlet valve cage. As a point of identification, the outlet valve cage on HP pumps has four holes in the side, while the cage on L pumps has only two.

Unless the valves are in perfect condition, it's advisable to fit new ones. The inside of the outlet valve cage, where the disc valve seats, is unlikely to be corroded but, if it is, renew the cage. More serious is deep corrosion and pitting inside the body where the inlet valve disc seats. Discoloration and very tiny surface pitting that you can scarcely see after cleaning probably won't stop the pump working, but if the pitting is deep, to the point where petrol will leak through when you hold the disc down on its seat, the pump won't deliver fuel reliably, and you will need to look for another one. We have heard of people getting a local precision machine shop to lightly reface this seat, but haven't tried it ourselves. We have also heard of people fitting the later plastic valve assemblies to L and HP pumps, but again we haven't tried it.

If the seatings are OK, give the body a clean in methylated spirit or carburettor cleaner, and put it safely to one side where it won't pick up dust and dirt.

On AUF and AZX pumps, which are more often found nowadays, you don't get valve seat trouble because the valves are self-contained Melinex plastic discs in pressed steel housings and are renewed as assemblies. The inlet and outlet valves are identical, except that the outlet valve fits with its tongue-side downwards, and the inlet valve fits with its tongue-side upwards. The valves, and the filter on the inlet side, are held on their seatings by a plate and washers inside the body.

On the AUF 300 and higher numbered pumps, if you have to take off the outlet flow-smoothing dome for cleaning, note that on the AUF 300 and 400 there is a hole in the top of the dome. Take this dome off carefully, because there's a spring underneath it which you don't want to lose. When you come to reassembly, you need a special tool, but this is easy to make, and we'll deal with it in a moment. If there isn't a hole in the top of the dome, there isn't a spring underneath it.

If you disturb the domed delivery flow-smoothing chamber, the pump should be pressure tested after rebuilding, so unless you're certain it's giving trouble, or the inside of

the pump is so full of muck that the dome needs to be taken off for cleaning, it's best to leave it alone. We're not saying that the pump will give trouble if you have to take the dome off for cleaning, and fit new sealing washers and a diaphragm, but both SU, when the company was in existence, and Burlen Fuel Systems who took over manufacture of SU pumps, recommend that the pump is pressure tested if the flow-smoothing chamber has been disturbed.

Fig. 6.3. There is a gauze filter under the inlet valve.

When you're satisfied that the body is quite clean, reassemble it with new gaskets and washers, and new valves if necessary. We usually renew the valves as a matter of course. Make sure you get all the washers in the correct order, and the domed washers the correct way up.

Now for the special tool that you need to reassemble the outlet flow-smoothing device on AUF 300 and 400 pumps. This is just a simple piece of 1/8in (3mm or 10swg) wire with flats filed each side of the last 1/8in (3mm), and a 1/16in (1.6mm) notch filed in the side near the end. Replace the sealing washer, the dished plate, the rubber diaphragm and the O-ring in the chamber, but don't put the spring on top or you'll damage the diaphragm. Put your 'special tool' through the hole in the dome, thread the spring on and hook on the retainer plate. Now hold the spring compressed up in the dome while you fit it back on. It needs very little pull on the wire. Then, without poking the wire tool about inside, turn it gently to let the spring and plate down on to the diaphragm.

Returning now to the solenoid part of the pump, lift up the edge of the diaphragm and take out the nylon guide by easing the end lobes up from the recess in the solenoid body. Now you can unscrew the diaphragm and it will lift out complete with its spring. The spring fits with its smaller end towards the diaphragm, and there is a small neoprene washer between the end of the spring and the diaphragm.

Now turn your attention to the other end of the solenoid. Early pumps had a Bakelite cap screw, later ones a plain connector. Take off the Bakelite end cover which should be sealed either with sticky tape or with a wide rubber band, or sometimes both, to stop moisture getting inside and condensing. If, as we do, you prefer the look of a rubber band on a pump that's on show under the bonnet, you won't do much harm if you leave the sticky tape off, but we like to fit both if the pump's mounted in the open under the car.

On the long terminal screw which also holds the cover, there are a number of washers, including a lead one. This will have squashed out when the nut was tightened and you'll have to cut it off with a knife. You get a new one in the repair kit. When you take the nuts and washers off, be careful not to damage one of the two leads which run to the solenoid. They're quite fine and easily broken. On all except possibly the earliest pumps, you'll have either a capacitor or a diode resistor to reduce arcing at the points and cut out radio interference. It doesn't matter which way round you fit the capacitor because it isn't an electronic one and isn't polarity conscious (to use the electronics term) but the diode resistor is. To be on the safe side, make a note of which way round this component is fitted and refit it, or its replacement, the same way.

Undo the screw which holds the spring blade contacts and which also carries two leads, the second one from the solenoid and one from the capacitor or diode resistor. Now you can undo the two larger 2BA screws which hold the Bakelite pedestal, but take care not to break the braided earth lead which runs

Fig. 6.4. Take the cover off the sediment bowl and clean inside thoroughly.

Fig. 6.5. If you have to disturb the flow-smoothing device for cleaning, or to replace the plastic diaphragm, the pump ought really to be flow tested.

Fig. 6.6. Older pumps had a ring of 11 spherical-edged brass rollers under the diaphragm.

Fig. 6.7. On all later pumps, including rebuilt ones, the brass rollers were replaced by a nylon guide.

down to the toggle of the moving points. You get a new lead with new points, but you might want to use the old points again. If you tilt the pedestal slightly, you can feed down the long main terminal screw to free the solenoid lead, and then lift the pedestal off complete with toggle rocker mechanism. Push out the hardened steel pin on which the toggle mechanism pivots, and you can lift it off.

Don't immerse the solenoid in any sort of cleaning agent or you'll

ruin the insulation. Apart from cleaning the outside, which you should have done before you started dismantling, wipe it clean and make sure that the small air vent at the base of the solenoid, if fitted, is free. If your pump is mounted under the car, and has an air vent, pipe the vent to a dry place such as inside the boot. Some pumps have a vented elbow on the cap with a ball valve inside it instead of a vent on the solenoid. Make sure the ball valve is free.

To reassemble the contact end of the solenoid, fit the rocker assembly to the black plastic pedestal and push in the hardened steel pin. The centre toggle should be set so that, with the inner rocker spindle in tension against the rear of the contact point, the centre toggle spring is above the spindle on which the white rollers run. In words this sounds complicated, but it all fits together logically. Make sure that the rockers are free to swing on the pin, and are not

Fig. 6.8. With the guide (or rollers) removed, unscrew the diaphragm.

Fig. 6.9. The pump could have one of two types of arcing suppressor. One type, as here, fits in a wire clip.

Fig. 6.10. The second type of suppressor is suspended by its own wires.

Fig. 6.11. The top points blade has a slotted end and can be slid in or out without taking the screw right out.

Fig. 6.12. Tilt the Bakelite plate slightly to withdraw the threaded terminal post.

binding on the legs of the pedestal. We've sometimes found that, after being handled in their plastic bag, new rocker assemblies are slightly distorted. If you find one like this, straighten it with a fine pair of pliers till it swings freely.

Push the square-headed terminal post in from the back of the pedestal, and fit the various leads and washers in the correct order. Make sure the nut with the recessed cone is fitted with the recess facing the lead washer. Fit the pedestal to the end of the solenoid, remembering that, if you haven't got a suppression capacitor, the spring washer fits between the earthing tag and the pedestal, not directly under the head of the screw. If a capacitor is fitted, the wire tag of this goes under the earthing tag, and the spring washer isn't fitted. Be careful not to swing and break off the earthing tag when you tighten the screws, and don't overtighten them. Leave the spring contact blade off for the moment.

Fit the spring to the diaphragm remembering that the narrow end of the spring goes towards the diaphragm and that there is a thin neoprene washer between the spring and the diaphragm. Fit the diaphragm rod up inside the solenoid, and screw it in to the threaded hole in the rocker trunnion. Screw it in till the rockers just fail to 'toggle over'. Fold back the diaphragm and fit the plastic diaphragm centring plate or, if you've got an old pump and want to retain the 11 brass rollers, fit these. If you use the brass rollers, you'll need to wedge the rocker assembly by fitting a couple of matchsticks under it, otherwise the rollers will fall out as soon as you lay the solenoid down. SU manuals say use a bent wire fork, but we've found a couple of matchsticks serve just as well. Remember to remove them after you have assembled the solenoid to the body with the screws finger tight, and before you finally tighten them. The matchsticks, or the wire fork, are purely to prevent the rollers falling out, and are not intended to pre-tension the diaphragm as some people wrongly suppose.

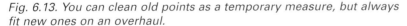

Fig. 6.13. You can clean old points as a temporary measure, but always fit new ones on an overhaul.

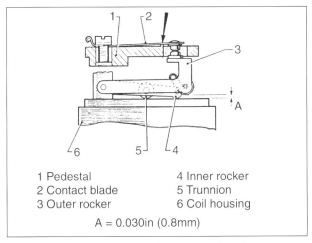

1 Pedestal
2 Contact blade
3 Outer rocker
4 Inner rocker
5 Trunnion
6 Coil housing
A = 0.030in (0.8mm)

Fig. 6.14. Settings for the older type of rocker assembly.

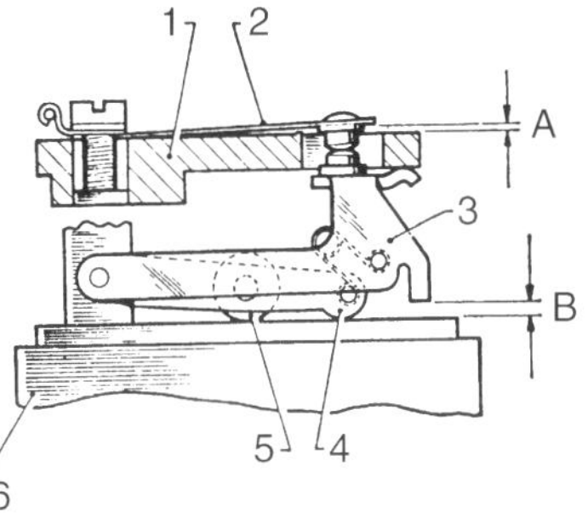

1 Pedestal
2 Contact blade
3 Outer rocker
4 Inner rocker
5 Trunnion
6 Coil housing
A = 0.035in (0.9mm)   B = 0.070in (1.8mm)

Fig. 6.15. Settings for the later type of rocker assembly.

With the points just failing to 'toggle' over, unscrew the diaphragm until the points just 'toggle' over, then unscrew it to the nearest hole *and for a further four holes*, two-thirds of a complete turn. The diaphragm is now set correctly and, despite what it says in some older books, doesn't need pre-tensioning when you fit the solenoid to the body.

There were two types of rocker assembly, an early type and a later type. You should get the later type as a replacement, but just in case you want to clean up and refit the earlier type, we'll run through fitting and adjusting both types.

Before you fit the solenoid to the body, fit the spring blade contact and notice that it has a slotted hole for fixing. Use this slot to adjust the blade up or down till, when the points are closed, the points on the spring blade are just slightly above the contact points on the rocker. When you get the blade correctly adjusted, you'll see that, when you open and close the points by moving the diaphragm, the points 'wipe' over each other. This goes a long way to prolonging their life. Pull the outer rocker down towards the solenoid, and check that the spring blade rests on the small lip on the Bakelite pedestal. If it doesn't, slacken the screw, swing the blade to one side and bend it very slightly till you get it right. If you have to do

this, remember to adjust the 'wipe' action of the points again.

Now to the two different types of rocker assembly. The early type didn't have any stop fingers for adjustment. With the points closed, hold the spring blade against the lip on the pedestal and use a feeler gauge to measure the gap between the fibre rollers and the top of the solenoid. It shouldn't be less than 0.030in (0.8mm). If it's wildly out, you can set the tip of the blade up or down slightly, but make sure it still rests on the lip, and check the 'wipe' action. If the gap is anything between 0.035in (0.9mm) and 0.050in (1.25mm) on these early rockers, we usually let it go.

On the later type of rocker assembly, measure the gap between the tip of the spring contact blade and the top of the pedestal with the points closed. It

should be between 0.030in (0.8mm) and 0.040in (1mm). If necessary, you can adjust the gap by gently using pointed-nose pliers to bend the top stop finger which bears on the underside of the pedestal. When you get the top gap within limits, measure the gap between the lower stop finger and the top of the solenoid, if necessary bending the finger till the gap is between 0.065in (1.6mm) and 0.075in (1.9mm).

Fit the solenoid to the body, lining up the marks you made, and tighten the screws. With rollers, remember to remove the matchsticks or wire fork before tightening the screws. Make sure none of the wires at the top is catching on anything, and refit the Bakelite top cover. Fit the waterproofing rubber band and, if necessary, a layer of sticky tape, and the pump's ready for test.

Fig. 6.16. The flow-smoothing chamber with a spring, and (inset and enlarged) the wire tool for asssembling it, made from 1/8in (3mm or 10swg) wire: A, B and E = 1/16in (1.6mm); C = 2in (50mm); D = 0.090in (2mm).

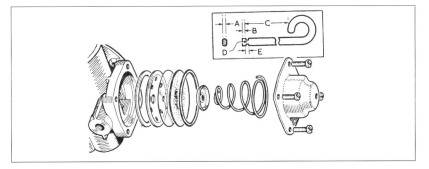

Chapter 7

Starter motors

Inertia drive starters

Unlike some later classics and most modern cars, which have pre-engaged starter motors, older classics are fitted with inertia starters. Just in case you're not clear about the difference, a pre-engaged starter has quite a large solenoid on the top, connected to a mechanical lever which moves the pinion gently into engagement with the ring gear on the flywheel before the motor begins to turn. On an inertia starter, the motor turns first, and when it gets up to speed the pinion flies along a helix and whangs into mesh with the stationary ring gear.

At least, that's what's supposed to happen. If, with a pre-engaged starter, you just get a click and nothing else happens except that the dash warning lights go dim, either there's an electrical connection fault or a motor fault. With an inertia starter, if you just get a whirring sound the pinion is sticking, and if you get a chattering sound, either the pinion or the ring gear (or both) is worn.

Before we go into stripping down the motor itself, it's as well to make sure that the fault isn't elsewhere, so we'll run through a series of checks. First, make sure that the battery is fully charged by testing with a hydrometer, and then check the battery terminals, the earthing strap where it goes to the body or chassis, the earthing strap between the engine and the chassis and the connections at the starter and solenoid. It's surprising how many 'dead' starters

magically come to life when these connections are cleaned and tightened.

You can check quite a lot just by physical inspection, but to check properly, and isolate the problem so you don't spend a lot of money just changing things and hoping for the best, there's nothing to beat a good multi-meter.

You can get cheap meters with an impressive selection of ranges, and for the sort of readings we're talking about here, they do an excellent job. But, as with all things, you get what you pay for, and it pays to fork out that little bit extra for a good quality instrument. Treated properly, it will last almost a lifetime. Whether you go for one with a pointer or one with a digital read-out is a matter of preference, but we prefer a digital one for most work, except possibly for checking the smoothness of variable resistors, because it's accurate, easier to read and it's generally more robust. With most analogue pointer-type meters, the more accurate and versatile the meter is, the more delicate the finely balanced movement.

You want to check voltages in the starter circuit when the starter is turning the engine, so take one of the low tension leads off the coil so the engine won't start. Set the meter to its voltage range on the setting covering 12 volts and hold the test prods across the battery terminals. With a fully-charged battery you should get a reading of 12 to 13.5 volts or 14 volts. Keep the meter connected, and get someone to operate the starter. You'll get a drop in the reading,

which will depend to some extent on the temperature, the rating of the battery and the size of the engine, but it shouldn't go much below ten volts.

If the reading drops right down, the trouble could be in the starter motor itself, but carry on with the other checks before you jump to conclusions. The next reading to take is with the meter connected at the starter, one of the test prods on the main terminal and the other on a clean part of the starter body. Which of the test prods goes to which point will depend on whether you've got a positive earth or negative earth system.

With the battery under the bonnet, and short main cables, the reading at the starter motor should be no more than half a volt less than the reading you got at the battery in your first test. With the battery in the boot, or under the seats, the drop will be a little more because of the voltage drop along the long cables, but certainly no more than one volt. If it's more, there's a high resistance (usually a bad connection) somewhere in the circuit. Check all the terminals and connections we mentioned, and clean them and tighten them if necessary. If this doesn't improve things, the trouble may be in the solenoid.

To check whether or not the high resistance is in the insulated part of the circuit or at an earth point, connect your meter between the battery live terminal and the main feed terminal on the starter. You should get the same reading as you got across the battery. Now get someone to operate the starter, and the voltage on your meter should drop to almost zero. A much higher volt reading means there's a high resistance somewhere in the insulated part of the circuit, either the battery, the solenoid or the starter. Check all the connections.

An inertia-drive starter will have a separate solenoid or starter switch in the main cable. To check the internal connection of the solenoid or switch, connect the meter across its terminals. Now get someone to operate the starter switch. When the solenoid operates, the reading should fall to zero if the internal connections in the solenoid or switch are perfect. At the most it should read less than half a volt. If it's much more than this, or if the reading goes up and down, the component needs overhauling or changing depending on whether or not you can get inside it.

The last check is for a high resistance in the earthing part of the circuit. Connect your meter between the body of the starter motor and the battery earth terminal. When someone operates the starter switch, the reading should stay at practically zero or, again, not more than half a volt. If the meter reads higher than this, either the starter body isn't making good connection with chassis earth (which indicates a bad connection at the engine earthing strap) or there's a bad connection between the battery earth cable and the body.

In summer, or with a warm engine, most starters will spin the engine if the total voltage drop is 1 to 1½ volts. To get the total, add the reading between the live terminal of the battery and the live terminal on the starter to the reading between the earth terminal on the battery and the body of the starter – both readings taken when the starter is being operated. On a cold morning with a cold engine, a total drop of much more than half a volt is likely to make the starter sluggish. The drop is more

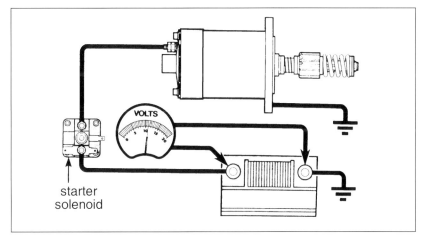

Fig. 7.1. With a fully charged battery, the reading across the battery terminals should not drop much below 10 volts when the starter is operated.

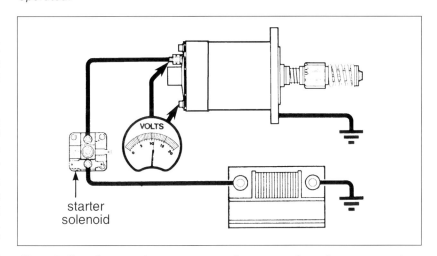

Fig. 7.2. Carrying out the same test at the starter, the voltage across the motor main terminal and the body should be almost the same as at the battery, probably half a volt less, but no more than one volt less.

Fig. 7.3. Using voltage drop to check for a high resistance in the insulated part of the circuit. The reading should drop almost to zero when the starter is operated.

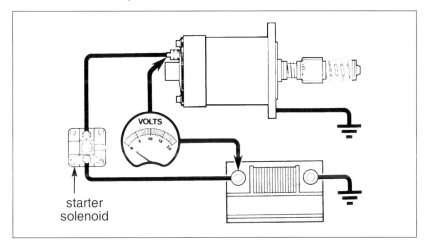

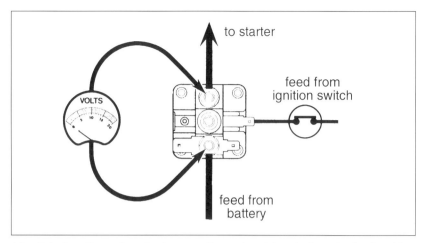

Fig. 7.4. A voltage drop test across the solenoid main terminals should also indicate almost zero, or at most half a volt, when the starter is operated. If it's much higher, the solenoid isn't operating properly.

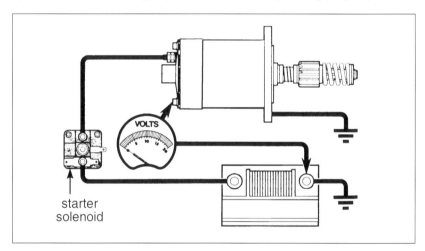

Fig. 7.5. Checking for a high resistance in the earth return part of the circuit. When the starter is operated, the voltage should stay at zero, or rise at the most to about half a volt.

Fig. 7.6. With a pre-engaged starter, you also start with a voltage check across the battery.

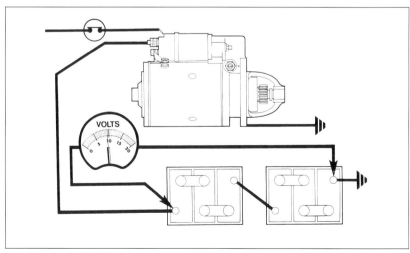

important than the actual battery voltage because a fully-charged 12 volt battery can be as low as 11 volts without any load when the temperature's way below freezing.

If all your voltage drop tests on the circuit came out right, but you still get a big drop in the first test you made (the reading across the battery terminals when the starter's operating), then the trouble's in the starter motor itself which is taking too much current.

With a pre-engaged starter motor, the readings are very similar, and you start with a voltage reading across the battery terminals. As with an inertia starter, when the starter is operated, the reading shouldn't fall below ten or so volts.

The solenoid for a pre-engaged starter is mounted on the motor itself, and is often fed through a relay. To check whether or not the relay is operating properly, connect your meter between the low-current feed terminal on the solenoid – that's the one with the thin cable going to it – and the body of the starter motor. When the starter switch is operated you should get the same reading here as you got across the battery terminals in your first test. If you get a low reading, or no reading at all, the relay is faulty, or the connections to it are faulty. If the relay is on its way out, you can often hear it clicking or buzzing as it tries to make contact, but it will also click and buzz if the connections to it, or the low-current connection at the solenoid, are poor.

Your next check is for the voltage across the starter. Connect the meter between the main starter feed terminal and the body of the motor. When the starter is operated, the reading shouldn't be more than half a volt less than the reading across the battery terminals. A low reading indicates a high resistance at the main solenoid contacts.

Now check the voltage drop in the insulated part of the circuit.

Connect the meter between the main terminal on the starter and the live terminal of the battery. You should get battery voltage. When someone operates the starter, the voltage should drop to almost zero. A high voltage reading means there's a bad connection somewhere in the insulated, or 'live' part of the circuit.

To test the internal switching of the solenoid, connect the meter across the two main solenoid terminals. You should get battery voltage. When the starter is operated, the voltage should fall to almost zero. A higher reading indicates a bad earth at the battery or the engine bonding strap, or a faulty solenoid.

As with an inertia starter, if your voltage drop tests come out OK, the trouble is most likely to be in the motor itself.

Assuming you have identified the trouble as being with the motor, we'll look first at inertia starters. As you'll appreciate, the pinion on an inertia starter has quite a hard life, not to mention the shock load on the starter motor, and it's a tribute to them that they keep working as long as they do. There comes a time, however, when they've had enough. In some cases, the starter's beyond economic salvage but, with a surprisingly high proportion, a little money spent on new carbon brushes and maybe cleaning the pinion and helix, plus a couple of hours easy work, will see it fit for several more years of service. It's a lot cheaper then shelling out for a replacement.

When you've got the starter off, move the pinion back and forth along the shaft. It should move freely and easily. If it feels sticky, gritty or notchy, it won't be reliable and it needs taking to pieces to overhaul it. This is about the only time you're likely to run into a snag because, unless it's a very early starter, you need a special tool to compress the large spring on the shaft. On early inertia starters, the pinion was held on the shaft by a

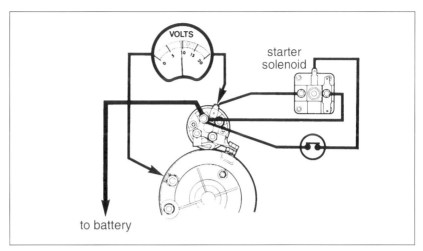

Fig. 7.7. The connections for checking whether or not the starter relay, if fitted, is operating properly.

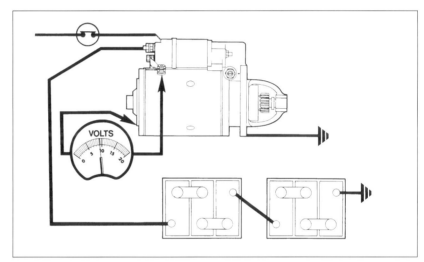

Fig. 7.8. Taking a voltage drop test on a pre-engaged starter. As with an inertia starter, the voltage should drop to half a volt or less.

Fig. 7.9. Checking the voltage drop on the insulated part of the circuit. It should drop to almost zero when the starter is operated.

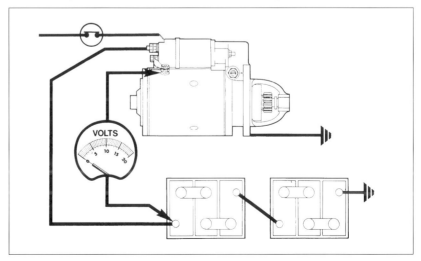

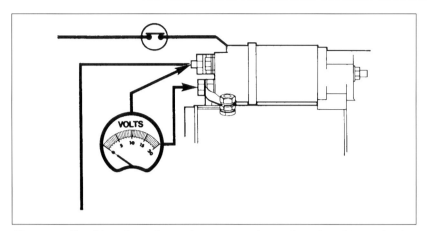

Fig. 7.10. Checking the voltage drop across the main solenoid terminals. Once again it should drop to almost zero when the starter is operated.

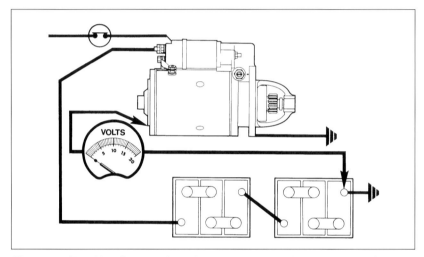

Fig. 7.11. Checking for a high resistance in the earth return part of the circuit. When the starter is operated, the voltage should stay at zero, or rise at the most to about half a volt.

castellated collar, nearly always with a left-hand thread, and locked with a split pin. With these, life is easy, you just take out the pin and unscrew the ring. On later models, which you've probably got, the collar is held by a circlip and you have to compress the spring to take the circlip off.

The compressor is quite a simple affair and you used to be able to buy them quite cheaply in most accessory shops, but we enquired at three shops in our area and they no longer keep them.

You might be lucky and find that your local shop still has a compressor in stock but, if not, it isn't difficult to make one, and we made one for this book (see *Fig.*

7.13). You need a couple of pieces of 6.5mm (1/4in) thick mild steel plate. The outside dimensions aren't critical, but we would suggest you make the plates at least 80mm (3⅛in) square. We made our tool from some 50mm (2in) wide plate that we happened to have handy, and we managed, using a socket wrench, to bend the plate with the arch-shaped hole on a very rusty and seized starter drive. Play it safe, and make the plates 80mm (3⅛in) square.

One plate has a 25.4mm (1in) hole in the centre, and two clearance holes for 8mm (5/16in) setscrews on the centreline 60mm (2⅜in) apart. The second plate is similar except that the holes are

drilled and tapped M8, and the centre hole is cut down to the base to form an arch shape. You also need two high tensile M8 setscrews 55mm (2¼in) long.

We haven't got a drill large enough to take a 25.4mm (1in) drill bit, though we could have got a local engineering works to drill the holes for us. Instead, we drilled a circular series of 4mm (3/16in) holes just inside the circumference, chopped out between them with a narrow cold chisel and filed the hole to size.

To use the tool, you wind the pinion down the shaft a little, slip the arch-shaped plate behind the spring, and the other plate on the end. Tighten the setscrews to compress the spring clear of the retaining collar. The collar usually sticks, so tap it down to expose the wire circlip which you can prise off with a screwdriver. Then the retaining collar, spring, helix collar and pinion all slide off the shaft.

If the pinion sticks, it's usually because of old oil, dirt or rust. If it's action is notchy, it's usually because of burrs on the splines of the shaft. Wash everything off in white spirit and try the helix collar along the shaft. If it doesn't slide freely you might have to dress the burrs on the shaft splines with a fine file or oil stone slip but, apart from that, the drives are usually in quite good condition. If the teeth on the pinion are worn, your best bet is to find a second-hand starter with a pinion in better shape and make one good one out of the two. The same pinions were used on quite a few different makes of car. Some drives were fitted with a very light gauge anti-rattle spring, and we've known these to come unwound at the end and jam the helix. If this happens, it's very awkward trying to reform the end of the coil, so look for another spring.

Check the armature shaft to make certain it isn't bent. A bent shaft isn't common, but it can happen if someone accidentally operates the starter switch while the engine is running and the pinion hits the flywheel ring gear while this is rotating at 1,000rpm or more. It could also happen if the ignition has been set much too far advanced and the engine has kicked back violently when someone tried to start it. Hold the body of the starter in a vice and turn the shaft. If the shaft is very badly bent, the armature core may even be rubbing on the yoke pole pieces. You can feel this and see evidence of the rubbing when you dismantle further. If only the long drive end of the shaft is bent, indicated by the extreme end rotating in a small circle instead of turning true, you may also find the pinion teeth badly worn. The bearing at the drive end may also be badly worn. The armature may turn freely, and the starter may even work, but a replacement pinion, and the flywheel ring gear, will have quite a short life. If you suspect a bent armature shaft but aren't sure, you can have it checked between centres in a lathe, but it's easier to look for another starter to get another armature.

Moving now to the other end of the starter, to the commutator and brush gear, you might have one of two types. The older type with an axial or in-line commutator often has a metal band clamped round the outside which you take off to get at the brushes. The later type has a face commutator on the end of the shaft with no band round the outside.

Dealing first with the older type, make a hook from a piece of fairly stout wire and, dealing with each brush in turn, lift the circular spring away from the brush and hold it while you lift the brush out. Then let the spring bear down inside the empty holder. Try to stop them uncoiling and running free but, if they do, use your hook to wind them back again. Take the nuts, washers and spacers off the main terminal post before you undo the two long through-bolts which hold the end plates to the yoke. These through-bolts can often be very

tight and you may have to hold the yoke in a strap in the vice and use a large heavy-duty screwdriver. When you pull the end-cover off, two of the brushes will come with it and two will stay behind attached to the field coils. The other end-plate will come away complete with the armature.

The inside of the starter body, or yoke as it is usually termed, will be covered in copper dust as the brushes are made from sintered copper with a small amount of carbon. Dust it all out because it's a conductor and can cause shorts. If the insulation of the field coils, or the terminal post, are in a bad way you might be better off looking for a starter in better condition but if, as is likely, they dust off OK, it's still worthwhile checking for electrical continuity and possible shorting.

Set your meter to continuity checking and, in the case of a series-parallel-wound starter test between the two tapping points of the field coils where the brush leads are fastened. In the case of a series-wound starter, test between the main terminal post and the common point where the brush leads are fastened to the field coils. Failure to get continuity means that one of the coils is open circuit. Next, test for possible shorting between the field coils and the yoke. Clean a part of the yoke body with glasspaper and test between the yoke and the field coil tapping points on a series-parallel starter or between the yoke and the main terminal post on a series-wound starter. If your meter indicates continuity here, the field coils are shorting to the yoke.

If you find either lack of continuity through the field coils, or shorting to the yoke, look for another starter. We have known people, even professionals, take the field coils out to re-insulate them by undoing the pole piece screws with an impact driver but we do not recommend you try it. The proper tool for undoing these screws is a wheel screwdriver mounted in a frame, and a pole

shoe expander should be used to hold the pole pieces in place when the screws are replaced. These tools are not normally found outside a professional reconditioning workshop.

Clean the commutator with fine glasspaper. Don't use emery paper or wet and dry rubbing-down paper as these contain carborundum which can short out the commutator segments. Unless it's badly ridged with a lip at the end, it will clean up well. If you are friendly with someone who has a lathe, even quite badly ridged commutators can be skimmed provided the skimming doesn't reduce the diameter so much that the brush springs can't put full pressure on the brushes. If the commutator is very badly worn, or if it has overheated to the point where the varnish on the windings has melted or the solder run, look for another starter in better condition. Don't undercut the insulation between the segments on a starter's commutator. You do this only on dynamos.

After cleaning or skimming, wipe the armature free of all dust with a petrol-moistened fluff-free rag and use your meter to check for any shorting between the commutator segments and the armature shaft. If you find any shorts, look for another starter motor.

If the brushes are worn down so that the circular spring hits, or almost hits, the metal brush holder before it puts pressure on the brush, you need new brushes. You can get them in accessory shops or from auto-electrical dealers and, if you can't get the exact ones because the starter's too old to be listed, look for ones which are slightly too wide or too broad. They can be filed down to size quite easily by rubbing them on a fine flat file. You can't solder the cables on your new brushes directly to the starter as the old ones are spot welded. What you do is cut the old brush cable about an inch or so from the brush, cut the cable on the new ones and solder the two cables together. Remember to slip a length of insulated sleeving on the field coil brush cables before you solder them.

Older books and manuals preach a counsel of perfection and tell you to bed in the new brushes using a piece of glasspaper wrapped round the commutator. What they don't tell you is the easy way to do it. If you just wrap the glasspaper round the commutator it slips and often tears. The easy way is to stick it on with an adhesive that's readily removable afterwards. It's easy, but time consuming. We've come across plenty of commercially reconditioned starter motors where the ends of the brushes have been left flat to bed themselves in. The starter will work OK if you do this, but you may get slight arcing at the brushes till they are at least partly bedded in, which shortens the time before the commutator needs cleaning again. We leave it to you whether or not you want to bed them in.

Putting things back is much the same as taking them apart. The armature will go in easily if you hold the brushes halfway out of their holders by wedging the

springs at their sides. Lucas used to say that the pinion and it's drive should be sparingly lubricated with a special grease but we've found that any grease tends to attract dirt which makes the pinion sticky. We always assemble them dry and clean and haven't found any adverse effects.

On most starters you will find a piece of insulating card inside the yoke to stop any chance of the terminal post shorting against the side. If this is in poor condition it needs renewing. Don't use any old piece of card, the proper stuff has high insulation properties and retains these in a damp atmosphere. Ordinary card is likely to short out if it gets damp. We once came across a home rebuilt starter where the original card had been supplemented by a piece of plastic cut from a washing-up liquid bottle. It worked for a time, before the plastic became soggy with heat and the motor shorted out. Always use the proper material. Some electrical wholesalers stock it in sheets, or you may be able to get a piece from a firm that rewinds electric motors.

On the later type of motor with the face armature, the pinion drive is the same, and attention to the

commutator and brushes is similar but much simpler. Here, you have a brush end-plate held by four small hexagon headed screws, or by a central spire nut. The spire nut will be damaged getting it off, so use a new one on reassembly. The teeth may also have raised burrs on the shaft, so clean these down with a fine file before you pull the end-plate off to avoid damaging the bearing.

The plate lifts off complete with two brushes, this time with the terminal post, and two stay behind, just like the older type. The brushes are triangular and sit in housings in a plastic moulding on the end cap. Pressure to push them against the commutator is provided by coil springs in the plastic moulding. Check that the coil springs have spring left in them, that the brushes are free in the housings and that they stick out far enough to press firmly against the commutator long before the springs are fully extended. If they are worn short, fit new ones. Once again, if your new brushes are too tight, ease them off with a fine file. In this case, the brushes do not need bedding in.

The armature comes out after you undo two screws at the other end and should be cleaned with

Fig. 7.12. An exploded drawing showing the essentials of an inertia drive starter except for the pinion drive.

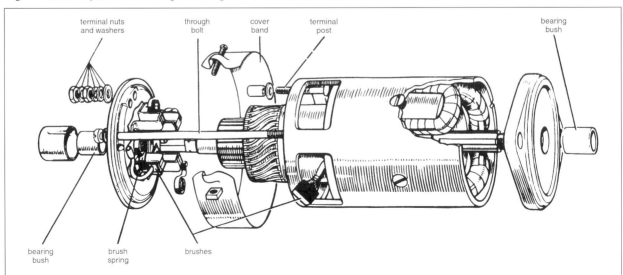

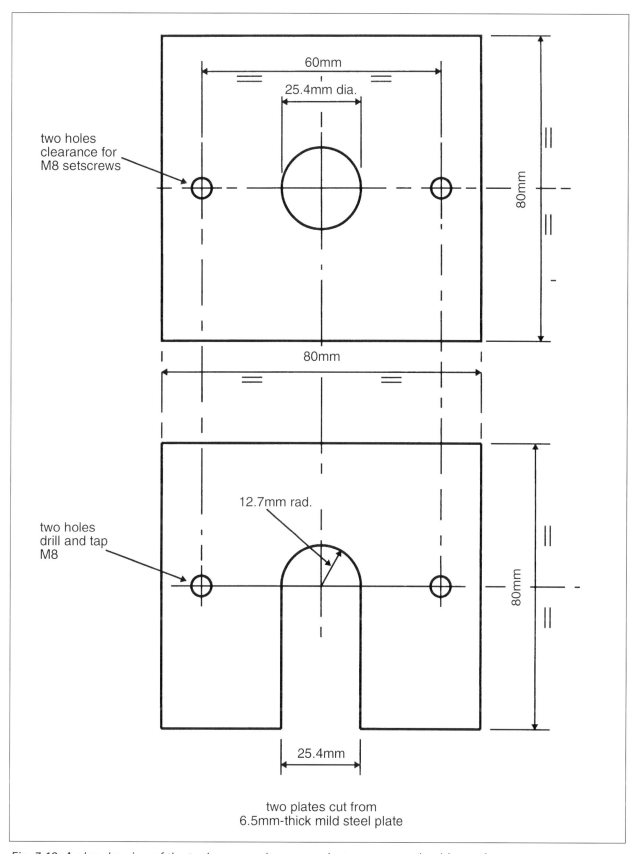

Fig. 7.13. A plan drawing of the tool you may have to make to compress the drive spring.

Fig. 7.14. We made this tool from a piece of stock plate 50mm wide, but it was possible to bend the arch using a socket wrench. We suggest you stick to the beefier sizes in the drawing.

Fig. 7.15. With the spring compressed, you may have to punch the collar down before you can lever off the circlip.

Fig. 7.16. The inertia drive in pieces. This one was sticking because of dirt and slight rust, but it cleaned up perfectly.

Fig. 7.18. The brushes on a starter with a face commutator are easy to get at after you undo the end-plate, usually held by four small bolts, but sometimes by a spire nut.

Fig. 7.17. With this type of older inertia drive you don't need a spring compressor, the castellated nut at the end usually has a left-hand thread.

Fig. 7.19. This face commutator was dirty, but cleaned up after only a rub with a petrol-moistened rag.

Fig. 7.20. With an axial commutator and windows in the yoke, use a piece of stout wire to hook the springs up from the brushes. When replacing the armature it helps to wedge the brushes as shown here.

fine glasspaper. The same remarks about skimming apply. Once again, get rid of all the dust and dirt before you reassemble things, and

check the condition of the insulating card.

The bearings in a starter motor don't wear very rapidly. The starter is rotating usually only for a few seconds while the engine is being started, and the rest of the time it's idle. Even assuming the engine has been started 20 or 30 times a week, using the starter for five seconds each time, that comes to only 150 seconds or two-and-a-half minutes a week, a little over two hours a year. Even so, it's worth checking them. Try rocking the end-plate at the drive end when the armature is out of the yoke, and also try the end-plate which carries the brushes. You are certain to find some wear, but we can't tell you how much is permissible. The makers will say 'none'. A starter with just a little wear in the bearing will probably go on working happily for years, but eventually it will become noisy, and the pinion wear will be more rapid than with new bearings. You might also find that the teeth on the flywheel ring gear wear more rapidly than they should.

New bearings aren't very easy to come by. You might be lucky and get some from a specialist classic auto-electrical firm, but some of them want to hang on to the stocks they've got for their own reconditioning. If you do get some, the old bushes are pressed out with a mandrel and the new ones pressed in with a shouldered mandrel to avoid burring the edges. You need a proper press for the job. You can't do it in a vice, so you may have to enlist the help of a friendly garage. If your starter's bushes are very worn, and your tool resources are limited, it might be better to look for another starter motor.

Pre-engaged starters

Pre-engaged starters are easily recognised because they have a large solenoid mounted on the top. As the term pre-engaged suggests, the solenoid pushes the starter pinion into engagement with the flywheel before it turns on the power. This is much kinder to both the pinion and the flywheel than the inertia type of starter.

Fig. 7.21. In this cutaway drawing of a typical pre-engaged starter, the solenoid is held to its lever by a nut and washer.

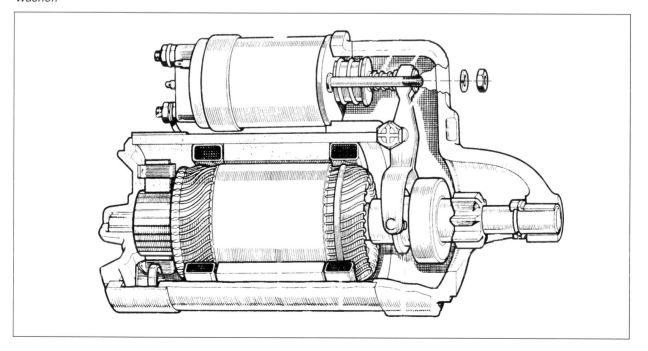

When you turn the ignition key to 'start', the solenoid pushes on a lever which, in turn, pushes the pinion along its shaft to engage with the flywheel. Then it moves a little further against a spring to turn on the power. There is a one-way clutch on the pinion drive so that if the key is held too long, the accelerating flywheel doesn't over-drive the starter motor.

If you were unable to make the meter checks we went through earlier, maybe because you have bought a second-hand starter, you can check the solenoid on your bench provided you've got a large vice to hold the starter, or a large G-clamp to clamp it to the bench. It needs to be held firmly because there is quite a big torque reaction when the starter turns, and it could easily damage your hands if it were not held securely.

Put a fully-charged battery on the bench near the starter and connect the earth terminal of the battery to one of the starter mounting holes. Use a nut and bolt, and a heavy cable, the battery's earthing strap is ideal. Now take a lighter cable from the positive terminal of the battery and touch it to the small push-on terminal on the solenoid. When you do this, the solenoid should work and the pinion should be pushed forward.

Now take another heavy cable from the battery positive terminal to the main terminal on the solenoid which normally takes the main lead from the battery. The starter won't turn yet because the solenoid hasn't completed the circuit. Now touch the lighter cable from the battery positive terminal on to the small terminal of the solenoid. This time, the pinion should move forward and, as it comes to the end of its travel, the starter should spin with quite a jump and plenty of torque. Keep your fingers well out of the way of the pinion. The fact that the starter spun with no load doesn't prove that it will generate enough torque to turn the engine, so it may still

need stripping, but at least you know the solenoid is operating properly.

To start dismantling, take off the short electric link cable that joins the starter and the solenoid. Then undo the bolts, usually two, which hold the solenoid to the starter. In most cases, you can unhook the end of the solenoid from its lever. Quite often you can't see what you're doing to unhook it, but all

that's needed is to push the solenoid in against a spring and lift it upwards. Don't lose the anti-vibration packing under the solenoid. In a few cases, you might find a plug at the end of the solenoid housing. Take out this plug, and take off the nut and washer which hold the end of the solenoid to its lever.

There will be a pin through the starter on which the pinion lever

Fig. 7.22. On this small French starter, the lever pin is held by a split pin. On others you may find a spire nut, the end may be peened over, or the pin may be eccentric and held by a nut.

Fig. 7.23. The solenoid just unhooked from the end of the lever.

Fig. 7.24. On the French motor, the forked lever wasn't attached to the clutch, it just sat in a groove.

Fig. 7.25. The brush end-plate is held by a spire nut and a spring.

Fig. 7.26. On this Lucas starter, the lever pin is peened over at the end, and the solenoid has to be pushed in against a spring and turned to free it from the lever.

pivots. Some pins, usually on smaller motors, are held by a spire nut, and some are peened over to hold them in. If yours is peened over, take off the peening with a drill. This will probably make the pin too short to use again, so find a close-fitting bolt to replace it. On more powerful motors the pins are often eccentric and locked with a nut. When you set up the pinion after overhaul, you use this eccentric to set the pinion clearance. Without an eccentric, the clearance is set by shims, so check where they go and don't lose them. With the lever and pin removed, undo the screws holding the large nose cover and bearing, and the armature will lift out.

Checking the armature, brushes and commutator are the same as on an inertia starter, but on a pre-engaged starter there is also the pinion clutch to check. You'll be very unlucky to find any appreciable wear on the pinion teeth, or in the clutch. But sometimes the clutch becomes sticky from lack of use and doesn't engage properly. Much more rarely, it fails to free when the engine fires, and the flywheel drives the starter at high speed. Treat this as a possible cause for a starter which is badly burnt inside.

Hold the body of the clutch and try turning the pinion back and forth. It should turn easily one way, and lock up immediately when you turn the pinion the other way. You can't buy clutches except from a firm that reconditions starters, and they will probably want to sell you a complete reconditioned starter. However, if you are cannibalising a couple of starters to make one good one, you can change the clutches on identical models. The assembly usually comes off after you undo a snap ring. Sometimes you can get at the snap ring easily, but on some heavy-duty starters you may have to first knock back a fairly tight collar using a piece of steel tube or an old long socket.

After overhauling the main body of the starter, fit the solenoid lever and pin. If it is the type held by a spire nut, or with a peened over end, that's all you have to do. If it's the type with an eccentric pin, you have to set the pinion clearance. Before you can do this, you have to refit the solenoid and hook its end into the lever. If you've got a six-volt DC supply handy, use this for

Fig. 7.27. The Lucas starter drive dismantled. Note that the solenoid lever is pivoted on a ring next to the clutch.

energising the solenoid to set the pinion clearance. If not, you can use 12 volts, but don't keep the solenoid energised for more than five seconds or so at a time or you could overheat it.

Energise the solenoid from a battery in the same way as when testing it, but without the heavy

power cable to the main terminal. When you energise it, the pinion will fly forward. You are looking for a clearance between the front face of the pinion and the thrust collar of about 0.005in (0.13mm) to 0.015in (0.38mm). Adjust the eccentric pin to get the correct clearance, and lock it.

Fig. 7.28. Test the clutch by turning the pinion. It should turn freely one way, but lock up instantly the other way.

Fig. 7.29. With an eccentric lever pin you have to set the pinion clearance. The setting is quite generous, 0.005in to 0.015in (0.13mm to 0.38 mm).

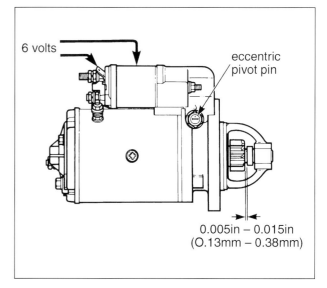

Chapter 8

Wiper motors

As with many small motors on a car, most of the problems with wiper motors are electrical rather than mechanical, though with wiper motors you may be confused by mechanical problems outside the motor, with the linkage or wheel boxes, so always check these before you start removing and stripping the motor.

Unfortunately, you can't get parts from Lucas agents any longer, but there are specialists who can supply. With other makes, availability is patchy, but again a specialist may be able to help. If all else fails, try cannibalising another motor.

Before you take the motor off the car, disconnect the motor's leads and check that you're getting voltage at the various feed colours at the main loom plug or the bullet connectors. Ideally you should get battery voltage, but there's bound to be a small resistance at the switch and a small voltage drop in the cables. However, you should get at least 11.5 volts with a fully-charged battery and nothing else except the ignition switched on (close the door and boot if necessary to switch off the courtesy lights). If you get a low voltage, or no voltage at all, check for a break in the wiring or something wrong with the switch and put this right before you go any further.

If the voltage feeds are OK, disconnect the wiper motor from the wiper blade drive. The method of disconnecting mechanical arm linkages varies but it's usually pretty self-evident. On linkages which have rubber housings over

ball joints, the link arms usually just lever off, but if you have difficulty, undo the nut and take the crank lever off the motor shaft.

On the type of motor which drives a tubular rack you take off the wiper blades, undo the knurled or sometimes hexagon nut which secures the rigid outer tube of the drive rack, undo the motor mounting bolts and pull the motor, complete with the inner rack, out of the rigid tube. Pull it steadily or you may damage the gears in the wheelboxes. If you can get to the wheelboxes easily, it's best to bring them out with the rack, or at least undo the back plates and lift the rack out. If you can't get to the wheelboxes, take the top cover off the motor, disconnect the inner rack and leave it behind.

With the wiper drive linkage disconnected from the wheelboxes you can check the current consumption of the motor under light running. Put the motor on the bench and run it somewhere where, if the rack is still attached, it isn't going to catch on anything. Take a lead straight from the live side of a battery and connect it, via an ammeter, to each of the feed wires in turn with the appropriate earth wire connected to the earth side of the battery. Remember that with the self-limiting and self-parking feeds, the motor may run for a little while, possibly one complete wipe of the screen, before it switches itself off. Checking these two feeds will ascertain the internal switching in the motor as well as continuity. With the normal-speed and high-speed feeds, leave the motor

running for about half a minute to warm up. When the motor warms up and the current settles down, it should operate with a current consumption not more than 3.5 amps, usually less with a wiper in good condition.

If the motor runs but is sluggish and the current taken is higher than this, it could be corrosion inside or heavy dried-out grease causing mechanical friction inside the motor, or it could be worn carbon brushes or a dirty commutator, possibly with carbon dust shorting out a couple of segments. If it runs well on some settings but not on others, it's probably poor connections or a fault with the switch. If it remains completely dead on any settings, you may be unlucky and find that the motor's burnt out in a big way, but don't discard it before investigating because it just might be a thermostatic overload switch which decided not to reset itself when it cooled down.

These overload thermostatic switches used to be fitted to a number of wiper motors. They were bi-metallic strip switches, often riveted to the body casing, or yoke, and cut out if the wiper got too hot. The idea was that if the rack linkage or wheelboxes got too stiff, or the wiper blades met really heavy resistance like packed snow, the wiper motor would stall and overheat trying to overcome this. The thermostatic switch would open and cut current to the wiper motor to prevent it burning itself out. It was a good idea if the thermostatic switches had been reliable. Unfortunately they weren't, they were cutting out at far too low a temperature and some motors were cutting out after a couple of hours or so use in normal rain.

The Lucas parts manuals listed the switches as factory-set and not suitable for individual replacement, which meant that the whole motor had to be replaced if the switches gave trouble. We suspect that Lucas was getting far too many motors back which were perfect except for the thermostatic overload switch, and they issued a service bulletin suggesting that Lucas agents could un-rivet the switch from the yoke and 'attempt to reset them by bending the moving contact'. This didn't prove very successful either, so around 1973 Lucas did away with them and issued a service bulletin saying that: 'Motors fitted with these devices can be brought into line with current practice by removing the two connecting wires, joining them together with solder and suitably insulating the joint.'

If you come across a motor with one of these thermostatic switches we suggest you do the same. Heat-shrink tubing would be a suitable insulation. Some other makes were fitted with similar switches and, as far as we know, they were dropped as well, but we haven't got any specific bulletins about them, so on makes other than Lucas, we leave it up to you.

If the motor performs faultlessly on these tests, yet the wipers still don't want to work properly, look for problems with stiff linkages, a worn rack or worn wheelboxes, or a faulty switch at the dash or steering column with corrosion causing a high resistance. If the motor doesn't pass the free-running tests, you need to strip it down to find out why.

There are too many makes and models of wiper motor for us to strip and photograph every one, but in principle they are all fairly similar and we've taken a representative selection apart to show how to go about it and included a couple of exploded drawings.

Lucas DR series

We'll begin with the popular Lucas DR series, in this case a DR3. Start by taking off the top cover to expose the gearbox. On some motors, though not on the one here, there's a dome which is separate from the top cover itself. This dome often carries a setting pip for the parking limit switch, so if yours has a separate dome, scribe a line across the dome and top cover before you take them apart so you can get them back in the same relative position, otherwise you may find the wipers stopping halfway across the screen instead of to one side and your having to experiment to find the correct dome position.

There will be big blobs of grease inside, so scoop and clean out as much of this as you can to make it easier to check on the position of things like shim washers and clips. You'll see that there's a large gearwheel driven by a shaft from the motor. Attached to the gearwheel is a crank arm connected to a link, often called the cross head (borrowing from steam engine terminology) attached to the inner part of the drive rack and sliding in a channel, often a nylon channel. As the gearwheel turns it gives a back and forth motion to the cross head and the rack.

On this type of motor the bottom of the cross head has a projection on it to operate the parking switch which is adjustable by a knurled nut on the outside of the gearbox. The parking switch

Fig. 8.1. Exploded view of the Lucas DR3 wiper motor.

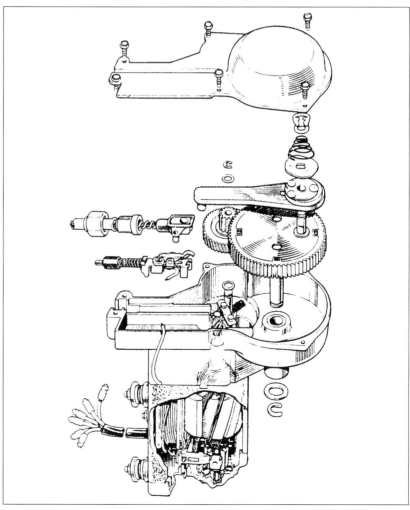

Fig. 8.2. When you take the top cover off the DR3, the inside will be full of old grease.

Fig. 8.3. A shorting point is where the parking switch cable fits in a groove in the housing.

Fig. 8.4. Check the condition of the wires where they pass into the yoke.

Fig. 8.5. With the grease scooped and cleaned out, you can check things more easily.

Fig. 8.6. Check and clean the contacts on the parking switch.

Fig. 8.7. The DR3 brushes with their tension spring and the red insulating retainer plate.

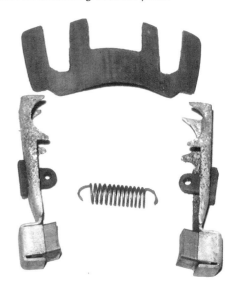

Fig. 8.8. Clean the commutator and check for shorts between the segments, and between the segments and the armature body.

has a cable coming from it which runs back down to the motor housing, and a possible trouble spot is where the cable passes through the housing. It can chafe, or the insulation can be hard and brittle, and it sometimes shorts out, so check its condition and, if necessary, make a note to renew it.

Before you can take the inner rack off you have to free the crank arm from the large gear, sometimes by undoing a nut and sometimes by taking off a circlip, and you can then lift the arm up and out of the hole in the cross head at the end of the inner rack, and lift the rack out. Watch the order of any washers or springs over the top of the crank arm and make sure they go back in the correct order.

The setting of the parking switch may not have been adjusted for years, and you may well find that the knurled nut, which should be finger tight, doesn't want to shift because the outside part of the thread is corroded. The inner part of the thread, inside the housing, is unlikely to be corroded because it's spent its life covered in grease, so after dosing things with easing fluid try screwing the knurled nut inwards to expose more thread which you can clean up with a wire brush. After you've got things free check that the switch operates

properly and doesn't stick in one position.

Take out the long bolts through the motor yoke, but don't take the yoke off yet. Take the end-cover off and take out the brushes. They're held by a shaped piece of red insulating card. Now you can take out the armature and take off the yoke. Check the wiring to make sure that it's not chafed. If you have to renew any wires, keep the colours the same. A couple of lengths of old loom from a breaker makes a good supply of various colour wires.

As with most wiper motors, unless the armature looks burnt and black there's probably nothing wrong with it except for a dirty commutator. Clean this with a petrol-moistened rag and fine glasspaper. Then get your meter and check that there aren't any breaks in the windings by going round testing for continuity between adjacent pairs of commutator segments. Then go round again with the meter set to ohms to check that the windings aren't shorting between turns. The windings should show a resistance reading of about 0.3 ohms to 0.5 ohms and it should be fairly consistent between each adjacent pair of commutator segments. If you get a reading much lower than 0.3 ohms, or no resistance at all, on any pair of segments it probably indicates a short in the windings and you will have got a high current consumption in the light running test. On the motor we stripped we got readings around 0.45 ohms. Lastly, check for any shorts between the commutator segments and the spindle of the armature. Strictly speaking you need an electrical test bench with 110 volts a.c. and a 15 watt lamp for this, but we don't advocate using mains voltages like this at home, and a meter check will show up a serious short.

Any shorts or open circuits on these tests means that the armature needs replacing. You might be lucky and get a new

armature from a Lucas agent, but don't bank on it, and in any case it will probably cost more than a second-hand motor with a good armature which you can cannibalise or restore.

Lucas 12W to 17W series

Another popular Lucas type of wiper motor on British classics is the 12W to 17W series (see Fig. 8.9). They were all two-speed motors and usually self-limiting, though the 16W was also available as self-parking. Externally they differ from the DL and DR series by having a round canister motor yoke held to the gearbox by two long through-bolts. They also have a nylon block switch assembly under the gearbox. We've taken a 14W as representative.

As well as giving the outside of the motor a good general clean before you start dismantling it, do any cleaning up you want to do on the cylindrical yoke canister before you take things apart. The outside of the canister is often quite rusty, and if you clean it with emery paper when it's off you'll get iron dust inside stuck to the magnets and you'll never get rid of it.

There's another very important point to watch when you're dismantling one of these motors. There are two marks, one on the yoke canister and the other on the gearbox housing which must line up when you refit the yoke to the gearbox. It's possible, indeed quite easy, to fit the yoke the wrong way round, 180° out of phase. If you do, the motor will run backwards when you start it and probably damage the switch assembly. The mark on the yoke is quite small, and if you can't find it because the yoke is rusty, as it often is, make some more marks after you've cleaned it up and before you take it off.

When you undo the through-bolts and pull the yoke off, the armature will probably come with it because it's held by the pull of the yoke magnets. Leave the

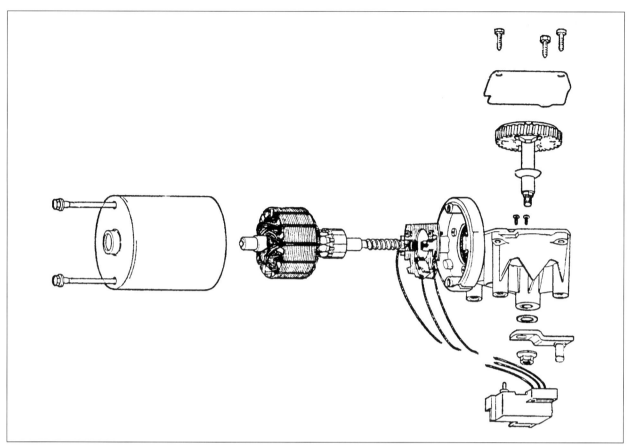

Fig. 8.9. This drawing is representative of the Lucas 12W to 17W series.

armature and yoke aside for the moment and deal with stripping the rest of the motor.

Taking the yoke off will have exposed the plate carrying the carbon brushes which has three leads coming from it, one for each brush, usually coloured red, blue and yellow. The red and blue leads normally come from the two full-width brushes opposite each other, and the yellow lead comes from the stepped brush which comes into circuit for high-speed running. Make a note of where they go, just in case your colours are different, and trace them back to the push-on Lucar connectors at the switch assembly. Make a note also of where each colour fits on to the switch, and then unplug them. Now you can undo the small screws which hold the brush plate and lift it off out of harm's way.

On the large gear wheel and crank arm, take off the circlip which holds the crank arm to the gearwheel. There should be a flat washer under the circlip and another flat washer between the crank arm and the gearwheel. They are different sizes, and the larger one should be underneath the crank arm. With the crank arm off try the slide of the cross head in the nylon channel to make sure the nylon isn't ridged and making it bind. It shouldn't be, but if it is it may account for a high current consumption, so make a note to do something about it before you put things together again. Check also that the large gearwheel turns freely without any binding or tight spots. The motor we stripped had been standing for some years and the gearwheel shaft was so dirty and dry it needed a little persuasion to get it to move at all. Turn the housing over and take off the circlip and flat washer that hold the gearwheel shaft. This is a blind

circlip with no ears for circlip pliers (should that be deaf circlip?). The easiest way to get it off is to put a screwdriver against one end and give it a sharp tap with a hammer. With average luck it will come halfway off and you can finish the job with a screwdriver, but sometimes it pings off with considerable force so direct it towards a rag on the bench because it's no fun crawling around the floor looking for a tiny piece of curved wire.

Before you lift the gearwheel out, wire brush the groove in which the circlip sat and check for any burrs which might damage the bearing when you lift it out. If there are any, take them off with a fine file. When you lift the gearwheel out take care not to lose the dished washer underneath it. This may come out with the wheel but it often sticks to the grease inside the housing and in either case it's easy

Fig. 8.10. Inside the gearbox, the 14W wiper is very similar to the DR3 except that there is no parking switch.

Fig. 8.11. When you undo the long bolts on the 14W, the yoke canister comes away, usually with the armature. Remember to mark the canister and the body before you take them apart.

to miss it. Finally, take off the nylon switch assembly by pushing sideways towards the end where the connectors fit and then downwards. At this stage there's no need to take out the screw which controls the armature end-float. If you leave it in it won't get lost.

The armature will be held firmly by the yoke magnets, and when you pull it out watch out for the small ball bearing on which it runs at the bottom of the yoke. The ball may lift out with the armature, it may stay in the bottom of the yoke, or it may come out of its seating and stick to one of the magnets.

Take care of it because the motor won't run without it. The ball sits in a hole in a small felt lubricating pad in a recess in the bottom of the yoke canister. The pad is probably safest where it is at the bottom of the yoke for the moment. Put the yoke in a plastic bag somewhere safe where it isn't going to get small pieces of metal or wires off wire brushes attracted to the magnets.

Clean the commutator with a petrol-moistened rag and fine glasspaper, and carry out the same meter checks on the armature that we went through on the Lucas DR. On the 14W motor we stripped we

got no indication of shorts, and resistance readings well within limits.

Next, check the brushes and brush plate. Clean away any old carbon dust because this can cause shorts between the brushes and all sorts of other problems. Check that the brushes are free to slide in their holders. If not, clean them. Check that the springs push the brushes well clear of the holders and haven't lost their tension. Lucas quotes a brush spring tension of 5oz to 7oz but we don't know of any restorer who checks this. Most go by feel. If they feel as if they'll exert a reasonable brush pressure

Fig. 8.12. Sometimes, as here, the ball end-bearing comes out with the armature, but it may stay behind, or stick to one of the yoke magnets.

Fig. 8.13. The brush carrier on the 14W is held to the top housing by three screws. Note that the speed control brush is stepped.

on the armature, they probably will. The two main brushes, the ones opposite each other, should be renewed if they've worn shorter than 0.2in (5mm). The third brush should be renewed if the narrow part has worn down to the full width of the brush.

These are figures quoted by Lucas and allow for the motor giving quite long further service. We've known motors run until the carbon is almost worn away, and we've known people get away with filing the third brush to increase the step slightly when it's almost worn level. It isn't something we advocate as general practice, but it might get you out of a hole. Worn down brushes may still work, but they won't give the motor its full restored life.

With the motor now completely in pieces, clean all the parts and check them for wear. You're not likely to find much, but it's as well to check. The large gearwheel is in two parts, a metal top-plate with a nylon gear underneath it. These motors were originally built for either left-hand drive or right-hand drive cars, and if you're restoring a second-hand motor there's just a remote possibility that you might have got hold of an imported one of the wrong hand. The only difference is in the relationship between the crank pin on the metal top-plate and the moulded cam on the underside of the nylon gear. On a motor for a right-hand drive car the crank pin should be almost above the cam. For a left-hand drive car the pin should be almost opposite the cam. If you fit a left-hand drive motor to a right-hand drive car, or vice-versa if you've got a left-hand drive car, the wiper blades will try to park on the wrong side of the screen.

AC Delco wiper motors

AC Delco wiper motors (see *Fig. 8.14*), fitted to most Vauxhalls and Bedfords, are also a tubular motor design and very simple to strip and

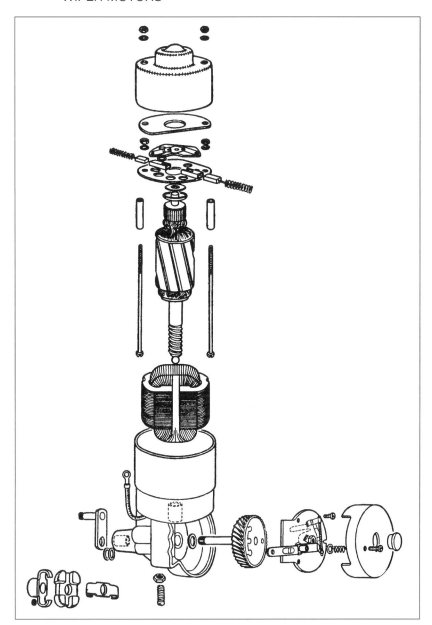

Fig. 8.14. A typical AC Delco wiper motor.

overhaul. The only points to watch out for are the end-float of the worm wheel shaft which is quite generous and should be between 0.002in (0.05mm) and 0.012in (0.30mm). If necessary, it can be shimmed. If you take the armature out to clean the commutator, be careful not to lose the thrust ball. The armature end-float is adjusted by its thrust screw until a 0.002in (0.05mm) feeler can be slid between the end of the thrust screw and the thrust ball.

Small Ford wiper motors

For its lighter cars, Ford used a series of small wiper motors (see *Fig. 8.15*) which were never intended to be repaired. If there were problems, Ford dealers always fitted an exchange motor. The motors were quite cheap and cheerful, but nonetheless gave good service. In almost every case where they give trouble, it's because of brushes and a dirty commutator.

Fig. 8.15. A cheap and cheerful wiper motor from Ford, not intended to be taken apart. Even so, you can do so, to check the brushes and clean the commutator.

Fig. 8.16. The bottom end-cover of the yoke comes off after you bend back three tags.

Vacuum wiper motors

Vacuum operated wiper motors go back to the 1920s when they were a tubular type, but these were ousted by the semi-circular paddle type in the 1930s, and were quite popular on small cars through to the late 1950s. Perhaps popular is an overstatement because although they were cheap and thus popular with manufacturers, owners weren't too keen on them as they tended to stop working at medium to high throttle openings when the depression in the inlet manifold dropped. The effect of this was later much reduced by fitting a reservoir tank in the vacuum feed line, and if you have one of these motors and want to keep your car original, we would advise fitting a tank as they were a popular after-

There aren't any screws to hold the end-cover on the yoke, just three bent-over tags. The metal is quite soft, and the tags can be straightened with a pair of pliers, but go easy because you can also break them off.

The brushes are held in the end-cover, one brush connected to the end-plate, and the other through a suppressor (which we've never known to give trouble) to a wire which runs back to the top plate. We don't advise trying to take the yoke

off as it's also held by bent-over tags, stronger than the ones which hold on the end-cover, and difficult to undo. In any case, there's no need to take the yoke off because you can pull the armature out. It helps to give a turn or two to feed it out of engagement with the main gear wheel inside the top cover. Clean and check the commutator as usual.

Problems under the top cover are rare. The only things that might possibly give trouble are the three spring contacts. Check that their pads are clean, and that they have a reasonable spring in them.

Fig. 8.17. Inside the end-cover are the two brushes and a suppressor, all held on an insulating plate supported by three rubber pillars.

Fig. 8.18. Clean and check the commutator in the usual way.

Fig. 8.19. Under the top plate, check that the three copper spring contacts have clean pads, and still some spring left in them.

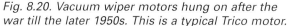

Fig. 8.20. Vacuum wiper motors hung on after the war till the later 1950s. This is a typical Trico motor.

Fig. 8.21. The slide control on-off switch on a vacuum wiper motor.

fitment. Many 'troubles' with vacuum operated wipers aren't the fault of the motor, they are caused by leaks in the vacuum lines, so make sure you check these before stripping the motor down.

The motor itself is robust and long-lasting, and most problems are caused by leaks, or dirt, at the sliding on-off control, or the kicker in the valve box not toggling over. The sliding control is in three parts, a lever, a leaf spring and a sliding control block with elongated holes to allow them to slide. When the control block slides, it either covers or uncovers vacuum ports in the body. The assembly is held on by two screws with plain shanks slightly larger than the threads so they are tightened without affecting the sliding operation. Between the control block and the body is a fairly thick rubber gasket with plain holes for the screws so that it doesn't slide. Take care of it, we haven't been able to find new ones, but they seldom wear.

Servicing the control is just a matter of cleaning, and when you put the gasket back make sure you get it the correct way up. We've come across them upside-down, but you can't go wrong if you line up the holes and slot in the gasket with the holes and slot in the body.

Don't put any grease or oil on this sliding mechanism, it should operate dry. Don't try bending the leaf spring to get more pressure on the slide. If you feel that it needs more pressure, use slightly thicker washers under the heads of the screws.

The mechanism inside the valve chest at the front of the motor looks quite complicated when you first take the cover off because it's usually smothered in grease and you can't see how it works. If you wash the grease out, and then turn the wiper spindle gently back and

Fig. 8.22. The toggle action in the vacuum valve box looks complicated, but it works very simply.

forth with a pair of pliers, you'll see that the valve has a simple toggle action rather like some electrical switches. Because it spends its life in a grease bath, the toggle mechanism seldom wears, and most troubles are caused by old grease which hardened when the motor stood idle for months, or even years. Under the gasket on the cover there's a square of felt which acts as a breather.

After washing out the old grease, take the mechanism out to dry out the chamber and make sure that none of the old grease found its way under the slide valve and blocked the three small ports in the body. First, look at the diagram (see Fig. 8.23) to identify the parts.

Use a small pair of pointed nose pliers to unhook the bottom end of the spring, lift off the valve kicker, then lift off the kicker yoke and spring without unhooking the spring from the yoke, and then the retainer. Finally, lift out the slide valve.

To get at the paddle, take out the six screws that hold the top cover and lift it off carefully to avoid damaging the two-piece gasket. Lift the gasket off gently with a thin knife blade, and take care of all the gaskets. We haven't found a source of new ones, and they can be fiddling to cut from gasket paper, though it can be done. The paddle is most unlikely to be worn, but you need to lift it out to clean the old grease from it and the chamber.

With everything clean and wiped off, make sure all the small ports in the body are clear, smear some good quality grease on the edges of the paddle, put it back in the chamber in the central position and fit the top cover. Reassemble the valve mechanism starting with the slide valve, then the retainer and the kicker yoke with its spring. Fit the valve kicker carefully, making sure that it engages properly with the yoke, and hold it down while you rehook the

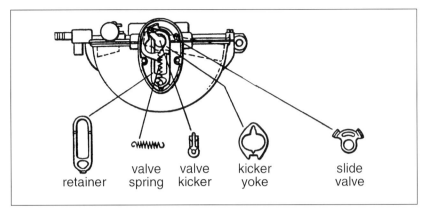

retainer   valve   valve   kicker   slide
   spring   kicker   yoke   valve

Fig. 8.23. Identifying the parts inside the vacuum motor valve box.

bottom end of the spring on the retainer. Keep a finger on the valve kicker to stop it jumping out, and work the spindle gently back and forth to check the toggle action. Finally, pack the valve chest with good quality grease and fit the cover.

Chapter 9

Trafficators

Electric direction indicators are quite an old idea and gained popularity, becoming a standard fitment, in the 1930s. Though there were one or two cars with illuminated arrows at the back, most indicators were quite thick semaphore arms appearing first in self-contained boxes mounted on a stalk at the bottom of the windscreen pillar. Although it was originally a Lucas trade name, the word trafficator became the common-usage name for all of them. These thick models gave way to slimline models which were usually mounted in the door pillars or, in the case of open cars, in the body just behind the driver's door.

As these were behind the driver, a regulation was introduced that if the trafficators were not self-cancelling, the car must be fitted with some form of indicator to let the driver know whether or not the trafficator was working and that he had remembered to cancel it. In most cases this was a warning light either built into the switch or mounted on the dash, though the Series One Morris Eight was equipped with a pair of tiny round mirrors mounted on the tops of the windscreen pillars. There were some clockwork self-cancelling switches, though they were not widely fitted.

Most self-cancelling switches of the later 1930s and early post-war years were mounted on the steering wheel hub, though one exception was Vauxhall which mounted the switch on an arm under the steering wheel. The switches were cancelled by a cam on the steering column which flicked them off when the steering wheel was returned to the straight ahead position. The steering wheel hub switch remained the standard form of switch till the introduction of the steering column stalk switch, though the Austin A30 hung on to a switch incorporating a warning light in the centre of the dash capping rail.

Even if, for safety on the road, you have fitted flashing direction indicators with a separate switch on the dash, it's nice to have the original semaphore trafficators working.

Trafficators are basically very simple but clever devices. The body is a solenoid wound with quite heavy gauge wire and with a soft iron rod down the centre. The rod is connected to the end of the semaphore arm through a linkage near its hinge. When current passes through the solenoid coil, the rod is pulled down and lifts the semaphore arm which drops under its own weight when the current is turned off. When the arm is down, the rod is held out of the solenoid core by a small coil tension spring. In this position the rod trips a locking catch at the hinge to stop the arm bouncing out with every road bump. When the rod comes down into the solenoid core it first unlocks the catch, then pulls the arm up. We have sometimes found this small coil spring broken or missing. They are quite unobtainable as a spare part, though you may possibly salvage one from a spare broken trafficator. We have successfully made them from the small coil springs often used to bias driving rollers and wheels in old record turntables, tape recorders and cassette players. Before you throw such things out it's always worth salvaging the screws, springs, copper contact strips and so on. We have an odds and sods box full of useful bits gleaned this way.

The solenoid body and the arm hinge are held in a metal frame, making an assembly for fixing to the car body. The arm has a translucent amber plastic body with a small festoon lamp inside and a detachable metal top. The metal top comes off after undoing a small screw, either at the tip of the arm or near its hinge. A connection from the solenoid takes current to the lamp so it lights when the solenoid receives current. On earlier trafficators this connection was a flexible lead and the lamp lit as soon as the trafficator was switched on and before the arm came up. With constant flexing either the wire inside the flexible lead broke or the insulation chafed giving a short. Later models were improved by having an internal switch. All this consists of is a spring metal strip riveted to the frame via a Paxolin insulating plate and connected to the feed terminal by a cable. The wire that runs down the arm for the lamp is soldered to an insulated button on the hinge end of the arm. When the arm reaches the up position, the button makes contact with the strip, so the lamp lights. If the arm comes up OK but the lamp doesn't light, look for a poor connection between the button and the spring plate. Earth return for the lamp is through the arm's metal

Fig. 9.1. Most British classics used this Lucas slimline Trafficator fitted in the door pillar.

Fig. 9.2. The top-plate on the arm must make good contact with the hinge for the bulb to light.

Fig. 9.3. On most Lucas Trafficators, the locking catch is a plate in the middle of the hinge. Push it down to free the arm.

Fig. 9.4. On later Lucas models, the bulb lights when the arm is up and this button makes contact with a spring plate on the body.

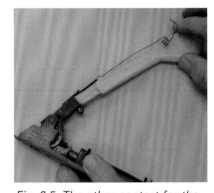

Fig. 9.5. The other contact for the bulb is a spring wire which sometimes gets corroded.

Fig. 9.6. This small coil spring operates the locking catch.

top. Usual faults with trafficators are short circuits, poor electrical connections, a sticking solenoid rod, corroded hinge pin, sticking locking mechanism or a bent arm – or a combination of any of these.

It's tempting to put your finger, or a screwdriver, under the arm to flip it up, but the locking-plate acts like a ratchet on Lucas trafficators, and on some others a positive lock that you can't force without breaking it. The Lucas ratchet lock will give, but continually doing this either breaks the plastic arm or weakens the mechanism which eventually binds and won't let the arm up. The proper way is to hold the locking-plate down with the end of a small screwdriver while you lift the arm. On some installations you can reach the locking-plate from outside with a long thin screwdriver, but on others you have

to take the trafficator out, usually from inside the car. On Lucas trafficators, the locking-plate is in the middle of the hinge sandwich assembly, but on some other makes it sticks out from the top.

Fig. 9.7. Check that the bulb wire isn't shorting where it goes under the hinge-plate. The insulating sleeve sometimes rots.

If the trafficator is completely dead, then first check the fuse. If it's blown, there could be a short either in the switch, somewhere along the cable or at the trafficator. Contrary to what some people may

Fig. 9.8. This is the detachable feed terminal on older models. The terminal below it is the earth return.

Fig. 9.9. This is a favourite place for chafing and shorting on older models.

turning in one direction, and not cancelling at all in the other direction.

If you're happy that there are no shorts in the cables, take the cables off both trafficators, in case there's a short in one of them, replace the fuse and check for voltage between the ends of the trafficator feed cables and the car body. If you get voltage each side here you can breathe a sigh of relief and check the trafficators themselves. Your first check is for a short between the feed terminal and the frame.

Unless you've got double-pole wiring, which is most unusual, the trafficator frame is the earth return. One end of the solenoid wiring is connected to the feed terminal and the other to the frame. Switch your meter to its lowest ohms setting and check between the feed terminal and the frame. On three trafficators we checked while writing this, we got readings varying from 5.1 ohms to 5.9 ohms, the resistance of the solenoid winding.

If you get a zero ohms reading, and you have one of the older trafficators with a flexible lead feeding the lamp, check carefully for a short between this lead and the frame. The lead is often trapped under the solenoid to stop it wandering about, and you have to take the solenoid out to free it

say, a sticking arm doesn't cause the fuse to blow because it doesn't affect the current passing through the solenoid. A favourite place for shorts (or breaks in the cable for that matter) on cars with the switches on the steering wheel hub is at the bottom of the long stator tube which runs down the steering column to carry the wires. This tube is usually held at the bottom of the steering box by a cap nut and an olive. When you take the nut and olive off, the stator tube pulls out from inside the car.

If you have to take the tube out for rewiring, put a drip tray under the steering box before you undo the nut because the oil will run out of the box. Remember to fill it up again when you finish. The cables at the bottom of the stator tube usually have bullet push-in connectors. The later plastic-covered ones lasted quite well, but the rubber-covered ones from the 1950s are usually soaked in oil and perished, giving ideal conditions for a bad connection or a short. When you put the stator tube back, make sure the self-cancelling cam is in the centre, or neutral, position and the wheels are pointing straight ahead. Otherwise you'll find the trafficators cancelling before you want them to when

Fig. 9.10. On older models, the solenoid lifts out after you undo a fixing screw. Check the cables and the card insulators.

Fig. 9.11. On some non-Lucas trafficators the locking catch is very positive. If you lift the arm without freeing it, something will break.

Fig 9.12. Grit and muck on the solenoid rod can make it sticky. Clean it with WD-40, but wipe it as dry as you can.

and renew it. You can take the solenoid off its frame by undoing a screw at the feed terminal and pulling the body of the solenoid down out of a tongue on the frame plate. The feed terminal is insulated from the frame by a Paxolin plate and a thin fibre insulator.

Check that the fibre insulator is in good condition and that the hole in the Paxolin plate for the fixing screw isn't oval and allowing the screw to short against the terminal plate. Quite often on these older trafficators you find a second terminal with its plate sandwiched between the body of the solenoid and the frame. This is an earth return terminal which proved more reliable than just metallic contact where the solenoid body hooked under the tongue on the frame. When you put the solenoid back, don't forget the thin fibre insulating cradle between the solenoid and the frame. Later trafficators with the built-in switch for the lamp don't have this second terminal. The solenoid body is riveted to the frame instead of using a screw and a tongue, which gives better contact. Earth return on these later models depends on good contact between the trafficator frame and the car body. Quite often there isn't good electrical contact here and a clean at the fixing screw does no harm at all.

Mechanical faults with trafficators are usually self-evident. Solenoid rods are sometimes reluctant to move freely because of corrosion and dirt. You can feel them grating when you lift the arm up and down. If the solenoid body is detachable, you can take things apart to clean the rod. If the solenoid body is riveted to the frame, a spot of WD-40 on the rod plus working the arm up and down and cleaning the rod with a rag will usually cure things, but don't flood it. Cleaning is better, and Lucas used to recommend that the rod ran dry.

The amber plastic part of the arm comes off for renewal when you undo a screw near its hinge. Just occasionally you come across a trafficator where the metal part of the arm, the hinge, is bent because someone walked into the arm while it was up, or even drove into a narrow garage with it up. If the arm hinge is bent it's almost impossible to straighten it while it's still attached. Even when you get it off, straightening is difficult, so it's best to look for a trafficator in better condition.

Sometimes, though, you may have two trafficators, one with a bent hinge-plate and one with a good hinge-plate but damaged in some other way or too badly corroded to clean. Provided the two trafficators are the same model you can swap bits over. The hinge pin is riveted so you have to file one end off before you can drive it out. You can try riveting in a new hinge pin if you can find a long enough rivet the right diameter, but it's much easier to use a small screw and nut and, when everything's back and working, solder the nut to lock it. If necessary you can file the head of the screw and the nut afterwards to give clearance in the car body opening.

Chapter 10

Horns

Most horns on classic cars can be divided quite handily into two types, the high frequency 'beep-beep' type and the musical 'Windtone' type.

One of the nice features on larger British classics from the 1950s and 1960s was a pair of Windtone horns, the ones which give a loud musical chord, a right royal and important-sounding warning of approach. They went with polished walnut dashboards, leather seats and the rest of the features which were essential on top-of-the-range 'luxury' models.

Strictly speaking the name Windtone should be used only for Lucas horns of this type as it's a Lucas trademark, but it has become almost a generic term like Hoover.

We're dealing first with the earlier Lucas Windtone horns which have a large detachable domed cover, and model numbers with the prefix WT. The model numbers are WT28, WT29, WT28U, WT29U, WT614, WT616 and WT618. All except the WT616 are quite compact, painted black and not really designed to be seen from the outside of the car. They all look similar, with a big domed cover and coiled cast trumpet underneath, and though they have detail differences inside, they all work on the same principle. The odd ones out for looks are those with U at the end of the type designation. These have short straight trumpets and were classed by Lucas as 'Extra Loud'. One on its own is the WT616, the show-off horn, with a long straight trumpet, usually chromium plated, designed

Fig. 10.1. The Model 618 is typical of the WT range of Lucas Windtone horns.

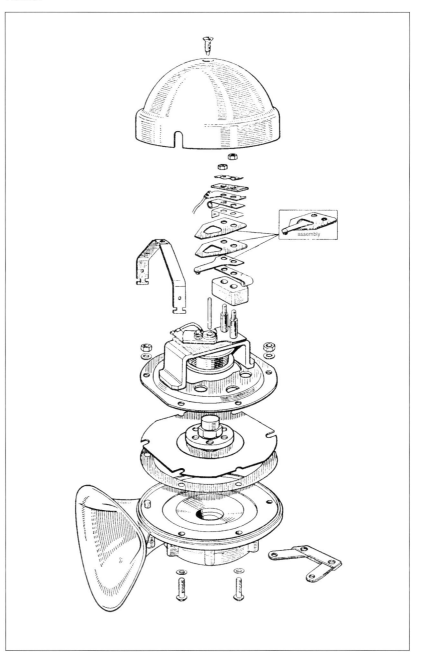

assembly

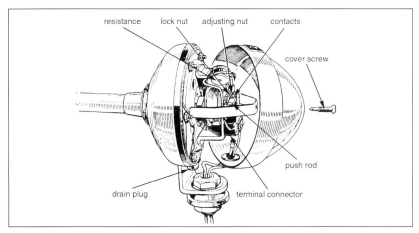

Fig. 10.2. The Lucas WT616 long trumpet is similar to the other WT horns except that the diaphragm is mounted vertically instead of being horizontal.

to be worn on the front of the car. A pair of these went with lots of other chromium plate like a big radiator shell, bumper bar and a badge bar with a row of club badges.

There was another, later series of Lucas Windtone horns, with H in their model designation, but they were a different design and we'll deal with those in a moment.

If you're looking for a pair of WT Windtones at an autojumble or, much more rarely nowadays, at a breaker's, try to get a pair of the same model because different models weren't always tuned to exactly the same pitch, and a pair of the same model blend better. You won't find the model number on the body. It was on a sticker inside the horn which is usually readable even after 40 years, but different models had different shaped lips to the trumpets; so, if a sticker's missing on one of a pair, you shouldn't get mixed up, but take a little care. Lucas made WT horns in 6 volt, 12 volt and 24 volt rating, and we were once offered a 'pair' at an autojumble, one 6 volt and one 12 volt!

We haven't come across the voltage marked on the body of WT Windtone horns. Like the model number, this was on the sticker inside. The vast majority on the British market were 12 volt, so you're pretty safe. However, if you're doubtful and the sticker's

missing, there is a way to check between the different voltage ratings. Open the points, or put a piece of paper between them, and take a voltage reading at the ends of the coil leads with your meter set to ohms. On 6 volt coils the reading should be 0.054 ohms, on 12 volt coils it should be 0.28 ohms and on 24 volt coils 1.4 ohms. You may not get these exact readings but they're sufficiently different to distinguish them.

Lucas Windtones, and most similar types by other makers, came in matched pairs, high pitch and low pitch. You should find an L or an H cast or stamped on the body, or cast inside the lip of the trumpet. In a few cases you might find LP or HP. The letters stand for Low or Low Pitch and High or High Pitch, and the direction in which the trumpet's coiled shows that they're handed, left and right. In most cases we've come across, the low pitch is the right-hand horn.

The low and high pitches are tuned a musical major third apart, the most common interval in musical harmony, to give a harmonious combined note. You can't alter the pitch by making adjustments, it depends on the thickness of the diaphragm. The adjustments are there to make the note nice and clear.

When you take the cover off a WT horn you find that the screw

fits in a stirrup which just unclips from the body to give you easy access to the contact breaker. There's an electromagnet with its coil fed through a pair of contact breaker points which are closed when there is no current passing through them. Through the middle of the coil is a push rod which sits on the centre boss of a spring diaphragm sandwiched between the body and the top plate.

When you pass current through the points, the diaphragm is pulled upwards and the push rod opens the points. This breaks the circuit, the diaphragm and push rod go down again and the points close. The sequence is repeated rapidly so the diaphragm vibrates to move the air inside the trumpet and give the note.

Parts for these horns are completely unobtainable now, but fortunately they very seldom need new parts. Most of them can be put back into good order by cleaning and resetting. If the mechanism is nice and clean inside, probably all you need to do is clean the contact points with a strip of fine sandpaper and, if necessary reset them. If, however, things look grotty and corroded, as they sometimes do, you may have to strip things down to clean everything. The design of the contact breaker mechanism and the way the cables attach varies slightly on different models, but it's pretty self-evident.

When you undo the sandwich plate that holds the terminals and one of the contact points you shouldn't normally have to unsolder the leads from the magnet coil. However, old wires often become brittle and snap off at their soldered joints while you're cleaning things, so it's wise to make a note of where each lead goes before you start. Also make a note of the order in which the sandwich plate goes together, and make sure you get things back in the correct order or you'll have problems.

At one time Lucas used to fit a

large resistor or capacitor across the points to suppress arcing when they opened, but we've found plenty of Windtones without one. We had a word with Ken Cox, of Cox Auto Electrical (01827 712097), a mine of information on all classic electrical bits. Ken reckons that the theory is good but with the amount of use a horn gets compared with the points in a distributor or a dynamo regulator, the points in a horn aren't going to burn very much over years of use, and Lucas didn't always fit a suppressor. Indeed, they issued a service bulletin saying that the suppressors were no longer available, and that agents could take them out and leave them out if they gave trouble. If your horns have got a suppressor, and it's in good condition, you can please yourself whether or not you leave it on, but if it's broken or damaged, leave it off and don't worry about it. You won't find a separate suppressor on a WT618 because if it had one it was built into the sandwich plate assembly where the black 'insulating' block is actually a resistor.

Quite often you find that the push rod in the middle of the coil is sticky. If it is, lift it out and clean it. When you put it back it should have just a slight smear of light grease. On all but the WT28 and WT29 models, look under the coil and you'll see that the boss of the diaphragm has a domed nut on it with a locking ring underneath. There was a Lucas special peg spanner and special cranked open-ended spanner to loosen this locking ring and adjust the domed nut when the horn was assembled, but we haven't seen a pair about for ages. Even Lucas agents weren't issued with them, they were expected to make their own from drawings supplied by Lucas. We haven't got these tools, and we haven't made them even though we've got the drawing. Fortunately, the need for adjustment is quite rare, but on a couple of occasions when it has been we've

successfully adjusted things without one, and we'll come to that in a moment. However, if you want to make a pair of special tools, we've included the drawing (see *Fig. 10.14*).

To find out whether or not it's essential to adjust the diaphragm nut, put the push rod in and connect a couple of 12 volt leads directly across the coil. Don't keep the leads attached for more than a couple of seconds or so at a time or there's a danger of overheating the coil. When you connect, the diaphragm should push the push rod up. Lucas gives figures for the amount the push rod should move, which varies between 0.045in and 0.060in, but it isn't critical. What is critical is that the diaphragm boss mustn't touch anything when the diaphragm flexes up. You can hear if this happens because you get a sharp metallic click.

If there's no clicking, leave the nut and locking ring strictly alone. If you're unlucky and the boss does hit something, then without the special tools you have to take the diaphragm out.

You might, of course, want to take it out anyway to clean the inside of the trumpet and paint it. The top-plate's held by a ring of six nuts and bolts, though on later models these were replaced by rivets. If you've got rivets you have to drill them out, or grind the heads off, and use nuts and bolts when you put things together again. Sometimes, if water has got in to the horn, the nuts will be rusty, and they can be swines to undo – not because they're too tight but because Lucas didn't put a screwdriver slot in the heads of the bolts. They're absolutely plain, and are supposed to grip by serrations under the head. If the nut binds halfway up, and the serrations don't grip, you might be able to hold the bolt head with a pair of pliers or you may have to cut a screwdriver slot in it. The really awkward one is the bolt head inside the trumpet. If the worst comes to the worst you have to cut

or grind the nut off. The average angle grinder is rather clumsy for this sort of work, but we've found a Dremel tool really handy.

After you've got the bolts or rivets out, the top-plate lifts off the body, and then the diaphragm lifts up. Try hard not to damage the gasket between the diaphragm and the body because this governs the height of the diaphragm, which is why there's an adjustment on the centre boss. You don't want to adjust this if you don't have to, but if you got clicking when you tested it, or if you have to make a new gasket and get clicking because it's slightly thinner or thicker than the old one, do it after you've cleaned everything.

On the two occasions when we've had to adjust the nut because we had made a new gasket, we gripped the sides of the locknut firmly in the edge of the vice and loosened the domed nut with a socket. We adjusted it a small amount at a time and had to make several attempts before we got the adjustment right, assembling the top plate and body and testing it each time. Old Lucas agents might scoff at doing it this way, but needs must when you haven't got the special tools, and it worked.

Clean the contact points by rubbing them on a piece of fine sandpaper or an oilstone, if you've got one, and when you tighten the sandwich block make sure the points are opposite each other and sit squarely.

There isn't a gap setting for the points. You adjust the fixed point till you get a reasonable note when you put 12 volts to the horn, and then make the final adjustment with an ammeter. When you're adjusting the points, either bolt the horn securely back on the car or clamp the mounting plate firmly in the vice. You won't get a true clear note if the horn's just sitting on the bench.

Use a fully-charged battery for setting the points, and put an ammeter in circuit with one of the

12 volt feeds. The current consumption should be as follows: WT28 and WT29, 5.5 amps; WT28U and WT29U, 12.5 amps (check your multimeter first, it may read only up to 10 amps); WT614, 6 to 7 amps; WT616, 8 to 8.5 amps; WT618, 7.5 to 8.5 amps. If the current is outside these limits, adjust the setting of the fixed point. Take the trouble to get the setting right even if the horns apparently sound fine.

Remember that with this sort of current the horns must be operated through a relay to avoid burning the points on the horn switch, and remember that a pair of horns take twice the current of a single one, so make sure the relay can handle it.

On WT28 and WT 29 horns, life's much easier if the diaphragm needs adjusting. There's a rubber bung under the horn, and under this is an ordinary slotted adjustment screw with a plain hexagon nut to lock it. All you need is a box spanner and a screwdriver. Seal the bung with rubber solution when you put it back.

The other series of Lucas Windtone horns, the H series, are much more squat in appearance and nothing like so imposing, though they give a similar sort of note to the WT series. They were considerably cheapened on production, not always a bad thing as much early Lucas equipment tended to be over-engineered.

The most popular of the H series was the 9H which, like the WT series were designed to be used in pairs, high note and low note. The bodies are riveted together but, what is nice if you don't need to take them apart is that all the adjustments are external and you don't need any special tools.

Provided the horn sounds and you don't feel the need to take out the rivets, there are two adjustments, one for the contact breaker setting and one for the armature air gap. You can't mistake them because the air gap adjustment is a large screw with a locknut, whereas the contact

Fig. 10.3. If your Windtone looks pretty grotty inside like this, you'll probably get a better tone if you strip, clean and adjust things.

Fig. 10.4. The stirrup which holds the domed cover unclips to give you easy access to the points.

Fig. 10.5. When you take the sandwich block apart, lay the parts out in order so you get them in the correct places again.

breaker adjustment is by a smaller screw, often serrated with a click action.

Dealing first with the contact

breaker adjustment, the first adjustment is very rule of thumb. You turn the screw anti-clockwise till the horn just fails to sound, then

Fig. 10.6. The points aren't usually badly burnt, and you can clean them on fine sandpaper or an oilstone.

Fig. 10.7. The push rod that opens the points is often coated in old hard grease. Clean it and lightly grease it.

Fig. 10.8. The top-plate lifts off after you undo a ring of bolts, or grind off a ring of rivets.

Fig. 10.9. When you lift the diaphragm off, try not to damage the gasket. Its thickness governs the height of the diaphragm, and if your new gasket is too thick you may have to adjust the diaphragm dome nut – not the easiest of jobs without a special peg spanner.

Fig. 10.10. In most cases, there's a sticker inside giving details of the horn. At the top is the Lucas part number, under that is the horn model number and at the bottom is the voltage.

Fig. 10.11. This windtone-type horn was made by Clearhoooters. In this case, the diaphragm is pulled down to open the points, and the points adjustment is by the big nut at the top. The wire coil at the front is a spark suppressor resistor.

turn it back clockwise between a quarter and half a turn.

You set the armature air gap in two stages. First, slacken the locknut and screw the centre core inwards (clockwise) till you feel it just touches the armature, then back it off one and a half turns.

These two coarse adjustments should get the horn giving a reasonable note, and you move on to fine tuning. Set your meter to amps and put it in series with the supply circuit. When you sound the horn you should get a current consumption between 3 amps and 3.5 amps. If not, adjust the contact breaker till you get within these limits. Now unlock the armature air gap screw, and screw it in till the note goes harsh, which will indicate that the core is just on the point of touching the armature. Then unscrew it 1/8 to 1/4 of a turn and lock it. This fine-tuning should give you a good note at anything between 10 volts and 14 volts supply – a fairly flat or a fully-charged battery.

If you can't get the horn to give

Fig. 10.12. This is the Lucas diaphragm adjustment. If you haven't got the special spanners you have to adjust it out of the horn. We've used the vice and a socket, but had to assemble the horn after each adjustment to test it.

Fig. 10.13. Using the Lucas special spanners to adjust the diaphragm.

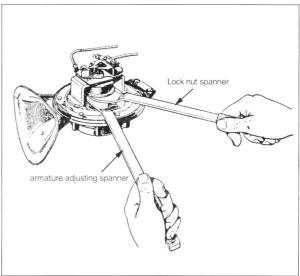

a good note with these adjustments, it's possible that the coil connections inside are corroded or that the contact breaker points need cleaning. In either case, you have to drill out, or grind off, the ring of rivets to take the horn apart.

Other makers made windtone-type horns which were different inside because they had to get round Lucas patents, but if you've got a non-Lucas pair, most of what we've said here applies, and overhauling them is very similar.

Right: Fig. 10.14. If you feel like making the special spanners, this is the Lucas drawing.

Below: Fig. 10.15. A dismantling flow chart for Lucas WT Windtone horns.

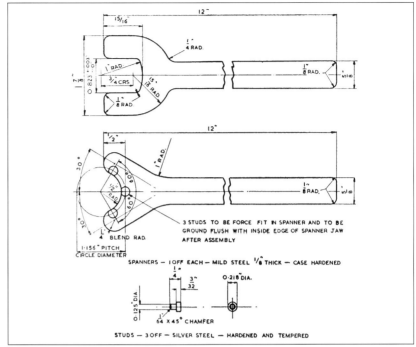

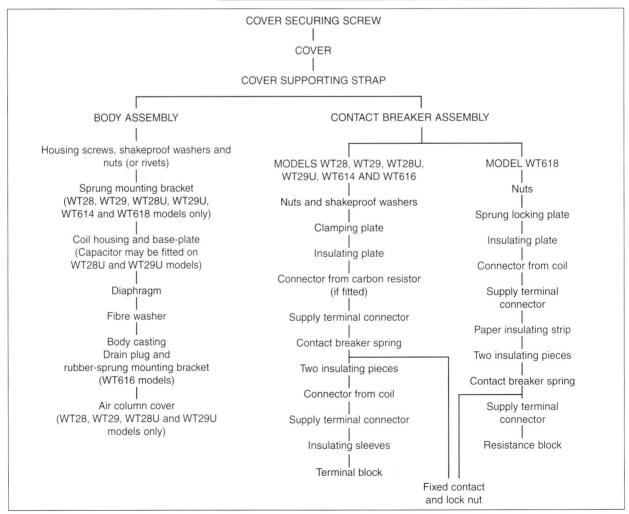

Fig. 10.16. When we first un-riveted this H series Windtone, it looked terrible where salt and muck had been thrown up inside the trumpet.

Fig. 10.17. However, under the diaphragm the mechanism looked in much better condition. All we had to do was clean the points and reset the adjustments.

High-frequency horns

Looking at high-frequency horns, we'll deal first with the cheap swaged together type. All you can see in the way of adjustment is an adjusting screw under a silicone rubber bung that's probably gone soft and soggy with age. If adjusting this doesn't bring the horn back to life, most people regard it as beyond repair. Cheap they may be, and it was never intended they should be taken apart, but they're very robust and not over difficult to restore if you want to. The main problem is

Fig. 10.18. This is the fibre insulating ring which opens the points on H series Windtone and Lucas high-frequency horns.

undoing the swaged ring that holds the horn together, but persevere with a large lever rather than a thin screwdriver and ease back the swaging from the back of the horn a little at a time. It takes about ten minutes or so of careful levering to open up the ring to the point where the back will lift off without having to distort the ring so much that you can't get it back again.

We've chosen as an example a Hella horn, not the highest quality, but robust and a very clever design from the production engineer's point of view. When the swaged ring is off you have a diaphragm riveted to a thicker resonance plate at its front and an armature at its back. The armature fits into a coil inside the body to form an electromagnet. One end of the coil goes to one terminal and the other to a contact breaker point mounted on a fairly substantial spring blade. The second contact point is mounted on a stiff bracket above it and insulated from it by a strip of Paxolin. One end of this bracket goes to the second terminal and the other to an adjusting screw and a substantial coil spring both of which are insulated from the body.

The points are normally closed and, when the electromagnet is energised it pulls the armature and the diaphragm inwards. As this

happens, a part of the armature which is wider in diameter presses on the Paxolin plate and pushes the spring blade contact down to open the points and cut the current. The diaphragm flexes back again, the points close and the cycle is repeated. Nothing to go wrong except dirty or worn points. You can take both the adjusting bracket and the spring blade off as an assembly to swivel them apart and clean the points, and you can take both terminals off for cleaning. We wouldn't advise separating the spring blade from the bracket, nor taking off the terminal block. There's no need to, and the short plastic tubes which insulate them harden with age and don't like being disturbed. While you've got things apart you can clean up and paint the body and diaphragm. Many were originally finished in a light silver-grey.

When you put things together again you can't adjust the armature air gap, but it's pretty generous. Turn the adjusting screw clockwise till the points make contact, which you can check with your meter, then one further turn. Put the diaphragm in position, then fit the swaged ring and go round gently tapping the ring down with a small hammer till it's properly seated, and finish off going round with a piece of wood between the ring

Fig. 10.19. On some cheaper high-frequency horns, like this Hella, the front is held by a swaged ring. With careful levering and lifting, it can be removed without damage and peened back after cleaning.

Fig. 10.20. Inside, the Hella horn is very simple. It ought not to present any problems other than cleaning the points.

and the hammer head. The ring must be tight or you'll get a buzzing sound instead of a clear note. Go for a large number of light blows rather than a fewer number of heavy blows. Make sure the ring and not the resonance disc is resting on the bench or a block of wood while you're hammering. With care, you won't distort the ring and, when it's painted, your handiwork shouldn't show. Test by connecting to a battery via an ammeter and turn the adjusting screw till you get a clear note with a current of about 3 amps to 4 amps. Seal the hole for the adjusting screw with a plastic bung and silicon waterproof sealant if you can find one the right size, or a plug of silicon bath sealant if you can't, and the job's finished.

Overhauling the better quality high-frequency horns is very similar, but a lot easier in most cases as the horn is held together by a ring of rivets which can be drilled out and replaced by bolts and nuts or, on older horns, the bolts and nuts are already there.

Quite a few Lucas high-frequency horns, like the popular high frequency 1849, come apart very easily. There's a cover on the back held by a single screw which

fits in a stirrup very similar to the WT types. At the front, there's a tone disc with a central nut, chromium plated on the de-luxe models. This nut locks a push rod which is screwed in or out to set the tone.

In most cases, all that's needed to get the horn working again is to clean and reset the contacts inside the back cover and reset the push rod. While you've got the cover off, test the continuity of the coil windings even though they seldom give trouble. With the meter set to ohms, you should get a reading of

about 0.85 ohms to 1.0 ohms. If it's much higher, look for corroded terminal connections.

To set the contact breaker points you need an 8 volt DC supply for 12 volt horns, or 4 volt supply for 6 volt horns. You can use dry batteries for this, though they drain quite quickly. It's better to use a variable resistor to tap off 8 volts or 4 volts from a normal 12 volt or 6 volt car battery. We have sometimes used a dimming adjustable resistor from a dash-board illumination circuit.

You can use a full-wave rectified

Fig. 10.21. On some Lucas high-frequency horns, the tone ring is riveted to the diaphragm, as on the left, but on others it is held by a nut.

Fig. 10.22. The points mechanism inside Lucas high-frequency horns differs in detail, but they all work on the same principle.

Fig. 10.23. Not all horns are restorable. The inside of this non-working high-frequency horn was a mess. We got it from a breaker's where it had been mounted under the bonnet, close to the exhaust manifold. Possibly the heat had melted the varnish insulation.

and smoothed DC from AC mains if you have a suitable power supply, but the DC output from something like a battery charger is not suitable because most of these are only half-wave rectified and not smoothed.

Unscrew the push rod and take it out, then connect the 8 volt or 12 volt supply, then adjust the contact breaker setting till you get a buzzing sound. This position is quite critical and happens when the points are just about to open.

With the contact breaker adjusted, screw the push rod back in and adjust it till you get a good clear note with the normal 12 volt or 6 volt supply connected to the horn. As a check, with the push rod properly adjusted, the current consumption of most Lucas high-frequency horns should be between 3 amps and 4 amps for a 6 volt horn and between 2.5 amps and 3.5 amps for a 12 volt horn.

Fig. 10.24. One range of Lucas high-frequency horns looks very similar inside to the WT Windtone. This type is easier to restore than the riveted together type.

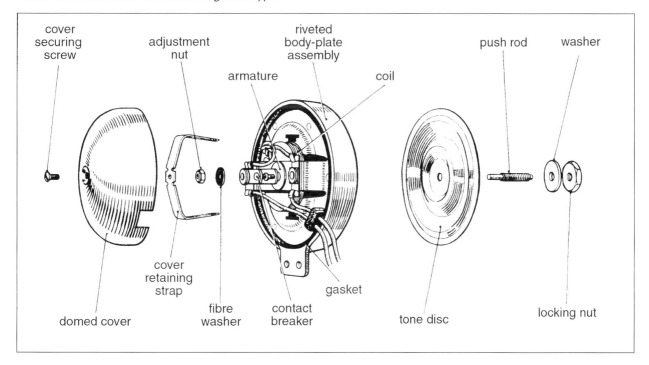

cover securing screw

adjustment nut

riveted body-plate assembly

push rod

washer

armature

coil

cover retaining strap

fibre washer

contact breaker

gasket

tone disc

locking nut

domed cover

Chapter 11
Carburettors in general

There are a number of things which apply if you're overhauling any carburettor, and we deal with these first before going on to different makes and types. It would be impossible for us to go through every type and model of carburettor fitted to classic cars, so we've taken a representative selection.

Most carburettors fall into two classes – fixed-choke and variable-choke. The single barrel fixed-choke carburettors are usually quite straightforward to overhaul, though twin-barrel carburettors are often thought to be complicated. They are more complicated in that they have more parts, but they are still straightforward if you go about things logically and keep all the parts in order. We deal in detail with two of the most popular, the Weber DGAV and the Weber DCOE.

In the variable-choke class, we have dealt with a representative selection of SUs, and a Stromberg CD150. Other models differ in detail, but are very similar.

All carburettors fitted to classics have a die-cast aluminium alloy or aluminium-zinc alloy body. It doesn't often corrode in service because it sits in an atmosphere where, except on a concours car, there's usually a fair amount of oil mist around. On a concours car the owner keeps the carburettor clean and polished. There are, however, two cases where you come across a corroded body. One is where the engine bay has been steam-cleaned with a strongly alkaline detergent in the steam. The residue from this will corrode any aluminium alloy parts in a few weeks. The second is where the carburettor has been sitting in a breaker's yard open to the elements. In this case, you usually find all the steel parts rusted, and the aluminium covered in white crystals. The carburettor isn't necessarily beyond reclaim, but don't pay a lot for it, even if it's a rare model.

Always check a second-hand carburettor carefully for damage, and to make sure it's complete. Some on autojumble stalls have had pieces taken from them. It's unusual to find the body damaged, but always check the mounting flange for cracks, both at the bolt holes and where the flange joins the body. It's surprising what some ham-fisted people can do with a socket set. A more frequent cause of damage is when the carburettor has been dropped or when an engine, complete with carburettor, has been lifted out of a car at a breaker's using a chain and hoist or a fork-lift truck and very little finesse. In some cases we've found not just the body cracked but other parts bent and damaged as well.

Don't force any corroded parts to get them to move, dunk the whole carburettor in a bath of white spirit overnight. The exception to this is if you're dealing with a thermostatically controlled starting device (such as the SU one fitted to Jaguars and a few other luxury cars), a solenoid anti-over-

Fig. 11.1. This carburettor looks pretty desperate, but with a good soak and scrub in white spirit it came up quite clean.

Fig. 11.2. This is how the carburettor looked after cleaning, but before restoration.

run valve or a throttle stepper motor fitted to some carburettors on later classics. In this case, remove the electrically operated part before dunking in white spirit as in most cases white spirit will attack the varnish insulation. On a twin-carburettor set-up it's best to dismantle and work on one carburettor at a time because things like throttle spindles, and jets on SUs, are often handed, and you don't want to get them mixed up. It also helps, if you forget which way round anything fits, to have the other carburettor as a mirror image.

Until you've tried it, you'll be amazed what a 24-hour soak in white spirit can do, even with a carburettor that's covered in white horrible-looking corrosion. After soaking, give the carburettor a good scrub in the white spirit with a nail brush, and an old toothbrush for the awkward parts. When you see how clean it becomes, it gives you new heart for tackling the job.

Let it dry off, then liberally dose all the screws with a freeing agent, such as WD-40, and leave it to soak in for an hour or so. It's the best way we know to avoid broken-off screws and stripped threads. Don't be in a hurry, particularly on a carburettor that's been standing for years. If you find something seized, don't force it. Die-cast zinc and aluminium alloy is very brittle, and forcing things leads to breakages. If something's really stuck, try more applications of freeing agent. If even that doesn't work, try gentle heat. Cook it in a medium oven for a quarter of an hour or so, or wave a butane or similar blow lamp gently over the whole carburettor long enough to warm it up.

Don't make it too hot, and don't hold the flame in one spot or you'll get differential expansion that could crack something. After you've warmed it, douse it again in a tub of white spirit. The expansion of heating and the contraction of cooling is usually enough to free even the tightest joints. Use force only as a very last resort, and only

then if you're sure that the component parts need to come apart, or if you've got a spare carburettor you can raid for anything that breaks.

In the vast majority of cases, things never get to this drastic stage, except possibly on vintage or veteran 'barn discovery' cars. After soaking and cleaning, the carburettor usually comes apart with a minimum of effort. Unless you're very familiar with the model of carburettor you're working on, don't just strip things out willy-nilly and dump them in a further cleaning bath. It would be impossible in a book like this for us to detail every carburettor fitted to every classic car, so make notes and draw diagrams as you strip things off. To repeat what we said in the introduction, the ideal is to get a cheap snapshot camera that won't be a serious loss if it gets dirty or damaged in the workshop, and take pictures as you go along. This applies particularly to throttle and other linkages. Sometimes, the various rods and levers can be a right Chinese puzzle to put together again. You might think you'll remember, but you won't; so make notes.

If the carburettor comes up nice and clean after its soak and brush in white spirit, you may decide that you want to leave the body as it is to keep the car looking original. On the other hand, you might decide you want things looking really spotless and either have the parts bead-blasted or polished to a high shine. (Many people use the term 'grit-blasted' because that's the generic term usually used to cover any form of cleaning with compressed air and some sort of abrasive.) Quite reasonably priced home blasting cabinets are available, and if you've already got an air compressor you could do the job yourself. If not you can entrust it to an outside firm.

Whichever you decide, don't let anyone near a die-cast carburettor, or any other die-casting for that matter, with the heavy coarse grit

used to blast flaking rust off iron seaside piers. It's far too coarse. You can get very fine and gentle abrasives which will get things clean without leaving the surface looking like the craters on the moon.

Perfectionists who are aiming for top concours honours often have carburettors polished till they look as if they're made of silver. Many carburettor bodies made from around the early 1950s onwards, notably SUs and Stromberg CDs, were made from an aluminium-based alloy, and these are the ones which polish well. Before then, and until much later, the bodies of some fixed-choke carburettors were made from a zinc-based alloy. You can easily recognise this because it will come out of the white spirit wash a slate grey colour. The material will polish, but it won't hold its shine, and within a couple of months it reverts to a slate grey, so you may as well just clean it thoroughly and leave it at that.

You may not want to go as far as those looking for concours honours, but you might decide that you would like at least a reasonable polish on the dashpot on SU and Stromberg carburettors. If so, you can do this in your own garage with a buffing wheel attached to your electric drill.

An electric drill isn't the ideal machine for buffing, and professionals use a powerful high-speed electric motor made for the job, which runs at anything from 7,000rpm to 10,000rpm, and a five-inch or six-inch buffing wheel. Nevertheless, with a smaller buffing wheel and plenty of patience, your 3,000rpm electric drill will do the job. All except very old electric drills have what is usually termed a Euro-fitting neck behind the chuck. This is a universal fitting for most types of attachments, and you can get an attachment to mount the drill in a vice. Get one and use it; don't attempt to clamp the drill in a vice by holding it on the body.

Some people like to strip everything down to the last nut and split pin before polishing, others do the majority of the polishing before dismantling because it's easier to hold a complete carburettor than lots of small pieces. If we're polishing, we usually strike a compromise, polish the main body first on a buffing wheel and then finish in the nooks and crannies with a smaller wheel, sometimes a very small one in a Dremel tool.

Buffing soap, as it's known, comes in a variety of grades ranging from coarse, which is usually a dark buff colour, through gradually finer grades which are light buff, yellow, white, pink and red. Usually, the colours run in that order, but check with the tool shop where you buy the buffing soap because the colour code isn't by any means universal, and different makers might have different ideas about grading.

You can save yourself a lot of time on the buffing wheel if you go over the body first with a brass wire brush, or even a very fine steel wire brush, getting it as clean as you can. This will leave scratches, but provided you're reasonably gentle, and don't go at things as if you're getting rust scale off an old garden gate, the scratches will polish out easily. After wire brushing you'll probably find rather unsightly casting marks, or even coarse grinding marks where the casting flash has been ground off. A high-speed large buffing wheel with a coarse soap will take these out, but again you can make life easier for yourself by dressing down the unsightly marks with a fine file. Remember to use chalk or washing-up liquid on the file to stop the swarf catching in the file teeth and leaving even worse marks. See the 'Files and filing' section of Chapter 1 about using files on aluminium.

The buffing is going to leave the carburettor with lots of dirt and muck in the crevices and probably down inside as well, so give it another thorough clean in white spirit both before you dismantle it, and afterwards, making sure nothing's left in the crevices of the parts.

We go through dismantling different makes and types of carburettor later, but for now we'll assume you've got the whole thing dismantled and all the parts cleaned. As well as checking the body for cracks, check the face of the mounting flange for flatness where it meets the inlet manifold. You can get an idea of the flatness by putting a straightedge across it, but this isn't always easy on an oval flange. A much better way is to use a piece of fine wet and dry rubbing paper upside-down on a perfectly flat surface such as an old mirror or piece of plate glass. Hold the flange firmly against the paper and rub it back and forth two or three times. Any lack of flatness will show up as highlights and hollows. Keep rubbing down till you get an even marking all over the flange.

You'll be unlucky if you find any stripped internal threads, but check them all just in case. There's just about enough metal round the tapped holes for the screws which hold, for example, an SU dashpot, to be drilled and tapped slightly larger, but if the threads holding an SU jet assembly or float chamber, or similar fixings on other carburettors, are damaged, the body is scrap. The same thing applies if any other tapped hole which takes a screwed-in fitted part, and not just a plain screw, is stripped.

In almost all books on car overhaul, and most books on carburettor overhaul, you will be told that if the throttle spindle is worn to the extent that it shows any discernible play in the carburettor body, you'll never get the engine to run properly, and the carburettor needs replacing. This is a counsel of perfection that has been preached for decades, and many writers follow it so that no-one can later write to the publisher and say that an important point like this hadn't been covered.

So, how much difference does a small amount of wear on the throttle spindle and body make to the running of the engine? It's a thorny question because rebushing the throttle spindle bearings of a worn carburettor body at home isn't practicable. You need quite sophisticated equipment to make sure that, when the body is reamed to take bushes, it is reamed absolutely concentric with the original hole. With a normal hand reamer, the hole tends to wander because of the oval wear, and then the butterfly never seats properly against the venturi.

An air leak at the throttle spindle makes a difference mainly on tick-over and very small throttle openings when the depression in the inlet manifold is high, and the small amount of air that can be sucked past a worn spindle is a sufficient enough portion of the total air going in to affect the mixture. As soon as the throttle butterfly starts to open, the depression falls, so the suction at the worn spindle is less, and the amount of air sucked past it is small compared with the total amount of air going through the carburettor. At about a quarter throttle the effect of the air leak is very small. Even at tick-over, a very small amount of play in the throttle spindle isn't going to make a fantastic difference to the slow-running mixture; certainly not as much as a badly adjusted slow-running air bleed screw. Indeed, you can often adjust an air bleed screw to allow for slight throttle spindle leakage.

Does this mean that you can ignore wear on the throttle spindle? No, it doesn't. If you find that there is play between the throttle spindle and the body of the carburettor, and you've just spent a large amount of money having the engine rebuilt to new condition, then we would advise either buying a new carburettor, or getting someone like Burlen to ream and bush the existing carburettor body. However, all things are relative, and you may not fancy shelling out for a new carburettor for an engine that's done quite a few thousand miles, but still runs well, particularly when a new spindle might almost cure any play.

If the spindle is really wobbly in the body, whatever the mileage your engine has covered, either get a new carburettor or look for one on which the spindle play is near negligible. If, however, you can't feel any sideways play in the throttle spindle, or there's so little that you have a job to discern it, we'd advise you to leave it alone and not even take the throttle butterfly screws out.

That leaves the problem case where there is some play in the spindle, but maybe not enough to reject the carburettor out of hand. In this case, undo the throttle butterfly screws, but before you do, mark the top of the butterfly with a lightly scribed 'T' to make sure you get it back the correct way up. The butterfly fixing screws are bifurcated and opened out to stop

any chance of their coming loose and being sucked inside the engine. Close them with a pointed-nose pair of pliers before you undo them, and never try to use them again because when you open the bifurcation a second time, the ends will be weakened. If a broken end, or the whole screw, goes inside the engine it can cause catastrophic damage.

Pull the spindle out, and wipe it clean. A visual check will show you if it is badly worn where it's been running in the body, but as a test put it back in, but not the whole way. Leave it out far enough for you to be able to try the play on an unworn part of the spindle. If the play is now so slight that you feel it's acceptable, then a new spindle, and new bifurcated screws, will go a long way towards curing the problem, at a considerable saving.

We have seen it advocated that you can cure a leak at the throttle spindle by counterboring the bearing holes in the carburettor slightly, and putting close-fitting nylon washers in the counterbores. We haven't tried it so we can't talk about its effectiveness, but if you

can find some suitable soft nylon washers, and want to try it, it's up to you.

You may wonder why we haven't included any Ford carburettors. The three reasons are: first that on many classic cars Ford fitted proprietary carburettors; second, Ford's own fixed-choke carburettors, often labelled Motorcraft, are simple robust units that seldom need anything more than a clean and new gaskets until they're worn out; third, and the exception, is Ford's VV carburettor, VV standing for Variable Venturi. This is a clever design of carburettor and, when working properly, a very good one. Unfortunately, it is very complex and subject to numerous ills when it gets older. It is also very tricky and difficult to overhaul and set up properly. Most Ford owners who have a worn VV carburettor change it for an appropriate Weber, and this is also what we would advise. Quite often, a Weber was fitted by Ford as an option. If it wasn't, you can find a direct replacement carburettor in the Weber catalogue.

Chapter 12

SU carburettors

There's one big advantage when it comes to overhauling SU carburettors, you should never be stuck for new parts. The SU company was wound up in 1996, so it doesn't make or service carburettors any more, but Burlen Fuel Systems did owners of classic cars fitted with SUs a great service by acquiring the old SU company and carrying on manufacture. They keep a full range of parts and overhaul kits in stock, and even remanufacture new carburettors to the original specifications ranging from modern ones back to about 1930.

There are four main types of SU carburettor used on classics: H, HS, HD and HIF. Quite a lot of overhaul procedures are the same for all four. So, after a few words about SUs in general, we deal first with an overhaul of the H-type, and then go through the differences with other models.

SU carburettors are handed left and right depending on the position of the choke and throttle levers. Looking into the inlet, if the choke and throttle connections are on the left, it's a left-hand carburettor. If they're on the right, it's a right-hand.

People often refer to the carburettors on a twin-carburettor longitudinal in-line engine as front and rear, but in SU's parts lists and manuals they are are always called left-hand and right-hand, the handing being as viewed from the carburettor side of the engine. On a transverse in-line such as in Austin and Morris cars, or a vee-form engine with twin carburettors, such as the Rover V8, the handing is

always as viewed from the driving seat. In other words, if you're standing in front of the car looking at the engine, the carburettor on the left is right-hand and the one on the right is left-hand. Confusing at first, but that's the way SU originally laid it down. The only time SU used front and rear to describe carburettors was on an in-line longitudinal engine with three carburettors. In that case, the one nearest the front of the car is the front carburettor, the one nearest the bulkhead is the rear carburettor and the one in the middle is, logically, called the centre carburettor.

In the parts manuals, the abbreviations are LH, RH, F, C and R. On the H, HS and HD types, the float chamber can be fitted on either side of the body, but on the HIF it can't because it's integral with the body. On some classics the carburettor or carburettors are mounted as a sidedraught set-up with the air intake horizontal and the float chamber parallel to the dashpot. On some, it is a semi-downdraught set-up with the air intake mounted sloping downwards, usually with an adaptor plate between the carburettor and the inlet manifold. In this case, the float chamber is mounted at an angle to the body to keep it upright. It's worth keeping these points in mind when you're hunting for a less-worn replacement carburettor at an autojumble or in a breaker's yard.

All SUs are classed as variable-choke carburettors, choke in this context meaning the cross-section area of the inlet passage, not a

strangler flap to cut down the air and give a rich mixture for cold starting. On the SU there is only one jet which is partially closed by a tapered needle. The needle is fixed in the base of the piston, a round block of alloy which closes the air intake passage and has a wider piston with an oil damper as its top part. The piston works in a chamber, usually known as the dashpot, connected to the inlet manifold suction. The more fuel mixture the engine needs, the higher the piston rises in the dashpot, and the larger the area of the intake passage. At the same time, the tapered needle rises in the jet and allows more petrol to be drawn in to compensate for the extra air. An extra rich mixture for cold starting is, in most cases, obtained by lowering the jet down the taper of the needle. We say 'in most cases' because some SUs have a small auxiliary carburettor just for cold starting. We'll deal with this separately.

The jet needle is held by a small set-screw in the side of the piston. When this is slackened, the needle should lift out, but sometimes they stick. Don't rock it from side to side to try to free it, you're more likely to bend it. Give it a couple of very light taps straight towards the piston with the handle of your screwdriver, and it will come free. SU fixed needles were made in two types (one with a square shoulder and one with a tapered, slightly rounded shoulder), and it's important to fit each type correctly. The type with the square shoulder fits with the shoulder level with the base of the piston. The type with the tapered shoulder fits with the smaller end of the shoulder level with the base of the piston. The later spring-loaded needle always has a square shoulder and is fitted with the shoulder level with the base of the piston.

If you have a pair of SUs on your car, it's best to deal with them one at a time, and not strip the pair at once. This gives you the advantage that you have one complete carburettor to look at should you forget exactly how the various linkages went together, and there's no danger of accidentally interchanging parts which have bedded-in to their mating parts. You may also find that some parts, such as the throttle spindles, are handed on twin installations, and if you get them mixed up you'll never set the carburettors up on the engine. Those are the basic principles of all SUs, and we now start our overhaul first with the basic SU carburettor, the H series.

The H-type

The H-type was introduced in 1937, and stayed in production in bore sizes from $1\frac{1}{8}$in to 2in right through to the late 1950s when it was gradually phased out in favour of the HS-type. The H-type was a development of the pre-war OM-type and HV-type, and overhauling these is almost identical. The main difference you'll find on some early models is that the petrol inlet pipe fitted directly on to a brass tube in

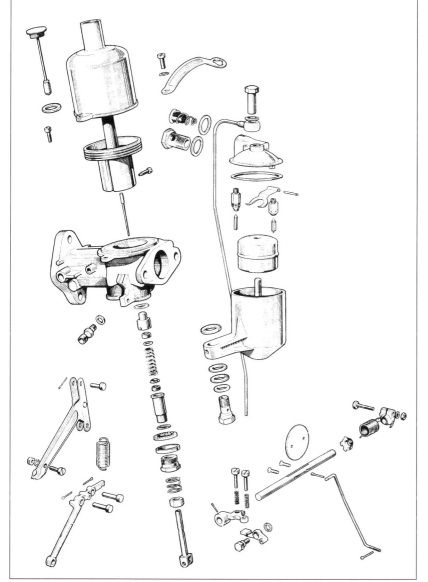

195 Fig. 12.1. The H-type SU is a pre-war design, but hung on well into the classic era.

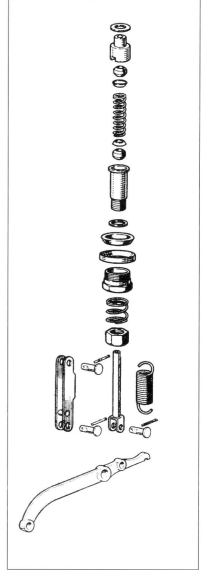

Fig. 12.2. A detailed picture of the numerous glands and washers on the H-type jet assembly.

the top of the float chamber lid, instead of via a banjo union and filter on later models (SU reverted to the brass pipe on the later HS-type). There were also various differences to the jet lowering lever.

After giving the outside of the carburettor a thorough clean, decide whether or not you want to do any polishing on the buffing wheel before completely stripping things down. If not, carry on by taking off the fuel inlet pipe and banjo union, and the inlet filter and spring. Notice that the filter sits inside the spring so that the spring keeps it pressed up against the inlet union. Take out the damper rod and tip any oil out, then mark the dashpot and the body so they go back in the same relationship. This is particularly important on dashpots which have only two fixing screws. The type with three screws usually has the screws offset so the dashpot fits back only one way, but with two screws you can put it back 180° out. If the dashpot doesn't want to come free after you've taken out the screws, give it a few taps with a wooden mallet or even the handle of your screwdriver.

If the carburettor's been standing a long time, the piston may stick in the dashpot and come out with it. Be careful, because the long spring under the piston may push it out suddenly so that it drops on the bench and bends the needle. Loosen the needle locking screw, take the needle out and put it somewhere where it won't get damaged. The piston spring may have a smaller coil at one end. If it has, this end fits towards the piston, and there should be an anti-skid washer underneath it. With flat-ended springs there is a washer with some models, but with others there isn't, so watch out just in case.

Turn the body upside-down, unhook the jet lever return spring, and take out the clevis pins that hold the lever and its bracket. If the carburettor is fitted with a piston

lifting pin you can either take this out now, or leave it till later. It's held by a small circlip, and we prefer to leave it in at this stage because the pin, circlip and spring are small and easily lost. You'll find it easier to get at the jet assembly if you first take off the float chamber. Notice where the washers go, and save them for identification even though you'll get new ones in the overhaul kit.

Next, you've got a choice. You can either pull the jet out and then undo the jet adjusting nut and its spring, or you can leave the jet in place and undo the large nut next to the body to take the whole lot out as an assembly. We usually do it the latter way because it helps to keep all the springs, gland washers and other bits and pieces in the right order. It's best to make a sketch or note about the order in which these bits go together, but in case you lose your notes, or didn't make notes and can't remember, we've included a line drawing showing the correct order of assembly. Once again, keep all the bits even though you get new washers and glands in the kit.

This is the time to decide whether or not you want to take out the throttle spindle and butterfly, see the section on general carburettor overhaul. If you decide you need to, follow the method we gave you there. If not, take off any remaining linkage and slow-running adjust-ment screw. Don't lose the locking spring. Finish dismantling by taking the lid off the float chamber and stripping out the inlet needle valve and float lever. The hinge pin for the float arm usually just pushes out, though it may be a little tight if the carburettor's been standing dry. The needle valve unscrews as an assembly. Some float chamber lids have a small spring-loaded plunger, or 'tickler' as it was popularly known, to depress the float and flood the carburettor in extremely cold weather. If you've got one, take it out and clean it, and make sure it's free so that the

spring never fails to push it up. If it's sticky, it's going to stick when some curious person asks what it is and pushes it down. Then you'll have to take the lid off to free it.

SU used two types of float, a brass one and a plastic one. All H-type and earlier models are fitted with a brass float. On later models this is identical top and bottom, but on some early floats one end was domed and one flat. Before you take the float out, scribe a light T on the top face to make sure you put it back the same way as it came out.

On some SUs, when you look down where the dashpot fits, you may find that there are a couple of screws holding what looks like a seating ring for the piston. It is, but don't try to take it out. You won't gain anything by doing this, and you're unlikely to get it back dead true. Also, on some models, there's a detachable tongue over which the groove in the lower part of the piston fits. If it's perfectly tight, leave it alone, but if someone's been fiddling with it, it will invariably wobble, with the result that the piston will be stiff and jerky. If you're unfortunate enough to have one that wobbles, make sure the screw thread in the body isn't stripped, clean it and tighten the screw with a dose of Locktite or similar thread-locking compound. On other SUs, you don't get this problem because the tongue is cast in the body.

With all the parts dismantled, use a small polishing mop, or a brass brush, to clean up the last of the awkward corners and crevices, and blow air, or even push a pipe cleaner, through the hole between the float chamber and its fixing union, and between the boss where the float chamber union fits and the body of the carburettor where the jet assembly screws in. Both are favourite places for crud to collect in a dried-out carburettor. Then give all the parts another thorough wash, and leave them to dry off while you make sure you've got everything you need in the overhaul kit. If you haven't, order the parts now so that you don't have to stop halfway through assembly to wait for a new part.

If you renewed, or removed, the throttle spindle, start reassembly with this. Slide the spindle in position and fit the butterfly through its slot, making sure you've got it the right way up and the right way round. Put the screws in, but don't tighten them yet. Turn the spindle till the butterfly is closed, which will centre it in the spindle, and hold it there while you tighten the screws. Don't overtighten the screws, and put something through the body of the carburettor to support the spindle while you tighten them because it's very easy to bend the weakened, slotted part of the spindle. When the screws are tight, open the bifurcated ends just enough to stop the screws coming loose. You need open them only a small amount, don't bend them back like a split pin or they'll break off.

If the body has a piston lifting pin and spring, refit these and make sure that the pin doesn't show the slightest sign of sticking.

Put the jet assembly, together with all the washers and glands, in the correct order, remembering that the coned faces of the gland washers fit towards the gland packing washers, and that the top copper washer fits with its 'sharp' edges towards the top jet bearing. Screw the jet assembly into the base of the body, but don't tighten it yet.

Test the fit of the piston in the dashpot, and make sure it falls freely under its own weight. If it doesn't, or if it hesitates, there's still some deposit left inside the dashpot or on the rim of the piston, maybe only showing as a brown discoloration. The workshop manual will tell you that you must not use anything except a petrol-moistened cloth to clean the inside of the dashpot and the rim of the piston, but we doubt if the people who wrote it ever tried to remove a stubborn brown deposit with a petrol-moistened cloth. It doesn't

shift it. You must never use a hard abrasive such as rubbing down paper, because this will scratch and score the dashpot bore, but we've used both Brasso metal polish and Jiff Cream kitchen cleaner. Both these cleaning agents get the deposit off without damaging the bore. You'd need an electron microscope to measure the amount of metal, if any, that they take off during a few minutes' polishing. Make sure, though, that every trace of the cleaning agent is removed from the bore by washing it thoroughly in white spirit.

Some SUs, usually the ones with a brass cap to the damper, have an internal vent hole in the dashpot. You can recognise this because there is a rounded rib cast in the side of the dashpot where the neck runs up. Make sure that this vent hole is free. Other damper caps, usually the black plastic ones on HS-type carburettors, have a vent hole in the cap, and no internal vent.

Fit the needle to the piston making sure the shoulder is correctly positioned (see earlier), fit the piston in the body, put just a trace of oil on the piston (a smear with a oily finger is enough), and then fit the spring and dashpot and tighten the dashpot holding screws, but don't fit the piston damper yet. Remember that if you've got the type of spring that has a smaller coil at one end, the smaller coil fits towards the piston, and there should be an anti-skid washer under it.

The next stage, centring the jet, is important, so don't neglect it. Take off the jet, jet adjusting nut and spring, and refit the jet and adjusting nut without the spring. Screw the adjusting nut fully up, make sure the jet securing nut is slightly loose, and push the jet hard up against the adjusting nut. If you look into the bore of the body, you'll see that the top of the jet is protruding slightly above the jet bridge and holding the piston up. The taper of the piston will centre the jet, so hold things in this

position and tighten the jet securing nut.

Lower the jet slightly by undoing the adjusting nut till the top of the jet is level with, or very slightly below, the top of the jet bridge. Hold the jet in this position, and lift the piston a few times with your finger. When you let the piston go, it should come back down to the jet bridge with a nice sharp metallic click. If it doesn't, slacken the jet securing nut and go through the centring process again. It's important to get the jet truly centred, otherwise you'll never be able to set the slow-running mixture properly. When you're happy with the jet centring, take out the jet, unscrew the adjusting nut and refit them with the adjusting nut spring in place. Fit the jet lowering lever and its return spring.

Fit the piston damper in the top of the dashpot, but don't fill it with oil till you fit the carburettor to the car – but do remember to do it then.

Turning now to the float chamber lid, you have to set the petrol level. Fit the needle valve assembly and the float lever, and turn the lid upside-down so that the lever is holding the needle valve shut. Slide the shank of a drill bit between the curved parts of the lever and the underside of the float chamber lid. On most H-types the diameter of the drill bit should be 5/16in (or 8mm if you're using a metric drill bit). On some early H-types, and pre-war HV and OM-types, the dimension was 3/8in (9.5mm). The drill shank should slide in snugly without lifting the lever. If it doesn't, you have to bend the lever, but be careful to keep the part which bears on the needle valve flat and parallel with the underside of the lid.

Fit the lid back on the float chamber and fit the chamber to the carburettor, refit the various levers and brackets for the installation on your car, and put the carburettor aside till you're ready to fit it.

HS-type

In the late 1950s, the HS-type carburettor started to take over from the H-type and soon superseded it. It went through a few changes in its early life, the main one being a change to a plastic float. Later, in the 1960s and 1970s, other features such as a spring-loaded needle, over-run valve and temperature compensation were introduced, but overhaul of the various models is very similar.

There are two big differences compared to the H-type. The float chamber is mounted on the side of the carburettor body through a boss that allows the chamber to be mounted at different angles to suit horizontal applications with the dashpot vertical, and semi-downdraught applications with the dashpot at an angle. The second big change is the jet assembly. This is simplified to do away with the series of glands and washers on the H-type, which often shrunk and leaked when the carburettor dried out. Instead, the jet is connected by a flexible pipe direct to the bottom of the float chamber. There are different types of jet assembly for the HS-type, depending on the size of carburettor, the angle of the float chamber, the size of the jet and whether the carburettor is handed left or right. To be on the safe side it's best to take the old jet assembly with you when you get a new one. From about 1970, the spring-loaded, so-called swinging, needle was introduced; so once again make sure you get the correct one.

When you come to dismantle an HS carburettor you'll find in most cases that the throttle spindle return spring is a fairly large torsion coil spring attached to the operating lever. You may also find coil springs on the fast-idle cam and the jet return lever. There are quite a few different arrangements of these springs and levers, so to save a lot of experimenting and puzzle-solving later, make a note of

how things go together before you take them apart.

With the main external linkages and levers removed, you can take out the damper, undo the dashpot screws and lift it off. On most HS-types, the damper cap is black plastic and has a vent hole which must be free. Don't be tempted to fit a damper with a non-vented brass cap just for looks, the carburettor won't operate properly. Remember to look for an anti-skid washer under the long piston spring. Take out the piston, remove

the needle and put it carefully to one side.

Most HS-type carburettors are fitted with a piston lifting pin which may be one of two types. If it has an external spring, remove the circlip and spring and push the pin upwards to remove it. If it has a concealed spring, push the pin upwards, take off the circlip and remove the pin downwards.

Loosen the screw which holds the jet lever linkage and release the tension of the lever return spring, then undo the brass sleeve nut

Fig. 12.3. The HS-type was very similar to the H, but had a much simplified jet assembly.

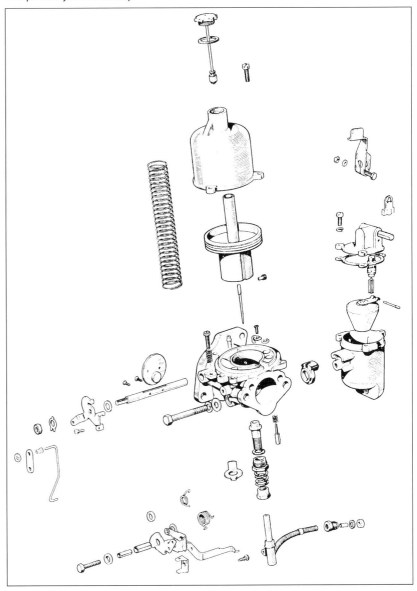

Fig. 12.4. Start dismantling by undoing the clip which holds the jet to the choke lever.

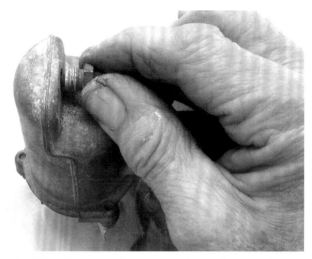

Fig. 12.5. Go easy when you undo the flexible pipe from the float chamber.

Fig. 12.6. When the pipe is undone, you can lift the jet out of its housing.

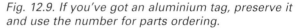

Fig. 12.7. Undo the jet adjusting screw and spring.

Fig. 12.8. The jet housing usually leaves its aluminium washer behind. Don't lose it.

Fig. 12.9. If you've got an aluminium tag, preserve it and use the number for parts ordering.

Fig. 12.10. Mark the float chamber lid before you take it off so that you get it back with the inlet pipe pointing in the correct direction.

Fig. 12.11. Make sure that the piston locating tag is securely screwed down into the body.

which holds the end of the jet flexible pipe to the bottom of the float chamber. Go easy with this nut, it's got a delicate thread, and it's easily stripped. When the pipe is free you can pull the jet assembly out of the body. Undo the jet adjusting nut and locking nut and take the jet bearing assembly out. Make sure you know how the pick-up lever return spring and the fast-idle cam spring fit, and take these off making a note of where the various washers and spacers fit.

Mark the float chamber and body so that you can put them together again at the correct relative angle. When you undo the bolt and take the float chamber off, you may find that there are rubber anti-vibration bushes between the chamber and the carburettor body. If there are, make a note of where and how they fit. Mark the float chamber and its lid so that you get the petrol inlet pipe pointing in the right direction when you come to put the carburettor back on the car, take the lid off and pull out the float lever pin. On most SUs after the mid 1960s, one end of the float lever pin is serrated, and this is the end you pull to take it out. Unscrew the petrol inlet needle valve

assembly and, except for the throttle spindle, the carburettor is in pieces. See the section on general carburettor overhaul to decide whether or not you need to remove the throttle spindle.

Reassembly is very similar to the H-type carburettor except that the jet centring is slightly different. Fit the jet bearing, washer and locknut finger tight, and fit the adjusting nut without its spring. Screw the nut fully up, and slide the jet in position. Fit the piston and needle, watching carefully that the needle slides down into the jet, and fit the damper spring, anti-skid washer (if one is fitted), and fit the dashpot but not the damper. Make sure the jet bearing locknut is free. Hold the piston down with a pencil or something similar in the top, and tighten the jet bearing locknut. Now when you lift the piston it should fall back to the jet bridge with a sharp metallic click. If it does, lower the jet adjusting nut fully, and try the drop of the piston again. The piston must fall freely with the jet adjusting nut in both positions. If it doesn't, slacken the jet bearing locknut and start again.

When you're happy with the jet centring, take the jet and adjusting

nut off, and refit them with the adjusting nut spring in place. Fit the jet lowering lever, and then connect the end of the jet flexible pipe to the base of the float chamber. Fit the nut, washer and seal on the end of the pipe and make sure that 3/16in (5mm) of pipe is protruding from the seal. We like to put just a trace of petroleum jelly (Vaseline) on the seal before fitting it in the base of the float chamber. Be careful that you don't get the fine thread of the nut cross-threaded, and don't over-tighten it.

Early HS-type carburettors had a brass float, and the petrol level is set in the same way as on the H-type. Later HS models used a plastic float with the float lever riveted on it. In this case you hold the lid upside-down and measure the distance between the face of the lid and the underside of the float lever. It should be between 1/8in (3.2mm) and 3/16in (4.8mm).

If you have a flexibly mounted float chamber, fit new rubber washers, line up the marks you made to get the angle between the float chamber and body correct, and tighten, but don't overtighten, the bolt.

Refer to your notes and refit all

the linkages, levers and springs that suit the installation on your car, and put the carburettor aside till it's time to refit it.

HIF-type

The last SU carburettor we want to cover is the HIF (Horizontal Integral Float chamber). Although it works on the same principle as other SU carburettors, the HIF is different because, as its designation implies, it hasn't got a separate float chamber. The float chamber is built into the base of the carburettor body. The cold-start arrangement

is completely different, and is built into the body.

You may also have three different types of piston and dashpot assembly. The first one is the same as on other SUs, then you have two variants of the type known as the ball bearing dashpot where the piston runs on two rows of ball bearings, six in each row. The piston is held either by a retainer or a circlip. On both types, you take off the dashpot complete with piston and damper. Then, on the type with a retainer, you loosen the damper, undo the dashpot, then hold the piston and pull on the

dashpot till the retainer pops out of the top of the piston. Lift out the damper with the retainer and take the piston out of the bottom of the dashpot. Don't try to pull the retainer out by pulling up on the damper rod. On the type where the piston is held by a circlip, the damper lifts out, then you push the piston up in the dashpot until the circlip is exposed, and take it off.

HIF carburettors also have what's often called a swinging needle which was also fitted to some late models of earlier carburettors. The needle is held in the piston by the usual screw in the

Fig. 12.12. An exploded view of the later HIF-type.

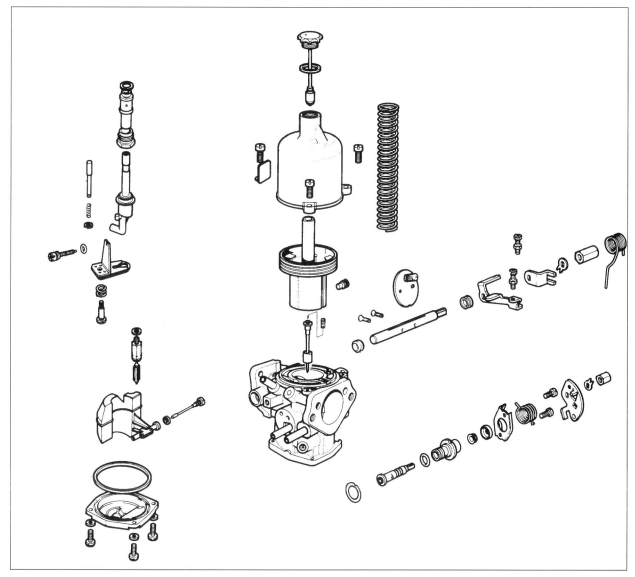

side, but doesn't bear on the needle. It bears on a guide into which the needle fits, and there's a small spring above the needle to keep it pressed down in the guide.

Start dismantling by taking off the dashpot and piston, then mark the bottom cover on the body so you get it back the correct way round. You'll realise why when you look inside the cover as it's shaped to fit round the jet and float. There isn't a normal gasket under the cover – it has a large rubber O-ring recessed into it. On the side of the body at the bottom there are two screws, one exposed and one sunk deep into a counterbore. The exposed one is the float hinge pin, and the sunk one, which you want to remove first, is the jet adjusting screw. You may find that there's an anti-tamper aluminium plug hiding it. Take out the jet adjusting screw and its O-ring. Then look inside the base where you'll find a jet-adjusting lever held by a screw with a locking spring. When you remove this screw, you can lift out the jet complete with the lever and unhook the lever from the jet.

Take out the float hinge pin screw complete with its sealing washer, lift out the float, and tip the carburettor the right way up for the needle valve to fall out. Then take

Fig. 12.13. On the HIF, take the dashpot and piston off together with the damper.

out the needle valve seating which, on later HIFs, has a filter with it. Undo the nut locking the jet bearing, and take out the bearing and its fibre washer.

The cold-start assembly is behind the fast-idle cam, and before you take this off, make a note of where the ends of its quite strong coil return spring locate. If you don't, you can puzzle for quite a time till you get it returning

smartly. The nut holding the fast-idle cam is locked by a tab washer which you have to bend down before undoing it. Use a screwdriver to hold the spring against the carburettor body while you prise off the cam, then lift off the spring.

Under the fast-idle cam is the starter unit cover plate, and note that this also locates the end of the throttle lever return spring. Undo

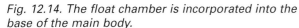

Fig. 12.14. The float chamber is incorporated into the base of the main body.

Fig. 12.15. The float hinge pin is screwed in from the side of the body.

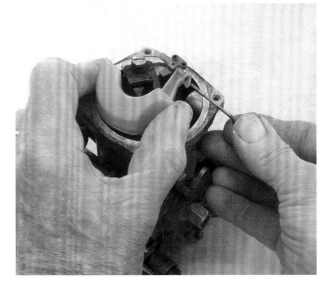

Fig. 12.16. The screw in the side which is sunk deep in the body is the jet-adjusting, or CO, screw.

Fig. 12.17. The jet lifts out after you release the adjusting screw and fixing screw.

the screws holding the cover plate, and take out the starter assembly. On early HIFs, the cover plate and starter body are quite separate, but on later models the plate and body are designed to stay together and shouldn't be pulled apart. You may also find different arrangements of seals inside. Early models have an O-ring and a gasket; later models have two O-rings and no gasket.

The throttle spindle on the HIF runs in ball bearings and very seldom gives any problems. Our

advice is that, unless it's absolutely essential, which it probably isn't, leave it alone on the basis that if it ain't bust, don't fix it. Make absolutely certain that you've got the correct repair kit for your model of HIF, with the correct washers, seals, O-rings and needle valve, before you start putting things together.

After thorough cleaning, start assembly with the dashpot and piston. On the ball bearing type, make sure all 12 balls are in

position, and put the piston in the dashpot without the damper or spring. Then hold the dashpot horizontal and give the piston a spin. It should spin quite freely. If it doesn't, look for rough spots or deposits in the dashpot that you haven't cleaned out.

On the pre-ball bearing dashpots and pistons, make sure the piston is free in the dashpot. You can, if you want to for peace of mind, carry out a drop time test, though SU used to say that this was necessary only if

Fig. 12.18. Note that the jet housing is in two parts, and also has an aluminium washer under it.

Fig. 12.19. The cold start device is held by its cover plate under the fast-idle cam spring.

the carburettor was misbehaving itself and you couldn't find any other reason.

To do the drop time test, plug the two air transfer holes in the base of the piston. SU used rubber plugs for this, but a couple of blobs of Blu-Tak do just as well provided you don't leave any behind afterwards. Put the piston in the dashpot without its long spring, and fit a bolt, washer and nut through one of the fixing holes so the washer overlaps the inside of the dashpot to stop the piston falling out. Fit the damper without any oil and make sure the piston is right at the top end of the dashpot.

Now turn the dashpot the correct way up, and measure how long it takes for the piston to drop down till it hits the washer. It should fall steadily and evenly and, according to SU, take between four and six seconds, though half a second either way is OK. If it doesn't fall steadily, or hangs about for eight or ten seconds, you need to do some more careful cleaning. If, on the other hand, it whizzes down in a couple of seconds, either you haven't plugged the transfer

holes properly or someone has cleaned the inside of the dashpot, and possibly the edges of the piston as well, with a scraper or emery paper and ruined it. We've come across only one HIF where this had been done, and it was impossible to get a clean engine pick-up or proper fast-idle. The dashpot and piston were scrap.

When you fit the piston needle, SU used to recommend that you always use a new locking screw. We must admit that we haven't always followed this when we've been changing needles for tuning, but it's still good advice. Look for an etched line on the needle guide. The guide fits with this line pointing towards the two air transfer holes in the piston. Push the guide fully home till it's flush with the recess in the piston, and tighten the screw. In this position, the shoulder on the needle should be level with the base of the piston.

When you refit the starter unit, remember that the valve fits with its cut-out towards the top cover retaining screw hole, and that the cover fits with the flanges that anchor the return springs facing

towards the throttle. Put just a light smear of oil on the starter unit O-rings before fitting the valve. If you fit them dry, there's a danger of damaging them on the edge of the hole as you push the unit home. Also, when you fit the jet, make sure the jet head moves freely in the cut-out. As a starting point, set the jet head flush with the top of the jet bridge, and carry out final mixture adjustments on the car as detailed in your car handbook.

After fitting a new inlet needle valve, and refitting the float, make sure that the float moves freely, then hold the body upside-down and measure the distance between the highest point on the float and a straight-edge held across the bottom of the carburettor. It should be between 0.020in (0.5mm) and 0.040in (1.5mm). If it isn't, gently bend the small brass tag that bears on the needle valve.

When you refit the dashpot, line up the fixing holes and the slot in the piston before you lower it down so you don't have to twist it too much to align it, with the attendant danger of winding up the large spring.

Chapter 13
SU auxiliary starting carburettor

SU auxiliary starting carburettors are found on a number of classics fitted with SU carburettors, notably classic Jaguars. You might find them described as starting enrichment devices, but they are a simple form of carburettor.

Fuel from the main carburettor float chamber comes in at the base and passes up through a jet where the flow is restricted by a tapered needle. The needle is normally held in the open position by a coil spring which pushes on a collar near the top of the needle. The needle runs through an adjustable stop screw and ends in a flat head so that the screw governs how far the needle can be moved down to close off the jet.

Alongside this assembly is a solenoid and plunger, and at the base of the plunger is a ball jointed disc valve and a light coil spring. The disc valve shuts off a connection to the inlet manifold. Current to the solenoid is controlled by a thermostatic switch in the cooling system, often in the inlet manifold water jacket, so that it comes into operation at coolant temperatures below about 85°F (30°C) to 95°F (35°C).

When the solenoid is energised, the plunger and disc valve move upwards allowing the depression in the inlet manifold through to the needle assembly where it pulls down on the needle collar to overcome the spring and pull the needle down into the jet. At the same time, air is sucked in through a passage alongside the needle so you get extra mixture sucked into the manifold. There's a rather primitive little dust shield over the air intake to deflect most of the dust or grit that might be floating about under the bonnet. How far the needle moves down, and thus how rich the extra mixture is, depends on the setting of the stop screw.

Apart from a burnt-out solenoid, which is rare, and general muck, corrosion and old gummy fuel deposits inside, there's almost nothing to go wrong on these quite simple and robust devices. If you get poor cold starting, and the stop screw isn't screwed down so far that the needle almost blocks the jet completely, the chances are that the solenoid disc valve isn't opening. This could be because the solenoid isn't getting current (check the connections and thermostatic switch), the solenoid is burnt out or the plunger is sticking.

If the solenoid appears to be working (you can usually hear the disc valve click if you put 12 volts across the terminals), and your fuel consumption is horribly high (or you fail the MOT emission test miserably), the chances are that the thermostatic switch has failed in the 'on' position so the solenoid is energised all the time, or the disc valve isn't shutting off properly. To settle a popular misconception, if everything else is correct, altering the needle stop screw affects the mixture only when the engine is cold. It won't affect the mixture or the fuel consumption once the engine's up to operating temperature.

If the threads for the petrol unions are stripped there's nothing you can do about it. The carburettor's scrap, so check carefully if you're buying one second-hand at an autojumble or a breaker's.

Apart from the stop screw, the only adjustments that can be made to the carburettor are to change the needle assembly and its spring. You find the size for the needle stamped on its collar. In the example we stripped for this book, the code number was 425, which is the needle for a Mk2 3.4 litre Jaguar, but if you pick up a second-hand carburettor, check the needle size for your particular car in the workshop manual specification or with a fuel system specialist. The needle comes complete with its bridge piece and stop screw, you can't separate them. So far as we know, the needle springs don't have any identification on them.

Stripping down is quite straightforward except that the solenoid sometimes sticks in the body. Tap it very lightly with a small hammer. It sits in a recess about an eighth of an inch deep, and hitting it too hard is likely to break the flange. Treat it with copious doses of WD-40 and, after gentle taps, keep trying till it comes free.

As we said, solenoids very seldom burn out, but the electrical connections are push-on Lucar type, and we've seen quite a few broken off. Provided a meter check shows that the solenoid winding is OK, you can solder new Lucar tags on to the stubs of the broken ones but you have to take care because the terminal posts which come out

Fig. 13.1. SU's auxiliary starting carburettor is simple, but after drying out it can give problems until it is cleaned and reset.

Fig. 13.2. There should be a number stamped on the collar of the needle, though it is sometimes faint. This identifies the engine to which the carburettor was originally fitted.

of the top of the solenoid aren't solidly fixed in the Bakelite top-plate. You will also find that the heat necessary to solder on new tags will probably melt the original solder connecting the terminal posts to the solenoid windings. Too much heat will melt the Bakelite top-plate; not enough will give a dry joint and a bad connection. It's a question of judgement, so if you're not used to soldering, perfect your technique on other components first.

We've never found a broken disc valve spring, but we have found plungers that stick in the solenoid core, and we've found gummy deposits and white crystals on the disc valve and its brass seating ring. Clean both of them with a spot of metal polish or Duraglit but take care not to damage the tiny ball joint on the disc valve

Apart from that, the usual cleaning methods apply, soaking in white spirit, treating the insides to a good dose of carburettor cleaner and brass brushing to make the body look smarter. The solenoid stirrup originally had a thin galvanised coating but this has often gone rusty. However, it looks quite smart if it's rubbed down with wet and dry paper, primed and given a couple of coats of aluminium wheel paint.

On a couple of occasions we've found stripped threads in the top of the body where the needle

assembly bridge piece sits, and in the top of the stirrup which holds the solenoid. If you're unlucky enough to find the threads in the body stripped, or the screws sheared off, go very gently when drilling to the next size and retapping. There isn't a lot of metal to spare, and old aluminium die-castings can get rather brittle. A stripped thread in the top of the stirrup is no problem, even though there isn't enough metal to drill and retap. The answer is to drill the hole a size larger and solder a thin nut on the underside. If the internal threads are OK but the screws have gone rusty and horrible, replace them. They should be cheese-headed, and are usually BA sizes.

Take care when you replace the Bakelite top-cap on the solenoid. There are two indentations inside the cap which fit over the terminal

posts. If you get the cap on the wrong way round and tighten the stirrup you'll crack the Bakelite.

Setting up the carburettor is quite simple. First let the engine come up to operating temperature, which takes longer than you might think, so it's best to do this immediately after a run. Energise the solenoid by connecting a couple of leads from the battery and then adjust the stop screw till the engine is running rich just short of the point where it starts to hunt and get lumpy. Disconnect the leads and give the engine a blip for a second or two to clear the manifold, and it should settle down to its normal tick-over. Next time you cold start, the carburettor should come in automatically. You may have to make a slight adjustment of the stop screw, but not more than a quarter of a turn.

Fig. 13.3. When you clean the solenoid plunger, be careful not to strain the ball joint at the disc.

Chapter 14
Weber DGAV and DGV carburettors

Weber's twin-choke DGAV was fitted to hundreds of Pinto-engined classic Fords and various other makes, as well as being a favourite on tuned Ford Crossflow engines and, though it looks complicated, it isn't a difficult carburettor to overhaul. The A, by the way, stands for automatic choke, which most of them had. Overhauling the DGV, with a manual choke, is much the same, and you can get all the bits you need for either model from your local Weber agent.

Before you start stripping down, clean the outside of the carburettor and identify it so you can get the right overhaul kit. It's no good just saying 'It's a DGAV.' There have been lots of models of DGAV over the years, so you need the other identifying numbers. You'll find them all stamped on the carburettor main flange. It does no harm to quote the serial number as well, but the Weber agent probably won't need this.

Carefully save all the washers, circlips and other bits and pieces you take off. You'll get new circlips, split pins and rubber O-rings in the kit, but little circlips have a habit of pinging off across the garage and it's handy to have a few spares. Another tip is to replace all the screws in their holes after you take something off. That way you don't lose them or get them muddled up. Some are the same thread but different lengths.

The first job, as usual, is to check the base flange for truth. If it's warped you'll get air leaks. To true it after dismantling, rub it on emery paper held against something flat like a piece of plate glass.

Start dismantling by prising off the small circlip and lifting off the top choke operating link, the one that's attached to the throttle spindle. Then you can undo the six screws holding the top of the carburettor and lift it off. Put the main body to one side for the moment.

Inside the top you'll find the float with its needle valve. You take the float off by pushing out its hinge pin, after which the needle valve just lifts out or, more likely, is pulled out by the float as it has a small wire on top into which a tag on the float fits so that it never sticks up when the float drops. If you've got an overhaul kit don't bother to inspect the needle valve or the brass valve seating into which it fits. You get new ones in the kit, but you don't get a float hinge pin, so save that carefully.

Just in front of the needle valve is the power valve, held by three screws and with a tall spring sticking out the top. Take this off carefully because you don't get a new one in the kit. If the diaphragm is OK and the valve spindle isn't seized you can use it again. The diaphragm is distorted by the spring when you lift the valve out, so ease the spring pressure to check it. If the diaphragm's had it, you can get a new valve from your Weber agent. You should find the part number on the leaflet that goes with the kit.

Behind the float, under a hexagon nut, is the fuel filter. You used not to get one of these with the kit, but they are now included. Check the kit when you buy it just

in case it's old stock and doesn't have a filter in it. Once you've got all this off the carburettor top you can dunk it in a tub of white spirit for an hour or so to loosen the muck and give it a good scrub off. If you've got an air line, blow through all the holes and passages to make sure they're free. If you haven't got an air line you can get a useful jet of air by clamping the body of an old ball point pen in your footpump line.

Now turn your attention to the main body and take out all the jets. Start with the two on the top of the body, the primary and secondary air correction jets. They've got brass emulsion tubes under them and these sometimes stick. The easiest way to get them out is to fish them up with a small piece of wood. Don't use a screwdriver or you might damage them.

Keep all your jets strictly in order so you get them back in the same places. Later, when you've cleaned them, you can identify them by their numbers, but it's difficult to read these when the jets are covered in muck, as they probably will be. Keep all the washers with the jets, even though you get new ones in the kit. They're useful for identification.

Next to the air correction jets is the accelerator pump jet which holds down a Y-shaped delivery piece overhanging the main venturis. This has got tiny little holes in it, and they must be free.

While you're at the top of the body there's another piece to take out so you can clean out internal passages. It isn't a jet, it's the brass blanking plug for the accelerator pump and it sits in the top flange of the float chamber.

Now look down in the float bowl. The two main jets, primary and secondary, are set at an angle in the back of the chamber. The big one on the floor of the chamber is the full power needle valve, and the needle must be free inside the valve.

Next, go down to the sides of the body where you'll find two fairly large brass screws, one each side. These are the primary and secondary idle jets and, when you take them out, you'll find they're in two pieces, a jet and a jet holder.

The last brass bit to take out is the idle mixture adjusting screw, sometimes called the CO screw. This sits horizontally at the bottom of the carburettor body just behind the lever where the accelerator control sits.

Now its time to take off either one or two diaphragms, depending on whether or not you've got an anti-stall device. If you've got only one it will have a lever under it, and it's the accelerator pump diaphragm. If you have a second one connected back to the carburettor via a rubber pipe, it's the anti-stall device, but this wasn't fitted to all DGAVs. You get new diaphragms in the kit, but remember which way round they fit.

Last to be dismantled is the automatic choke. Start by undoing the three screws which hold the ring clamping the thermostat housing. You won't be able to get at one of them with a screwdriver because the water pipe is in the way, but they have hexagon heads as well as screwdriver slots to you can loosen the last one with a small spanner.

Once they're loose you can rotate the housing, but before you take it off, identify the two scribed lines at the top which make sure you get it back in the correct position. As you lift the housing off you'll see that the coiled spring inside fits over a brass peg. Make sure it fits there when you put it back. Don't bother to take the

domed cover off. There's nothing under it except a water passage, and the screw often seizes and shears off, which can be a nuisance to say the least.

Under the housing is a plastic heat shield and under that is the horizontal choke diaphragm rod. Undo the three screws at the end of the choke body and have a look at the choke diaphragm. You don't get a new one in the kit, but if it's at all suspect get a new rod and diaphragm from your Weber agent. It's held inside by a small circlip, a spring and a washer. Make a note of the order in which they come off.

At the end of the diaphragm cover plate is a small central adjusting screw under a brass or plastic plug. Don't dig the plug out for the moment, you may not have to adjust the screw. The plug usually gets damaged when you dig it out, and it's another part you don't get in the kit. If you have to dig it out to adjust the choke setting later on, you'll need a new one.

If you want to take the automatic choke right off, as you might do if you want to change it for a manual one, it's held by three more screws. After they're undone, you can either twist it to disengage the connecting link to the throttle lever or take the small split pin out of the other end of the link.

Unless you want to change the main venturi sizes (which you won't unless you're playing about with advanced power tuning) that's all you need to take off. There's no necessity to take off the various links and levers if you don't need to clean them. Also, unless they're seized or badly worn, there's no need to take out the throttle or choke spindles. Open the primary throttle a few times to make sure that the secondary throttle follows it easily without sticking, and that both throttles snap shut when you let go. If they don't, a good soaking in cleaner, or a squirt or two of WD-40, will usually free them off.

Before you leave the body, check the security of the two

auxiliary venturis, the 'bridge pieces' which fit in the top of the main venturis. They should be tight, but if one is loose it can cause uneven running and is a very tricky fault to spot later on. Tightening them isn't easy, but we've done it in the past by lightly knurling the side edges of the lugs which fit in the carburettor body. If you haven't got a knurling tool you can do it by holding a sharp file against the side of the lug and squeezing it gently in the vice. This isn't recommended by Weber, who say that if they're loose you should replace them, but it's worth a try before you do. Don't, however, squeeze them too hard or you'll buckle them, and don't try to modify the carburetor body to tighten them.

Now you can give the body of the carburettor a good soaking and scrub and blow through the drillings to make sure everything's clean and free of gunge. This is where an aerosol of proprietary carburettor cleaner comes in very useful. It's surprising how much muck it shifts out of the drillings.

When you put back the idle mixture screw, screw it home and then undo it three full turns. This will give you a basic setting to get the engine started.

Putting everything back together again is pretty well the reverse order of taking things apart. Then you're ready to set the choke plate pull-down and the choke phasing. However, before you put the top back on the body, you have to check the float level. There are two settings. For the first one you hold the top vertically so that the float is just resting on the needle valve, and measure the distance between the machined face of the carburettor top and the bottom of the float. If it isn't right you bend the small brass tag on the float, the one which fits in the little wire on top of the needle valve.

For the second setting, Weber tell you to hold the whole thing upside down and let the float hang, but we find it's difficult to measure

Fig. 14.1. Start by removing this circlip from the end of the choke spindle.

Fig. 14.2. Check the spring and the diaphragm on the power valve.

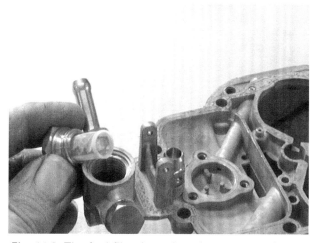

Fig. 14.3. The fuel filter is under a hexagon nut just behind the float.

Fig. 14.4. The primary and secondary air correction jets have emulsion tubes under them. Lift them out using a thin stick of wood.

Fig. 14.5. The accelerator pump jet holds down a Y-shaped delivery piece. The tiny holes in this must be clear.

Fig. 14.6. Down in the float bowl, the primary and secondary main jets are set at an angle. The big jet on the floor of the chamber is the full power needle valve.

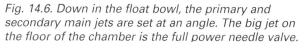

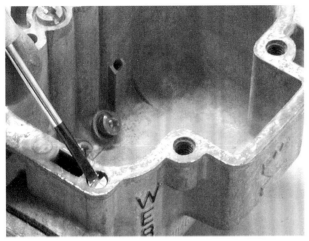

Fig. 14.7. Take out this blanking plug for the accelerator pump so that you can clean the internal passages.

Fig. 14.8. The primary and secondary idle jets are in the side of the body, one each side.

Fig. 14.9. Under this housing is the accelerator pump diaphragm. You get a new diaphragm in the overhaul kit.

Fig. 14.11. The choke diaphragm is under a cover at the end of the automatic choke housing, and is attached to an internal rod. You don't get a new one in the kit.

Fig. 14.10. Before you remove the automatic choke housing, note that there are scribed lines to use when you replace it.

Fig. 14.12. Before you replace the top of the carburettor, check the upper and lower float level limits.

things upside down, so we lay it on the bench with the float uppermost and lift the float gently till it stops. Then you again measure the distance from the flange to the bottom of the float. This time if it isn't right you bend the small tag on the float which stops it coming down too far by hitting the needle valve housing. The float settings vary with different engines but they'll be in your workshop manual, or you can get them from your local Weber agent.

To set the choke plate pull-down you need a special tool which Weber doesn't supply but most stationery shops do – an ordinary rubber band. Before you fit the choke thermostat housing back, hook a rubber band over the choke plate lever, the small brass pin into which the coiled spring fits, and hook the rubber band so that the chokes are closed.

Now open the throttle so that the choke plates close fully, and then let it go. The fast-idle screw should now be sitting on the top step of the fast-idle cam. Use a small screwdriver to push the choke diaphragm rod outwards against its stop and measure the gap between the bottom edges of the choke plates and the walls of the air intakes. You'll find the correct gap specified in your workshop manual, or your Weber agent can tell you, and you measure the gap with a drill shank of the correct diameter. If the gap isn't correct, you have to dig out the plug from the choke diaphragm cover to get at the adjusting screw.

To set the choke phasing, partly open the throttle so that the fast-idle screw is on the lower step of the cam and then let the throttle go. Push the choke plates down till the fast-idle screw jams up against the step in the fast-idle cam, then let them go. Again check the clearance at the bottom edge of the choke plates using a drill shank. Once more you can consult your workshop manual or a Weber agent for the correct gap.

There isn't a screw to adjust if the clearance is wrong. It's adjusted by bending the tag on the choke spindle lever with a pair of pliers. Brutal, but effective.

It sounds very complicated and technical, but it's all logical and straightforward when you come to do it. Bolt the carburettor back on the engine and set your slow-running, fast-idle and CO mixture in the usual way.

Chapter 15
Weber DCOE carburettor

Start talking about classic performance carburettors, and the first name that comes to mind is Weber's DCOE. It looks a complicated animal, but it isn't a complicated carburettor to work on. Weber designed it as an out-and-out performance carburettor, so they made it easy to strip and service, and easy to set up to match a performance-tuned engine without even taking it off the car.

However, If you've picked up a second-hand DCOE, or it came with the car and looks as if it could do with a thorough clean, it's best to take it off and work on the bench. With a second-hand DCOE, be prepared to fork out for a complete jet, emulsion tube and venturi change to suit your engine, especially if the carburettor came from a multi-carburettor set up. Unless you have one of the following makes, it's best to avoid second-hand carbs which came from Alfa Romeos, Maseratis, Lamborghinis, Renault Gordinis and Coventry Climax GTs, especially the turbocharged versions. Some of these can be difficult to adapt and set up on other engines.

There have been a number of detail changes over the years, but stripping and cleaning all DCOEs is basically the same, and the latest service kit will suit most of them. Even so, when you order a kit from a Weber agent it's as well to quote the type number to make sure you get a kit with everything you need. You find this type number stamped on the top of the carburettor in a panel marked Tipo. The one we took apart for photographing was

labelled 40DCOE 151. As the service kit is packed to suit a range of DCOEs, you may find a few washers and locking plates you don't need.

Before you start dismantling, wash the whole carburettor off in white spirit to get rid of all the old grease and crud. When the body is stripped, soak it and brush it in white spirit and use an aerosol of carburettor cleaner to squirt through all the internal passages. Check the flatness of the flanges that fit to the inlet manifold and, if necessary, true the face by rubbing it on emery cloth held on a flat surface.

The DCOE is basically two separate carburettors, handed left and right, built into one body with a common float chamber. Almost everything on one side is mirror-imaged on the other. Start dismantling by taking out the fuel filter which is under the big brass cap on top of the fuel inlet. Don't bother to clean it, you get a new one in the service kit. Next to this is a domed cover with a captive thumb screw. Underneath are the two main jets, the big ones, and two smaller jets which are the idle jets. For trying different size idle jets, main jets and emulsion tubes on a rolling road, you can change these without taking anything else off, but on a complete strip it makes things easier to get at if you take off the top cover first.

This is held by five screws, which are identical so you don't have to keep them in order, but keep them separate from the screws holding the bottom cover which are the same thread but

shorter. When you lift the top cover off, the gasket should come with it, but quite often parts of it stick to the body. Before you lift the top cover clear, go round with a blunt knife easing the gasket away from the body because the gasket doesn't come completely free until you take the floats off. If you yank at the top cover when the gasket's stuck, you might bend the float arm, and then you'll have a hell of a job getting the petrol level right.

On earlier DCOEs the gasket was paper, but on the later ones, and in the later service kit, it's rubber. The change was made to turn it into a pressure carburettor for car makers like Alfa Romeo who wanted to turbocharge it. The rubber gasket is completely interchangeable with the old paper one. The pivot pin holding the floats just pushes out, and you get a new one in the kit. On early DCOEs one of the bosses holding the float pin was split, and one solid. The pin comes out of the solid boss. Later carbs have two solid bosses, so if the pin doesn't want to come out one way, don't force it. Try it the other way. You also get a new needle valve inside a small plastic tube so the needle doesn't get separated from its housing.

Floats on earlier DCOEs were brass, but the later ones are black plastic, and there's a different height setting for each type. You measure the float height by holding the top cover, complete with its gasket, with the floats hanging vertically and the float lever just touching the needle valve when it's closed. Measure the distance between the top of the float and the face of the gasket. With brass floats this should be 8.5mm. With black plastic floats it should be 12mm. You adjust it by bending the small brass tab on the float lever which bears on the needle valve. Weber used to specify a float drop distance, but they no longer do. All they say is that the floats must not drop down so far that the needle comes out of its housing. The drop is governed by the other tab on the float lever, the one which hits the needle valve housing when the floats are fully down.

Underneath the carburettor, on the bottom, is a plate which you can take off to clean out the bottom part of the float chamber which acts as a sediment trap, so it usually gets quite a lot of crud in it.

Back on top of the carburettor, next to the main and idle jets is a flat metal plate pushed into the body of the carburettor. This is a baffle plate to lessen the chance of fuel being slopped up and into the air correction jets. It just levers out, but be careful not to bend it.

The main and idle jets unscrew as assemblies. The main jet assembly is made up of the top threaded holder, the air correction jet, the emulsion tube and the main jet. If necessary, they can be taken apart for cleaning, though after years of service you may find them a little tight. If you have to use pliers to take them apart, please pad the jaws. The idle jet assembly has just two parts, the threaded holder and the jet. All the jets have their sizes stamped on them. As with all carburettor jets, clean them only with carburettor cleaner and compressed air, or by blowing through them. Never poke any wire through them. Please use the proper size screwdriver to take out and refit the jets, to avoid chewing up the head of the threaded holders.

Towards the back of the carburettor you've got a cluster of the accelerator pump circuit and the starter circuit. The accelerator pump lifts out for cleaning after you

prize up its retaining plate with a small screwdriver. Be careful not to bend the plate. The piston comes off its rod after you push and twist it. Hooking it back on is easy if you hold the coil spring back, but try not to distort the spring. On each side of the accelerator pump is a blanking plug under which is a square section spacer and a small steel ball. Turn the carburettor over gently to tip these into your hand. The accelerator pump jets aren't in the cluster, they're under the large screwed caps on each side. The caps have rubber O-rings to seal them. The jets just lift out, and you can't put them back the wrong way because there's a flat on the collar halfway down to position the jet so that the hole discharges downstream.

The accelerator pump discharge valve is buried deep down at the bottom of the float chamber. This is a one-way valve which you test by blowing through it.

Now, at the back of the carburettor, take off the block which holds the starter circuit lever. There's a fine gauze air intake filter at the bottom of the block. Take care of this because you don't get one in the service kit (you have to get it from a Weber agent). Check that the lever and its quadrant gears move freely. If necessary, give them a squirt of WD-40. On older DCOEs the lever is held by a nut, and you can take it off to clean the shaft or renew the spring, if necessary, but on later models the lever is riveted on.

Two small arms on the quadrant gears engage with grooves in the starter valves which are under two retaining plates. Prize out the retaining plates with a small screwdriver. On some DCOEs the caps are in two parts, on others just one. Lift out the springs, then either turn the carburettor upside down or push the starter valves up with a small screwdriver to get hold of them. It's best to keep the starter valves separate so they go back in the same bores, but with jets it doesn't really matter.

Remember to put the valves back before you refit the starter lever block. Also in the cluster are the starter jets which again consist of a threaded holder and the jet.

In the middle and just in front of the starter valves is a round brass plate which anchors the top end of the throttle return spring. Don't disturb this unless you have to because the bottom end of the spring can be very awkward to hook back on the collar on the throttle shaft. If you have to unhook it, possibly to renew it, you get to it by taking off the flat plate on the back of the carburettor just under the starter lever block.

The throttle shaft runs in ball bearings which very seldom show any signs of wear and we don't recommend taking the shaft out unless it's absolutely necessary, mainly because of the distinct danger of bending the shaft when you peen over the small screws which hold the butterfly throttle plates. We've come across more than one where this has happened. The ball bearings will probably have had all their lubrication washed out when you cleaned the body, so take off the throttle lever and the washer at the other end of the shaft, wash the bearings out and, when they're dry, pack them with grease and check that the shaft turns and returns smoothly. You get new lock washers in the service kit.

The idling mixture adjustment screws are either side of the starter lever block on the sides of the manifold flanges. The taper on these differs with different model DCOEs, so if you renew them for any reason make sure you get the correct ones. When you reassemble the carburettor, screw the idle mixture screws right home, but don't force them, and then undo them one-and-a-half to two turns as a starting setting.

Just in front of each idle mixture screw are two screwed blanking plugs, one large and one small. Under the large one are three small progression holes which must be kept clear. The smaller blanking plug

Fig. 15.1. Weber's DCOE is a no-frills, no-nonsense performance carburettor.

Fig. 15.2. When you take off the domed cover the main and idle jets are exposed for changing without any further dismantling.

Fig. 15.3. The gauze fuel filter sits under the top brass plug next to the inlet.

Fig. 15.4. The main jets are the larger ones in the small cluster. They unscrew as assemblies.

Fig. 15.5. Just in front of the main jets are the idle jets which also unscrew as assemblies.

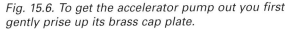

Fig. 15.6. To get the accelerator pump out you first gently prise up its brass cap plate.

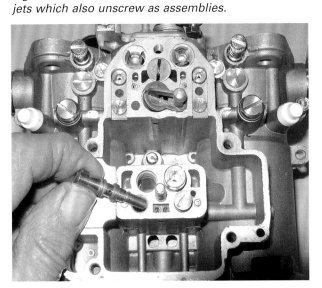

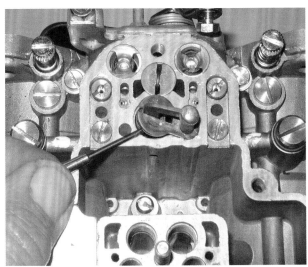

Fig. 15.7. After that, the pump piston, spring and guide lift out.

Fig. 15.8. The starter circuit jets are in recesses either side of the throttle spring.

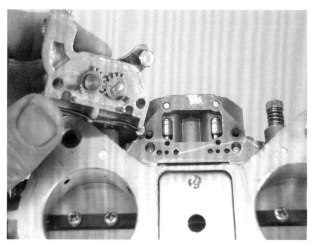

Fig. 15.9. At the back of the carburettor, unscrew the starter lever block and its gears to expose the starter valves.

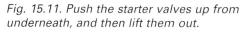

Fig. 15.11. Push the starter valves up from underneath, and then lift them out.

Fig. 15.10. To take the starter valves out, first prise up the caps retaining the springs.

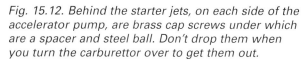

Fig. 15.12. Behind the starter jets, on each side of the accelerator pump, are brass cap screws under which are a spacer and steel ball. Don't drop them when you turn the carburettor over to get them out.

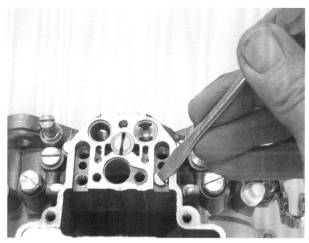

Fig. 15.13. The accelerator pump outlet is deep down inside the float chamber. After unscrewing it you need long-nose pliers to lift it out.

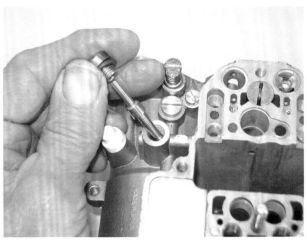

Fig. 15.14. The accelerator pump jets are under cap screws just outboard of the rear cluster. Don't forget the O-rings under the cap screws.

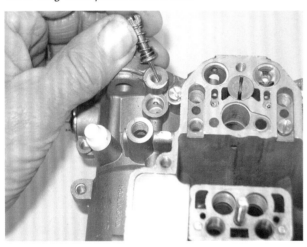

Fig. 15.15. The idle mixture screws are in bosses attached to the rear flanges. The small brass caps just beside them are vacuum take-off points.

Fig. 15.17. Later DCOEs have flow-balancing needle screws with locknuts under white plastic covers outboard of the accelerator pump jets. They also lock the venturis.

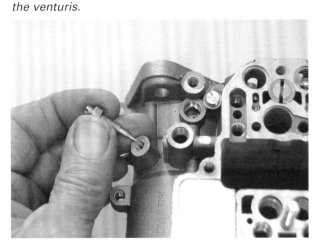

Fig. 15.16. Under larger brass caps in front of the idle mixture screws are three compensating holes which must be kept clear.

Fig. 15.18. Locking screws with locknuts for the chokes are three-quarters of the way round the two barrel housings.

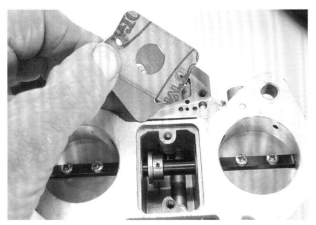

Fig. 15.19. Don't unhook the throttle return spring unless you have to, but if you do, you get to it behind a cover plate on the back of the carburettor.

Fig. 15.20. A cover plate underneath the carburettor is a sediment trap. It needs periodic cleaning out.

is to take a vacuum connection which you will want to use when you set the carburettor up on the car.

Lastly we come to the venturis and chokes. Because the DCOE is a performance carburettor, these are made easy to change for tuning to suit engines in various stages of tune. The air intake trumpets, if fitted, come off after undoing their clamp plates, but the venturis and, on later models the chokes as well, are locked.

The locking screws and locknuts for the venturis are three-quarters of the way round the body. Slacken the locknut and remove the screw, and the venturi just lifts out. You can't put it back the wrong way round because there's a dimple to take the point of the locking screw.

On earlier DCOEs, the chokes weren't locked, but on later ones they are because Weber introduced idling air flow bleeds. These are at the top of the carburettor body, just outboard of the accelerator pump jets, and should have white plastic covers on them. When you take the screws out, you'll see that they have long tapering points which pass through holes in the wall of the choke to give an air bleed past the throttle at idling to balance the idling flow of both barrels. The chokes just pull out after you take the screws out. Before the air bleed screws were fitted, it was common practice

Fig. 15.21. With the air flow balance screws and choke locking screws out, the venturis and chokes come out and can be changed if necessary for tuning.

for tuners to drill a tiny hole in one throttle butterfly to balance the flow.

When you set the carburettor up on the car, connect a vacuum gauge, or preferably a pair of vacuum gauges, in place of the plugs we mentioned earlier, and adjust the air bleed screws till the vacuum on each barrel is the same.

Reassembly is, in the time-honoured phrase, the reverse of taking things apart. There aren't any snags, and nothing like choke phasing. Apart from the float level, idling air bleed (if fitted), idling mixture screws and idling throttle stop, there's nothing to adjust.

Weber lists a wide range of sizes of emulsion tubes, jets and

Fig. 15.22. Before you can change the top cover gasket you have to take the floats off after pulling out the hinge pin.

venturis for DCOEs, and because even small changes can make a big difference, it's impossible to give lists of sizes for different engines, particularly with different air filters, exhausts or head porting. Sizes which are ideal for one engine may not be the best for a similar engine with nominally the same power uprating. A tuning firm, or a Weber agent, should be able to give you a list of sizes which will get the engine running well, and an experienced tuner can often make changes when road testing, but to get the best results when setting up a DCOE, a session on a rolling road is highly recommended.

Chapter 16

Zenith carburettors

Simple Zenith sidedraught carburettor

Probably the simplest Zenith carburettor is the basic sidedraught model with an external strangler for cold starting. It was fitted to quite a few pre-war and early post-war 8hp and 10hp classics. Simple it may be, but its very simplicity can be frustrating because there seems to be nothing that can go wrong with it, yet it sometimes misbehaves.

The external strangler can also be something of a Chinese puzzle to put together if you don't remember how it came apart, so we'll deal with this first. There isn't an air filter, so you get a typical carburettor roar when you accelerate, but the body of the strangler forms a dust protecting shield for the air intake. The strangler has a lever at the top which connects to the choke cable, and another lever with a bent flange sticking out of the side which, when it moves down, pushes on the throttle lever via an adjusting screw to set the fast-idle. The whole assembly is held to the carburettor by a screw and a nut. When you take the assembly off, hold the choke lever and the strangler plate against the cover, or pieces are likely to fly apart and springs come unhooked, which can damage your fingers.

The easiest way to explain how the strangler works is to look at the photograph. A peg on the choke lever fits in a small hole in the strangler plate and, when the lever

is pulled backwards, it brings the strangler plate down to cover the air intake. There's a small hole in the centre of the strangler plate to stop the engine being completely starved of air. A projection on the strangler plate buts up against a shouldered brass nut which stops its travel when the air intake is closed. At the same time, a cam attached to the choke lever pushes down on the fast-idle lever which is pivoted on the cover plate and has its own return spring.

Problems, apart from general rust and stiffness, can be breaking of the light coil spring on the fast-idle lever, or the much stronger coil spring on the choke lever. The light coil spring is easy to replace, and it isn't all that difficult to find a coil spring that can be adapted. If you've got an old-fashioned ironmonger's near you, such shops often stock a variety of coil springs, or you may find one by looking at various components in a breaker's, or even in your odds and ends box.

A more difficult problem is when the strong coil spring on the choke lever breaks. It's not the difficulty of finding a suitable spring, the problem is that the spring was put on before the lever and the cam were riveted together. We're not saying it's impossible to take them apart and re-rivet them, but it's a very difficult job to get them tight again. Even if you tack weld them together, the heat of welding is likely to take the temper out of the new spring. We've seen a couple of classics on which this spring has broken, and the owners had fitted an external tension spring to the lever to take its place.

In common with most Zenith carburettors with this type of float chamber, or float bowl as it's sometimes called, one of the bolts has a square key on the end which fits into the two jets in the bottom of the bowl to undo them for cleaning. You won't get these two jets, main and progression, mixed up because the outside threads are different sizes. The slow-running, or idling, jet is the small one at the top of the float chamber. The slow-running mixture screw is an air bleed valve on the top of the carburettor and is locked by the usual type of coil spring. It has a long tapered nose, and governs the amount of air bled in for slow-running through a side drilling in its housing. The idle speed adjusting screw is above the throttle lever and also has a locking coil spring.

At the back of the float chamber, where it pokes into the inlet venturi, is the emulsion block. This is an essential part of these Zeniths as it blends the fuel from the three jets and presents it into the venturi as a fine mist. There is nothing to go wrong with the emulsion block, unless possibly one of the passages getting blocked with dirt, which is rare, except when it's been disturbed. If someone has taken it off and put it back without a new gasket, it's odds-on that there are air leaks, or fuel leaks between the passages in the block and body, and you will never get the engine to respond as it should.

Overhauling the carburettor is basically a question of checking the flatness of the flange where it bolts to the inlet manifold, and cleaning all the muck out of the float chamber and from the internal drillings and passages. An aerosol of carburettor cleaner is invaluable for this job.

The throttle spindle and bearings seldom seem to wear much on these small Zeniths, and in any case, as we said in our introduction to carburettors, the effect of a slightly worn throttle spindle on the general running of the engine is often over-rated. You can usually compensate for slight wear by adjusting the slow-running mixture screw.

There isn't any adjustment for the level of petrol in the float chamber other than varying the thickness of the washer under the inlet needle valve. The level is quite critical to good running, which is why the washer under the needle valve is aluminium and not fibre. Fibre washers are not easy to mass-produce to a standard thickness, and they squash and flatten if the valve is removed and replaced. Always use the specified aluminium washer, usually 1mm thick. The brass float fits with its domed side uppermost and, just so you don't make a mistake, Zenith marked this side of the float 'TOP'.

Very similar to the sidedraught model is the downdraught version, either with an external strangler or with an extra cold-start jet which comes into operation when you pull out the choke. The choke wire connects to a horizontal plunger which uncovers the cold-start jet. Nothing to go wrong with it apart from dirt or a sticking return spring. Overhauling the rest of the carburettor is the same as the sidedraught model.

'Tall' Zeniths

The VIG, sometimes called the 'tall' Zenith, was a popular carburettor in the 1950s and 1960s, and was made with a variety of model numbers to suit different applications, usually on medium performance family cars with fairly low compression engines,

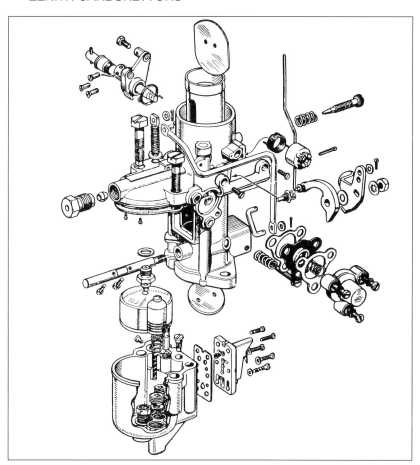

Fig. 16.1. The 'tall' zenith was fitted to a large number of British classic cars in the 1950s and 1960s. This is the VIG30.

light vans and some larger commercials. All VIG models are similar, and the same principles of overhaul apply to them all. We've taken a 30 VIG as being typical. Overhauling is basically a matter of cleaning and renewing gaskets and the economy diaphragm. All the adjustments are made on the external rod linkages, with only one of these being necessary before the carburettor goes back on the engine.

After cleaning the outside, start stripping by taking off the float chamber which is held by two bolts, one of which might have a squared end which acts as a key for undoing the jets in the bottom of the float chamber. If not, the jets will have slots for a large screwdriver. The gasket for the float chamber should be fixed to the carburettor body by four small hammer-in drive screws, to stop it

falling down when you take the float chamber off. Invariably, on an old carburettor, the drive screws no longer hold the gasket which has pulled away from them. There aren't any slots in the heads of the screws to undo them, and the easiest way we have found to get them out is to use a pair of side cutters to lever them up. The inlet needle valve under the top of the float chamber housing has a 1mm thick aluminium washer under it. You should get a new valve and washer in the kit. There is no adjustment for petrol level.

The accelerator pump piston and its spring come out after you slacken a small pointed-nose screw at the side of the float chamber. Keep your hand over the piston as you undo the screw to stop the piston and spring jumping out and flying across the garage. Next to the pump piston, at the top of the float chamber, is the pump discharge valve, and next to that, just behind the emulsion block, is the slow-running jet. Down in the bottom of the float chamber there are two jets, the main jet and compensating jet. These may have a square hole for undoing them, in which case use the key at the end of one of the float chamber bolts, or they may have large screwdriver slots. You can't get the two mixed up because the outside diameter of the compensating jet is larger. There are fibre washers under the main and compensating jets. Next to them is the accelerator pump inlet valve with a brass gauze filter over it. This undoes with a thin walled socket or a box spanner. Inside the valve is a steel ball which must be free. Take all the jets and the valve out for cleaning.

At the back of the float chamber is the emulsion block held by five screws. On the VIG, four of the screws are the same and one is longer. The three bottom screws, which sit below the petrol level, have aluminium washers. On other Zeniths with a similar emulsion block you may have two short screws at the top, one long screw at the bottom with an aluminium washer, and two countersunk screws in the middle with the countersink acting as a taper seal, so make a note, if only a mental one, to be careful when replacing them. The screws are usually very tight, so use a screwdriver of the correct size to loosen them. The emulsion block will probably stick hard even with the screws out, but don't lever at its sides, just give it a tap with the handle of your screwdriver to free it. You should get a replacement gasket in the overhaul kit.

Inside the emulsion block is the accelerator pump jet, and on the other side of the block, on the 'beak' that sits in the carburettor venturi, is a small triangular piece of brass held by a single screw. This is a deflector plate, sometimes called a dribble catcher, to direct the fuel from the accelerator pump

jet down into the centre of the venturi. The bottom part of the triangle should either be vertical or, at most, lean out about a degree from vertical, and if it looks OK there's no point in disturbing it. The channels on the inside of the emulsion block must be scrupulously clean, as must the three air bleed holes and the very small compensating fuel restriction hole. See *Fig. 16.12* for details of the emulsion block.

Make sure that the various passages on the back of the float chamber which connect to the emulsion block are free and clean, and check the small slow-running air bleed hole is clear, the one at the top of the slow-running jet housing which connects to a small notch in the top of the emulsion block.

Returning to the body of the carburettor, make a note of the external linkages because the details differ on different models. Basically, you have an accelerator connection lever with two linkages. One is a long rod which runs up and across in a bearing at the top of the carburettor, and then over the float chamber to operate the accelerator pump piston. There are two holes for this rod to connect to the accelerator lever, the inner one giving a short stroke to the accelerator pump piston, and the outer one giving a long stroke. In theory, the outer position is for larger capacity engines, but if you want to save fuel at the expense of a slightly slower acceleration pick-up, move it to the inner hole. If you want to take this rod off for cleaning or any other reason, you first have to take off the spring carrier which is held to the end of the strangler shaft by a split pin. The second link is a thinner rod which connects to the strangler butterfly to give you a fast-idle setting when the choke cable is pulled out. We'll deal with adjusting this when we come to reassembly.

The strangler shaft is biased by a coil torsion spring at each end. If you need to take the shaft out to

renew the springs, you have to undo the butterfly fixing screws and then take off the spring carrier at the end of the shaft opposite to the operating lever. Before you take the shaft out, make a careful note of which way the coil springs act, and the position of the tapered pin in the end of the shaft relative to the operating lever. It can be quite a game sorting this out if you forget.

On the side of the carburettor is the economy diaphragm held under a plate with three screws. Don't lose the spring when you take the plate off. You should get a new diaphragm in the overhaul kit. Make sure when you clean the body that the small air bleed hole, situated at about one o'clock when you look in the housing, is clear.

Take out the spring-loaded slow-running mixture screw at the back of the body and make sure the passage inside is clear.

After thorough cleaning, reassembly is literally the reverse of taking things apart. Start by putting back the external linkage rods, but leave the top end of the fast-idle rod finger-tight for the moment. Don't forget the aluminium washers under the emulsion block screws,

Fig. 16.2. On the small Zeniths, the only tricky part is the external strangler, if fitted. Later models had a plain dome and a cold-start valve operated by a cable.

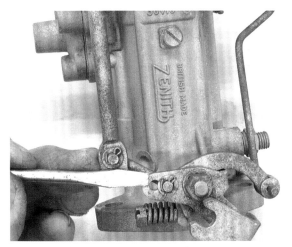

Fig. 16.3. If the tall Zeniths are fitted with an accelerator pump, there are two settings on the throttle lever link to vary the amount of fuel injected.

Fig. 16.4. This is the adjustment for the link which operates the fast-idle when the choke is closed.

nor the fibre washers under the main and compensating jets.

When all is assembled, you make the only adjustment setting that is necessary before the carburettor goes back on the car. This is to set the fast-idle throttle gap. This is the amount by which the throttle butterfly is held slightly open when the strangler butterfly is closed for cold starting. The gap varies with different model carburettors and different engines, but is usually in the order of 1mm to 1.5mm. To set it, slacken the pinch screw holding the fast-idle

Fig. 16.5. If there is an economy diaphragm fitted, it lives under this housing held by three screws.

Fig. 16.6. On some older Zeniths, the jets were outside the float chamber at the bottom.

Fig. 16.7. Most Zeniths have the main jets in the base of the float chamber. Next to them is the inlet for the accelerator pump. There are other jets in the top face of the chamber.

Fig. 16.8. The accelerator pump piston is held down against its spring by a small pointed nose screw.

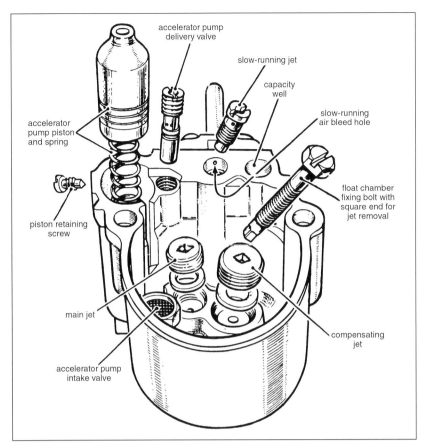

Fig. 16.9. Identifying the jets and other parts of the float chamber.

Fig. 16.10. Under the emulsion block, all the passages must be clean and free.

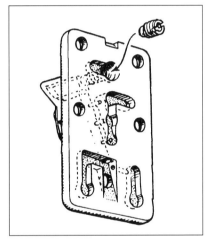

Fig. 16.12. The internal passages of the emulsion block are quite complex.

linkage rod and close the strangler butterfly. Then put a drill shank, or a piece of wire, the diameter of the specified throttle opening alongside the throttle butterfly in line with the flange mounting holes. Push the throttle butterfly closed so it grips the drill shank, and tighten the linkage pinch bolt.

Fig. 16.13. This small direction tag on the emulsion block should be pointing straight down or, at most, a degree or two leaning out.

Fig. 16.11. The accelerator pump jet sits in this small hole in the emulsion block. If it's tight, don't force it out because it's easily damaged. Blow through it to clean it.

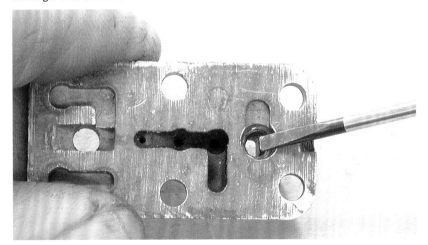

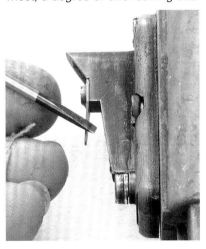

Chapter 17

Solex carburettors

As with most makes, various models of Solex carburettor were fitted to classic cars. As representative, we have chosen a PBI model, though other models are very similar to overhaul.

Dismantling starts with disconnecting the link between the throttle and choke levers, and taking off the top of the float chamber. This is held by two screws at the top and one underneath at the back. If the fuel inlet needle valve inside the top cover is recessed, it will be sunk quite deeply and if it's tight you will have to be careful about using a spanner if the cover is fitted with a small brass vent, as some are. It's not necessary to disturb this vent, and we'd advise against it as it's not easy to get it back tight. The needle valve doesn't come apart for cleaning, so test it by blowing gently though it while you push the needle plunger up. It should shut off cleanly and fall under its own weight without sticking. If it doesn't, renew it. There should be a size stamped on it, something like 1.6.

In the strangler butterfly there's usually a spring-loaded flap to prevent too rich a mixture when a cold engine first fires up. Provided the flap works freely, we would advise you not to disturb it. If it's sticky, you can release it for cleaning by taking out the small split pin on its underside. If you do, always use a new split pin as one which has been closed and opened again is weak and could drop bits down into the engine. The butterfly itself is most unlikely to need attention and we wouldn't advise trying to take it out as this means undoing the two screws which

hold it to its spindle. These are peened over underneath, and won't yield to a screwdriver. They have to be ground flush with a tiny stone in a flexible drive. In other words, to quote an American expression, 'if it ain't bust, don't fix it.' If the coil return spring for the choke butterfly is broken, you can replace it after taking off the lever.

On some Solexes, instead of a strangler butterfly at the air inlet, there is a cold-start device and a starter jet on the side of the body. These seldom give any problems, but if you need to clean the cold-start unit, it has a separate cast bracket on top (to take a choke cable) which must be taken off before unscrewing the unit itself. Under it, depending on the type of unit, you may find a small coil spring with a steel ball beneath it in a drilling down into the cold-start unit. This ball is a 'click stop' for the control and, if you unscrew the unit without first taking out the ball it is likely to fly out and get lost.

Carrying on with the main body, if the model is a later one it will have a hinged float. The hinge pin sits in a recess and the float just lifts out complete with its hinge pin. On older models, with a central inlet needle valve, the float is a loose drum.

Right in the centre of the air intake venturi is the air correction jet, and underneath this is a brass emulsion tube pushed down into the central pedestal. The emulsion tube may come out if you turn the carburettor upside-down and tap it. Most likely it won't, but if the inside of the carburettor is very dirty, the emulsion tube ought to come out for cleaning. Try fishing it out with

a piece of wood such as a toothpick or, if that fails, make a very small hook in the end of a fairly stout piece of wire (or paper clip), push this down the inside of the emulsion tube, hook it underneath and pull the tube out.

If the carburettor is fitted with an accelerator pump, the outlet for this, a thin curved brass tube, sits on one side of the venturi. It is in a brass block held by a small screw, and should lift out quite easily when this screw is removed. If it's very tight, be careful not to break the tube off, and never use a pair of pliers on it as these will squash the tube or break it. We have come across a couple of Solexes where this has happened, and the only way to get the block out to replace it was to drill and tap a larger hole where the fixing screw went (being careful not to drill into the body of the carburettor), and use an extractor screw to pull the old block out.

The accelerator pump is a diaphragm under a housing, with a spacer block, on the side of the carburettor. The lever is connected to the throttle spindle. Diaphragms don't normally come in gasket overhaul kits, but if yours is in poor condition you should be able to get a replacement from a carburettor specialist such as Burlen Fuel Systems.

Most of the jets on this type of Solex are external, and their positions vary depending on the model. Take out every brass jet or plug you can see, making a note of where each fitted, so that you can clean the internal passages as well as the jets. You shouldn't be able to get them back in the wrong place

Fig. 17.1. Start by disconnecting the link to the choke butterfly.

Fig. 17.2. The choke butterfly has a spring-loaded air vent. Make sure it is free.

Fig. 17.3. After taking off the top cover, remove the inlet needle valve.

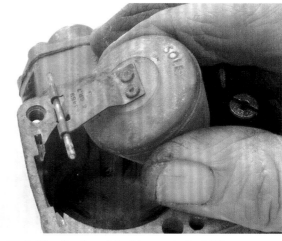

Fig. 17.4. The float and its hinge pin just lift out.

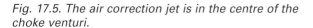

Fig. 17.5. The air correction jet is in the centre of the choke venturi.

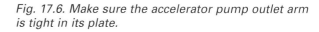

Fig. 17.6. Make sure the accelerator pump outlet arm is tight in its plate.

Fig. 17.7. All the other jets on the Solex are external. Remove and clean any brass plug in sight.

Fig. 17.8. Remove this plate and clean out the passages underneath.

because, with one exception, they are all different sizes. The one exception is the cold-start jet on some models which is the same thread as a non-return valve. Remember that the starter jet fits next to the cold-start housing, and you shouldn't go wrong, but it does no harm to make notes if you're unsure. The two screws with locking springs under their heads are the throttle slow-running screw, which should be obvious, and the idling mixture air bleed screw. On some models there is also a full-throttle stop screw with a locking nut.

One screw which doesn't need cleaning out is a small one with a blunt point, usually a steel screw, just under the lip of the venturi. This is the holding screw for the replaceable venturi but, unless you

are playing with different size venturis for power tuning, don't take the venturi out.

With all the jets and blanking plugs out, immerse the body in a bath of white spirit for an hour or so to loosen internal dirt, then clean out all the passages and drillings with a toothpick, pipe cleaner or whatever, followed by a squirt of carburettor cleaner from an aerosol and, if possible, by a blast of compressed air.

Reassembly, using new gaskets, is quite straightforward. When you replace the air bleed screw, screw it home and then back it off one-and-a-half turns to give you a starting point for adjustment when you start the engine. Leave the adjusting screws for the link from the throttle lever to the strangler butterfly or cold-start unit finger tight, and adjust the fast-idle when the

carburettor is back on the engine.

On some Solexes fitted to cars which are just coming into the classic era, you may have extra fitments such as a solenoid-operated over-run cut-out valve or an automatic choke. The automatic choke is usually in a housing with a coiled bi-metallic spring inside. The housing is connected to the cooling system and, when the temperature of the coolant rises, the bi-metallic spring uncoils and shuts off the cold-start valve. When automatic chokes work, they're fine. When they get old and don't work, they are awkward to repair because internal parts are hard to find. Either fit a complete replacement automatic choke unit if you can find one, or take it off and convert to a manual choke. Many accessory shops sell conversion kits complete with choke cable.

Fig. 17.9. After undoing four cheese-headed screws, the accelerator pump diaphragm and spacer will lift off.

Fig. 17.10. Undo two more, curved-headed, screws, and the diaphragm plate lifts off.

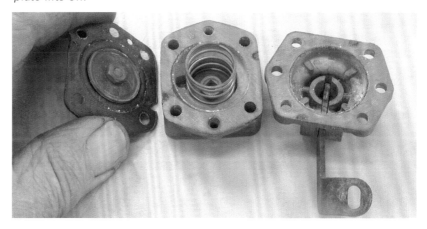

Chapter 18

Stromberg CD carburettors

The Stromberg CD carburettor looks somewhat similar to an SU in that they both have a dashpot with a damper, but there the similarities end. Some people find Stromberg CDs tricky to overhaul, but if you go about it in a logical way they are, if anything, easier to deal with than SUs. There are various models of CD, some of the later ones with emission control and temperature compensation, but we've chosen an ordinary CD150 from a Triumph as being representative of the ones used in the classic era.

Start dismantling by taking out the damper and marking the position of the suction chamber at the top of the carburettor relative to the body. Then undo the four screws holding the top of the suction chamber and lift it off. Be careful not to distort the long coil spring inside, it's quite delicate.

Inside, the piston is separated from the suction chamber by a large rubber diaphragm. This may be stuck to the body of the carburettor, so go round the edges carefully with a blunt pointer (the plastic type of screwdriver used for adjusting tuning coils in radios and televisions is ideal) and then lift the piston straight up to avoid bending the needle. On a general clean, there's probably no need to replace the diaphragm, but on a complete overhaul you get a new diaphragm in the overhaul kit from Burlen Fuel Systems. It's held to the top of the piston by a retainer plate with four screws, but take the needle out of the bottom of the piston before you undo the diaphragm screws as the needle is easily bent. It's held by a

Fig. 18.1. The Stromberg CD looks somewhat like an SU from the outside, but inside it's totally different.

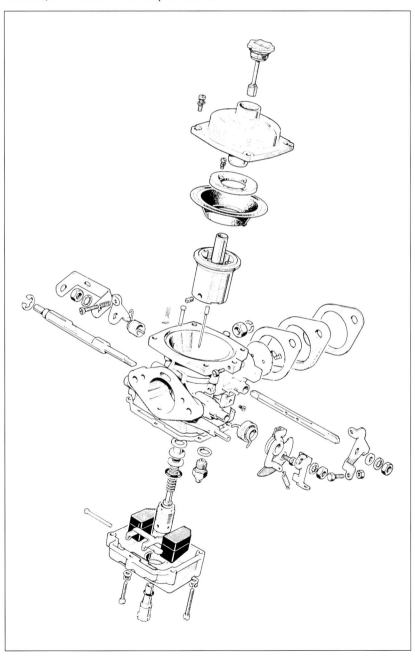

130

grub screw in the side of the piston, and you need a long thin screwdriver as the screw is quite deeply recessed.

Now turn the carburettor upside-down and take out the jet adjusting screw. On some CDs there's a small tommy bar in the bottom of this screw, but on others the head of the screw has finger grips in it and a slot in which you can use a coin, as it's sometimes very awkward to get a screwdriver in when the carburettor's on the car. Note that the screw has an O-ring in a recess. Then unscrew the large jet bottom housing, which also has an O-ring, turn the carburettor the right way up and catch the jet assembly and aluminium washer as they fall out. The jet assembly, which consists of the jet, spring, flat washer and top bush with a small O-ring recessed into its base, just pulls apart. With the O-ring removed, the jet ought to slide freely in the bush, but sometimes, if the carburettor's been standing dry a long time, the jet gets tight in the bush. If so, clean the outside of it till it slides freely or you'll have problems setting the slow-running mixture.

Six screws – three long and three short – hold the float chamber to the bottom of the carburettor. Don't lose the flat brass washers and spring washers on the screws. The float chamber will probably need a tap or two with a soft-faced hammer to free it, and the gasket will split as it comes off. Inside, there's a double float with a hinge pin that just pulls out, and the needle valve with an aluminium washer.

The rich mixture for cold starting on the CD is obtained rather differently from the SU. Instead of lowering the jet, the piston is pushed upwards by a rotating aluminium bar with a cut-out in it. The bar is turned by the choke lever and, at the other end is held by a circlip. This circlip can be a swine to get on and off, so don't try. Go to the other end of the bar and undo the cap nut which is locked by a locking tab. There are two ears on the locking tab, so you can use it twice. Make a note of which way round the choke lever fits before you take it off because you won't remember. Then slide the starter bar, complete with its awkward circlip, through the body of the carburettor. You may want to take the throttle spindle out, but, as we said earlier, there's no need to unless the bearings are badly worn. The last part you can take off, if you need to, is the piston lifting pin. If it works freely, there's no real need to take it out, but if it doesn't, take it out and clean it.

As always, reassembly after cleaning is the reverse of dismantling, but there are a few hints and tips which you could find useful. You get new rings and gaskets in a basic overhaul kit, but you don't get a diaphragm. These are available, but they seldom give any problems. On a carburettor that's been dry for ages you may find that the diaphragm looks distorted when you take it out, but if you clean it, rub some rubber lubricant over it and dry it off, nine times out of ten it will return quite happily to its original shape. It's easiest to clean the diaphragm after you take it off the piston. It's held by four screws and a quite heavy retainer plate. You'll notice that there are two locating bars moulded into the edges of the diaphragm, one on the outside and one on the inside. They fit into recesses in the body and the piston. These are the only means of locating which way round the piston sits in the body because, unlike an SU, there isn't a positive mechanical location for the piston. If you don't properly locate the bars, and thus the piston, you won't get the proper air transfer inside the carburettor and you'll wonder why the engine doesn't run properly. There isn't a locating bar for the diaphragm retainer plate, it doesn't matter which way round it fits.

Some people have problems getting the new O-rings on the jet housing and jet adjusting screw. They seem to be too small when you first try them. The easy way to put them on is to rub them with a little rubber lubricant and roll them on.

The older rubber floats must have a completely unbroken skin or they slowly absorb petrol and the carburettor will flood. If yours are damaged, replace them with the later plastic type. Make sure the twin floats are not twisted. They twist quite easily if someone gets ham-fisted with them. As well as looking, you can check for twist when you measure the float level. You do this by holding the carburettor upside down and measuring the distance between the bottom of the float and the face where the float chamber fits. On most CDs, this should be 18mm, but refer to your car's handbook to make sure before you alter it. You alter the float level, if necessary, by carefully bending the small tab which sits against the inlet needle valve. As a check for float twist, the height of both floats should be identical.

It's quite a fiddling business to drop the jet assembly through the hole in the bottom of the float chamber once the float chamber's on the carburettor, so put the assembly in first, then fit the float chamber with just a couple of screws to locate it, lightly screw in the bottom jet housing to make sure it locates properly on the jet and then tighten the float chamber and tighten the housing barely finger tight. You need it slightly loose later to centralise the jet. Fit the jet adjusting screw and leave that barely finger tight.

Fit the piston and diaphragm very carefully so as not to bend the needle, and make sure that the diaphragm locating bar sits in the recess in the body. When you replace the needle, or fit a new one, it sits with its shoulder flush with the base of the piston. Smear the tube of the top cover lightly with oil before you fit it, and be careful not to distort the long coil spring.

Fig. 18.2. When you take off the top cover be careful not to distort the long thin spring.

Fig. 18.3. Take the needle out to avoid damaging it. When you replace it, the shoulder fits flush with the face of the piston.

Fig. 18.4. The diaphragm is held by a retaining ring and has tags on it which fit into recesses in both the piston and the body.

Fig. 18.5. At the bottom of the carburettor, take out the jet adjusting screw and the housing.

Fig. 18.6. Remember the order in which the jet goes together. If it's stiff, clean it till it slides easily under spring pressure.

Fig. 18.7. For cold starting, there is a bar across the bottom of the body. A cut-out lets the piston right down, and the curved part lifts it for extra richness.

Fig. 18.8. Check the inlet needle valve, and the freedom of the float on its hinge pin.

There isn't anything to locate which way round the top cover fits,

Fig. 18.9. The last job before reassembly is to check the float level. Both floats should be at the same level.

but you marked it before you took it off, didn't you? Before you fully tighten the top cover screws, check that the piston falls easily and cleanly down on to the jet bridge, and check this again after the screws are tight. Leave the damper out for the moment.

The last job is to centralise the jet. Screw in the bottom jet housing almost fully home, hold the piston up and screw in the jet adjusting screw till you can see the end of it just above the jet bridge. Now let the piston down so that the needle drops down into the jet to hold it central. Hold the piston down with a rod or screwdriver pushed down where the damper fits, and gently tighten the bottom jet housing, checking frequently that the piston is free to fall cleanly after you lift it. If it doesn't, slacken

the bottom housing, give the side of the carburettor a few light taps and try again.

When you're happy that the piston falls freely with the housing tight, unscrew the jet adjusting nut till its end is below the jet bridge, hold the piston firmly down on to the jet bridge with a rod or screwdriver in the top, and screw in the jet adjusting screw till you feel it touch the bottom of the piston. Then back it off three complete turns. This won't be the final setting, but it will set the jet accurately enough to get the engine started and warmed up before you do the final mixture adjusting. Remember to fill the damper orifice in the piston with light engine oil to within a quarter of an inch of the top after you fit the carburettor back on the engine.

Chapter 19
Mechanical fuel pumps

Your classic will be fitted with either a mechanical fuel pump (usually an AC, or possibly an SU, or a pump very similar to these) or an electric pump (usually an SU). We dealt with SU electric pumps in Chapter 7.

Mechanical pumps are quite simple in operation. A spring-loaded diaphragm between the two halves of the body is flexed up and down by a link and arm which bears on an eccentric lobe on the camshaft. The camshaft runs at half engine speed, so every second revolution of the engine the diaphragm is pulled down and lifted again. When it is pulled down it sucks petrol into the pump body through a one-way disc valve. When the diaphragm moves up, the pressure of the petrol forces the inlet disc valve shut and opens another disc valve on the outlet side so petrol is pumped to the carburettor. When the carburettor float chamber valve is full, with its needle valve closed, there is back-pressure on the petrol in the pump and this back-pressure holds the diaphragm down so that the operating arm is held free of the lobe on the camshaft. As soon as the back-pressure is released, the pump starts working again.

Some pumps have a hand pumping or priming lever, sometimes with a wire rod attached to make it easier to reach. If the carburettor float chamber is empty you can save battery power (that which it would take to crank the engine over to fill it) by using the hand primer. When the carburettor float chamber is full and the back-pressure holds the diaphragm down, you will feel the hand primer go slack. All AC pumps are self-priming, either by hand or by cranking the engine, so there's no need to fill the pump with petrol before you bolt it on.

Some later mechanical pumps, like those fitted to some Fords from the later 1970s, are sealed and you can't take them to bits. All you can do is clean the filter. That doesn't matter too much though because, at the time of writing you can still get new pumps. If you can't, there are plenty of good second-hand Ford pumps around, or you can try one of the many independent Ford specialists.

For many other classics, you can't get a new pump unless you find a 'new old stock' one because AC-Delco, the company which made most of them, doesn't exist any more. It's been broken up into parts, none of which makes mechanical fuel pumps.

They are, however, fairly easy to overhaul and, though it isn't all that easy to find overhaul kits any more, some accessory shops still have a few in stock, or sometimes you can find them at larger autojumbles on one of the new-old-stock stalls. Burlen Fuel Systems keep parts for SU mechanical pumps. Even if you

Fig. 19.1. Mechanical fuel pumps come in a variety of sizes. Most are by AC, but SU also made them.

can't get hold of a kit, don't despair. In a very large number of cases, all that's needed to get them pumping happily again is a strip and clean. What's more, if you're unlucky enough to find bits inside that are beyond salvage, many of the wide variety of AC pump models within each group used the same internal bits, so you can hunt out another couple at an autojumble and make a good one out of the lot.

Before you buy a pump second-hand, there are a few things you should check to minimise the chance of paying out for one which is fit only for scrap or parts. In a few cases of pumps which are less common, you might be forced to do some reconditioning work on the body, so we will cover that later in this chapter.

The first thing to do when you pick up a pump at an autojumble or a breaker's is to work the operating arm, or try to work it. If it's so stiff that it either won't move or moves reluctantly and doesn't want to return under spring pressure, it doesn't necessarily mean that the pump is scrap but it does mean a lot of careful stripping and cleaning, so the less you force the lever the better. If the arm works freely against its spring, you may hear a sucking sound as you move it and, if you put a finger over the outlet union, you will probably feel slight air pressure. You may also feel suction with a finger over the inlet union. If so, the pump is probably in pretty fair condition, but it's still wise to strip it and clean out any deposits or old dried gummy petrol before putting it into service.

On the types which have a glass or metal bowl held by a stirrup, the wire stirrup may be bent, but it can be straightened if necessary. However, if the thumb screw and cup is bent (as sometimes happens when someone has used a pair of pliers to undo a tight screw, or tried to make the bowl seal against a worn-out cork washer), it's very difficult to straighten, so you may have to salvage one from another pump.

If the heads of the screws holding the top and bottom parts of the pump together have been mauled by ill-fitting screwdrivers, it's worthwhile paying a few pence for a scrap donor pump to get some in better condition. They are usually BA (British Association) form threads, and though some specialist tool shops still stock BA screws, many tool shops these days stock only metric thread screws, so you may have a little difficulty in getting new ones, at least with the type of heads you want. Check round the pump where the diaphragm fits, looking for signs that someone has been levering it apart with a screwdriver. It's possible to lightly reface the mating surfaces to take out raised pips, but if the damage is deep the body is scrap. After the screws are out you should use only a hide-faced hammer to jar the two halves of the body apart.

It's unusual to find any of the circle of threads in the bottom part of the pump stripped, but should you be unlucky there's enough metal to drill and tap them to a larger BA size if you can get the screws, or to a metric size which makes getting new screws easier. On pumps without a filter bowl (the ones with a domed metal cap over a flat gauze filter) you quite often find the thread for the central holding screw has been stripped. We've come across pumps with a coarse-thread screw or self-tapper forced in the top in an attempt to cut a thread, and even found fuse wire, solder or thread wound round the original screw to try to get it tight enough to seal the cap. This is useless bodging, but unless the bodging has enlarged the hole too much there's usually just enough metal to reclaim things by drilling and tapping a new thread. Watch out for this because a pump with stripped threads on an autojumble stall is worth only a few pence as spares.

If the screw threads in the inlet or outlet ports are stripped or damaged, things are more serious.

They are more likely to be stripped on an installation with copper pipes or steel Bundy pipes than one with flexibles. It can sometimes be very awkward to line up the threads properly with fixed pipes and there is always the temptation to get the union started and force it home with a spanner.

There's just about enough metal round the inlet and outlet ports on most pumps to let you drill and retap if you are careful, but you're faced with having to be very careful indeed not to damage the taper seat and, not a minor consideration, you have to find a pipe union that will fit your new thread. Always find the union first, before tapping. With a fixed union on a flexible pipe this can be quite difficult. If you're forced to retap on a pump that's difficult to find in better condition, it's often easiest to use a union with a short copper pipe and attach a flexible hose to this with a Jubilee clip. If you are hunting for a pump at a breaker's or autojumble it's worthwhile carrying a couple of pipe unions and a spanner in your pocket so that you can try the threads of the inlet and outlet ports on the pump.

AC pumps come in a variety of shapes and sizes but they can be split down into various groups, models Y, T, U and WE. Model Y, the baby of the family, was fitted to various smaller-engined cars, including many small side-valve Fords (the Eights, Tens, Populars and so on), though export models had a larger U-type. Most others had either a T-type or U-type, basically the same except for the top part. The exceptions are the WE, WH and WG pumps fitted to the Consul, Zephyr, Zodiac and some later Prefects. These pumps are a double-decker affair with the top part, the petrol pumping part, very similar to the T-types and U-types. The bottom part is a vacuum pump, its purpose being to keep the suction-operated windscreen wipers going during acceleration.

As AC pumps were fitted to hosts of cars, hunting at

autojumbles for pumps to recondition, or even to cannibalise for parts for types Y, T and U isn't difficult as the main differences inside each group are in the bottom part, the flanges for bolting it on to the engine and the shape of the arm that drives the pump from an eccentric on the camshaft. Fortunately, these parts seldom give any trouble because they're kept lubricated by oil mist from the engine. Most maladies occur upstairs in the diaphragm, valve and filter department, and it's here that you can swap bits from one to the other. Harder to find, but not impossible, are the WE-type because, so far as we know, they were fitted only to Consuls, Zephyrs, Zodiacs and later Prefects and to some Bedford S and TA trucks, so you may have to hunt around a bit.

As you may want to find a pump of the same family as yours to cannibalise it for spares, we've drawn up a table of the type of AC pump fitted to most cars and light commercials from the mid-1930s to 1960 (see *Table 19.1*). Also, for readers running a car with an AC pump from the early 1930s, we've drawn up a table of equivalent replacement pumps for types which were, by the mid-1950s, obsolete – types A, B and M (see *Table 19.2*). These equivalents have the same, or near enough the same, pressure and flow characteristics as the ones listed as obsolete.

Having got the types sorted out we can get down to overhauling. At the top, the main differences you'll come across are in the filtering arrangement. Some have a plain metal cap held by a central screw, while others have an inverted glass, or sometimes metal, bowl held by a wire stirrup and a thumb screw. A variation on this is the type which has an extended top part with the glass bowl sitting, not on top, but up the other way alongside the body.

We'll look at the plain type first. When you take the cap off, there's a flat gauze filter underneath which you take out and clean. The chamber underneath will probably have muck and rubbish in it and, if the pump's been standing dry a long time, white crystals where the die-cast body of the pump has corroded. Tip the rubbish out, but don't dig around too much till you've taken the valves out or you might damage them.

The next step is to separate the top and bottom parts of the pump, held together by a ring of screws. But, before you take them out, mark the flanges so they go back in the same position, otherwise your inlet and outlet unions won't line up with the pipes. The two parts of the pump usually stick together after you take out the screws, but don't lever them apart with a screwdriver or you'll damage the diaphragm. A few sharp taps with a hide hammer will separate them.

The diaphragm will stay with the bottom part and, underneath the top part, you'll find the valve assemblies held by a plate or, sometimes, two plates and screws. The valves are very simple hexagon-shaped discs of Paxolin (a sort of laminated plastic) with quite light coil springs to help keep them on their seats. The action of the pump holds them firmly. AC used to recommend that you cleaned the valve discs with paraffin, saying this helped them to seat, but we've found that almost any cleaning solvent works just as well.

The muck inside the body is often very tenacious, and white spirit (our favourite cleaning agent) has difficulty shifting it, but an aerosol of carburettor cleaner and a stiff brush usually does the job. Best of all, if you have one or have access to one, is a blast cabinet, but don't use a coarse blasting grit on the die-cast body or you will end up with a surface which looks like pebble dash. Suppliers of grit for blasting cabinets stock grit in various grades, including some very fine materials such as crushed walnut shells. Even with these, mask off the seatings for the valve discs. As these are on the underside of the body there ought not to be much muck around them, so go very easy with the scraping and blasting. Be careful, too, about the faces which clamp the diaphragm, and mask them off. We also like to put screws back in their threads, particularly where the thread is in a blind hole like the one that holds the metal domed top. Whether you use a solvent, scraper and brush or a blast cabinet, get the inside of the body where the petrol flows as clean as you can, and make sure there are no particles of grit or loose flakes of white corroded metal left behind. If there are, they will sooner or later wedge themselves under the disc valves and the pump will stop working.

The valve discs and springs will probably clean up well but, if not, this is where you can swap them for parts from a wide variety of other pumps. Make sure the valve seats are clean and undamaged, the discs aren't scored or damaged by grit and that the springs haven't been buckled by some ham-fisted mechanic who has been there before you. The inlet and outlet discs are usually interchangeable and, at a pinch, if one side of a disc has been damaged by grit you can turn it over and use the undamaged side against the seat.

The type of pump with the glass or metal bowl is different in that the filter isn't a flat one, it's a domed gauze that pushes over the raised outlet tower. The valve arrangement inside is either the same or very similar to the others.

There's a special point to watch on the Y-type pump. When you take the valve retaining plate off, the outlet valve comes with it but the inlet valve doesn't. It's held by a star-shaped piece of plastic (sometimes brass on older pumps) which is quite a tight fit in the body of the pump. Be careful how you dig it out as it's very easy to break off one of the arms. In an emergency, if you're stuck, the pump will still work with one arm missing from this plastic retainer but, if you break two of them, you'll have to hunt for another one because the valve disc won't stay central.

With the top part cleaned and reassembled you can turn to the bottom part with the diaphragm. If the diaphragm hasn't gone hard and stiff, or soggy and sticky, and if it goes in and out easily when you operate the lever, it will probably give further service after cleaning. If it's gone hard or very soggy and sticky, it needs replacing. If you can get hold of a repair kit, replace it anyway, but if not, you can use one in better condition from another similar pump. Except for the small Y-type pump, the diaphragm has a tag on the outside with a staple through the leaves of the diaphragm. We suspect that it's mainly to help manufacture but if, before you take the diaphragm out, you make a note of where the tag is pointing, it also helps you to position the diaphragm to make sure it locks properly. There's a metal rod with a flattened end and two slots attached to the diaphragm, and the slots fit in a fork in the operating arm in the body. If you hold the pump with the engine flange towards you, the tag on the diaphragm will be at about 7 o'clock. Push the diaphragm down slightly and turn it clockwise till the tag is at 10 o'clock and the big coil

spring underneath will push it out. On very early Y-type pumps the diaphragm and rod were separate, but most of these have been replaced with a diaphragm and riveted rod.

You might also find a second, smaller spring with an oil seal washer under it held by a twist and lock action. This is to save oil mist coming up and making the diaphragm soggy, but not all pumps have them.

You may not need to take the operating arm out except, possibly, if a screw thread in the bottom part of the body has stripped and you want to change to another bottom part you've found which is the same except for the operating arm. If you do want to take it out, the arm is usually held by a rod with wire circlips at the ends. You may sometimes find a pump where the rod holding the operating arm is staked in. The method of getting the pin out is to hold the operating lever in a vice and give the casing a sharp tap with a hide-faced hammer. At one time, service replacement retainers at the ends of the rod were available with a reduced shoulder so that they could be staked back in. These are no longer available, so you may have to grind or file a couple of bevels on the retainers to allow you to stake the casing back and hold them. The lever is in two

parts, one which bears on the camshaft and one which operates the diaphragm. There are washers each side, plus a fairly strong coil return spring. It helps, when you are putting things together, if you can find a rod the same diameter as the pin, usually 0.240in or, near enough for this purpose, 6mm. Use this as a mandrel and then feed the pin through while you draw the rod out.

When you have fitted the diaphragm in position and are ready to put on the top part of the body, push the operating lever in towards the pump till the diaphragm lies flat. Then put the top part on and tighten the screws until the heads of the screws are just touching the spring washers. Then push the operating arm fully in towards the body. This should pull the diaphragm edges in till they are flush with the body. Hold the arm in this position and, working diagonally, tighten down the screws.

When you have rebuilt a glass bowl pump and are trying it out on the car, don't worry when you see air trapped in the bowl. It's meant to be there as a compressed bubble to help smooth the flow of fuel to the carburettor.

The WE-type pump fitted to Consuls and Z-cars is very similar up top, where it pumps petrol, and you go about overhaul in the same

Fig. 19.2. On flat-top AC pumps, the disc filter sits directly under the top cover.

Fig. 19.3. The inlet and outlet one-way valves are flat Paxolin discs under a brass retainer. Be careful not to lose the small springs.

Fig. 19.4. The diaphragm comes out after you push it down and give it a half turn.

Fig. 19.5. Instead of a flat top, some pumps have a glass or metal dome cover.

Fig. 19.6. Pumps with a dome have a mushroom filter which just lifts off.

Fig. 19.7. Dome-topped pumps usually have the valves held by an H-shaped retainer.

Fig. 19.8. These valves are sealed units, they don't have separate springs.

Fig. 19.9. In pumps which have been left standing, you often find these white crystals. They must be cleaned out.

Fig. 19.10. The SU mechanical pump has a shallow dome with a disc filter under it.

Fig. 19.11. Instead of disc valves, the SU pump uses a single rubber flap valve.

Fig. 19.12. If you want to take the operating arm out, you have to prise off a circlip at the end of the shaft.

Fig. 19.13. If your SU pump has an AUF identifying tag, save it. Burlen Fuel Systems can probably supply parts if you quote the number.

VEHICLE	PUMP	VEHICLE	PUMP	VEHICLE	PUMP
ALVIS		**DAIMLER**		**ROVER**	
1951 3 litre (first 400)	UG	1938 15hp	T	1937-38 14hp	T
1951-55 3 litre, later	UE	1939-40 15hp	T	1939-47 10hp, 12hp, 14hp & 16hp	T
		1939-40 Light 20 & Light 8cyl.	T		
ARMSTRONG SIDDELEY		1939-50 20hp & 32hp 8cyl.	T	**SINGER**	
1936-40 12hp, 12 Plus & 14hp	T	1946-48 18hp & 2.5 litre	T	1938-40 Bantam & 10hp	Y
1935-36 15hp & 17hp	T	1949-54 18hp & 2.5 litre	U	1946-53 9hp & 10hp	Y
1937-40 17hp	T	1948 on, 27hp & 36hp	U	1955 Hunter & Roadster (UK)	FG
1939-40 20hp & 25hp	T	1952-55 Regency 3 litre			
1946-48 2.3 litre	T	& Conquest	UE	**STANDARD**	
1949-54 2.3 litre	U	**DODGE (England)**		1938 14hp	T
1952-55 3.5 litre	UE	1949-51 trucks	T	1939-40 8hp & 10hp	Y
		1952 trucks, Kew-built engines	UE	1939 9hp	Y
AUSTIN		1953-55 trucks, Kew-built engines	UE	1939-40 14hp	T
1935-38 7hp (747cc)	T			1939-40 others	T
1938-44 all except 7hp (747cc)	T	**FORD (England)**		1945-48 8hp	Y
1945-47 8hp & 10hp	T	1944 July onwards 8hp & 10hp		1945-46 12hp	T
1945-47 12hp	T	export	UF	1945-46 14hp	T
1945-48 16hp	T	1938-44 8hp & 10hp UK	Y	1947-48 12hp & 14hp	U
1948 A70, A90 & 25cwt	U	1945-53 8hp & 10hp UK	Y	1948-50 Vanguard, to	
1949-50 16hp	U	1954-55 Anglia & Prefect	Y	chassis No. 85000	U
1949-53 A70, A90 & 25cwt	U	1954-55 Popular	Y	Vanguard, later	UE
1948-51 A40 Devon & Dorset	U	1938-44 V8 cars & trucks	TF	1953-55 8hp & 10hp	Y
1952-54 A40 Somerset	U	1945-55 trucks	UF	1954-55 Vanguard diesel	Y
1955 A40 & A50 Cambridge	UE	1948-51 Pilot	UF		
1955 A90 Westminster	U	1951-52 Consul to engine No. 63026		**SUNBEAM-TALBOT**	
1948-50 Sheerline & Princess		& Zephyr to engine No. 18125	WE	1938-40 10hp	T
to chassis No. 4792	U	1952-55 Consul & Zephyr, later		1939 2 litre	T
1950-54 Sheerline & Princess	U	engine Nos.	WE	1946 2 litre	T
1952-55 A30 Seven	Y	1953-55 2/3 ton Cost Cutter (petrol)	UG	1946-47 10hp	T
1938-48 most trucks & coaches	T	1954-55 3 ton Cost Cutter (diesel)	Y	1948-50 10hp	Y
1949-55 trucks	U			1947-55 2 litre & Alpine	UG
1950-54 coaches	U	**HILLMAN**		1954-55 Mk III	UE
1953-55 Healey 100	U	1939-40 14hp	T		
1954-55 2 ton diesel	U	1939-40 others	T	**TRIUMPH**	
		1935-48 Minx	T	1946-48 Model 1800	U
BEDFORD		1949-52 Minx	Y	1949-50 Model 2000	
1936-38 all except light vans	T	1953-55 Minx (sv)	Y	to Chassis No. TDB 1947	U
1939-44 all except light vans	TG	1955 Minx (ohv)	UG	Model 2000, later	UE
1938-51 5/6 & 10/12 vans	Y			Mayflower	Y
1945-53 Models K, M & O	UG	**HUMBER**		TR2	UE
1952-53 CA van	Y	1938-40 all models	T		
to chassis No. 19142	U	1945-49 Hawk	T	**VAUXHALL**	
1954-55 CA van	UE	1950-53 Hawk	U	1937-38 12hp & 14hp Model D	
S Type to March 1952		1945-48 Snipe	T	& 25hp Model G	T
to engine No. 10958	UE	1945-53 Super Snipe (sv)		1938-40 10hp & 12/4	Y
S Type engine Nos. 10959 to 13354		& Pullman	T	1939-40 14hp & 25hp	TG
March-August 1951	WE	1953-55 Super Snipe (ohv)		1940-51 10hp, 12hp & LIX Wyvern	Y
S Type later models	WE	& Pullman	UE	1946-48 14hp	UG
1953-55 Model TA	WE			1948-51 18hp & LIP Velox	UG
		JOWETT		1951-53 Wyvern to Chassis	
BRISTOL		1937-39 two-cylinder	T	No. EX 44295	Y
1947-54 all models	UG	1939-49 van	U	1954-55 Wyvern	U
		1949-54 van model CC	U	1951-55 Velox	UE
CITROEN		1948-54 Javelin & Jupiter	U		
1935-36 10hp	T				
1935-37 12hp & 15hp	T	**LANCHESTER**			
1938-40 all models	T	1938-40 14hp	T		
1946-48 Light 15	T	1938-40 18hp	T		
1949-55 Light 15	U	1946-48 10hp	T		
		1949-50 10hp	U	**SUPERSEDED PUMPS**	
COMMER		1951-55 14hp	UE		
1935-48 8cwt	T			Pre-war model A was superseded by model U	
1949-52 Mk IV Express Delivery	Y	**MORGAN**		as a direct replacement.	
1953-55 Mk V Express Delivery	Y	1947-50 4/4	Y		
1938-40 15cwt & NI	T	1951-55 Plus Four	UE	Pre-war model B was superseded by either	
1938-40 all others	T			model U or YG as a direct replacement, except	
1945-51 15cwt & 25cwt	T	**RILEY**		that, in a few cases, an extra operating pushrod	
1945-51 others	T	1936-40 1.5 litre & six-cylinder	T	was required.	
1950-55 Medium Pick-up		1946-48 1.5 litre	T		
25cwt Superpoise Mk III	U	1947-48 16hp	UG	Model M was superseded by model T on the	
25cwt Forward Control Mk II	U	1949-54 1.5 litre	U	Austin 'little' Seven and by model U on the	
Other Superpoise Mk III	UE	1955 1.5 litre	UE	Austin 10hp as direct replacements.	
1948-52 QX Mk I	UG				
1953-55 QX Mk II	UE				

Table 19.1.

139

IDENTIFYING AC PUMP MODELS

pump model	position of filter	approx. pitch circle diameter of diaphragm screw holes (inches)
A, B, UE, FE & WE	at side of pump	2.75
T, TF, TG, U, UF, UG & FG	on top of pump	2.75
Y	on top of pump	2.25

Table 19.2.

way. The vacuum part is also similar, but it has a few awkward parts, and you really ought to have a repair kit. There are oil seals which should be replaced each time the diaphragm is removed because they usually get damaged doing so. If you can't get a repair kit, and the vacuum part is working well, just clean out the petrol part and leave the rest alone. If you get a repair kit it will have instructions inside for replacing the oil seals. Follow these carefully as there are two types.

On the earlier single-acting pump, the seals are a drive-in fit and are lightly staked to hold them in the body. On the later double-acting pumps, the seals have retainer plates. You also need a special flexing tool to hold the diaphragm against the spring pressure while you're putting things together. It's just a simple metal bar, about a quarter-of-an-inch by an eighth-of-an-inch, with one end turned up at right angles for a quarter-of-an-inch. You use it to hold the operating arm with the diaphragm spring in the compressed position. Again, the repair kit should have instructions. Dealing with the valves is very similar to dealing with those in the petrol part.

One point on which the repair kit instructions may not give warning is that the vacuum part of the pump has a very much stronger diaphragm spring than the petrol side. So, before you separate the vacuum part, get two screws 1.5in long and 2BA thread. Fit them diagonally in place of two of the ring of holding screws and, when the other screws are out, undo the long screws a few turns at a time to release the pressure of the spring gradually. Use them again when you're putting things together.

Before you reassemble any type of pump, check the inlet and outlet union seats. They're a taper seal and even a small amount of dirt will cause a leak. Clean inside the housing with petrol and a small brush.

Chapter 20

Locks

There are three basic types of door lock found on classics, the early, and quite simple, slam lock, the rotary cam lock and the rotary star wheel lock. Slam locks are simple enough to understand, and usually easy to fix when you take them apart, but rotary cam and rotary star wheel locks which don't operate properly puzzle many people.

There are so many variations of rotary cam and rotary star wheel locks fitted to different models of cars that there just isn't space here to go through each one in detail, but we'll cover the general principles which should help you sort out problems. Both types of lock will operate with a small amount of wear in the door hinge pins, but if the wear is so much that you have to lift the door to get the lock to engage, no amount of fiddling with adjustments is going to make the lock work properly. Put the hinge pins right first.

Rotary cam locks are easily identified by the forked latch on the door which engages with a striker stud on the door pillar. The stud swings the latch down, and this operates an internal cam and a two-position pawl mechanism which holds the door either on 'first safety', the position where the door is safe from flying open but not properly shut, and 'fully latched'. Rotary star wheel locks are very similar except that the star wheel is turned by a striker rack to operate the two-position pawl mechanism. There is usually a spring-loaded dovetail and wedge to restrain the door from moving up and down. Because the wedge positions the door when it's closed, the striker on the door pillar is held by a loose trapped plate inside the pillar. When you loosen the fixing screws, you can move the striker to obtain positive latching. If the dovetail and wedge are badly worn, there may not be enough adjustment of the striker to let the door latch properly, so once again, put this right first.

Provided the dovetail and wedge hold the door properly aligned when it's closed, adjusting the striker is very much trial and error, but never slam the door hard while you're adjusting it because if the adjustment isn't right, slamming the door can bend or break the lock.

Door locks are pretty robust mechanisms, and when you consider the amount of abuse they get by doors being slammed over the years, it's surprising that they last as long as they do. However, there comes a time when either the door doesn't come free easily when you turn the handle, click the trigger or push the button or, more serious, the door doesn't latch safely in the closed position.

Before you condemn the lock itself, make sure that there isn't excessive wear or misadjustment of any of the external linkages to it. There are dozens, hundreds even, of designs of linkages to operate the lock itself. There are internal levers or triggers to open the door, mechanisms to lock the door from inside, child safety catches, external push buttons and triggers, some of which lock and some of which go slack when you turn the key, external handles which lock

Fig. 20.1. The three types of door catch on classic cars, and their operation.

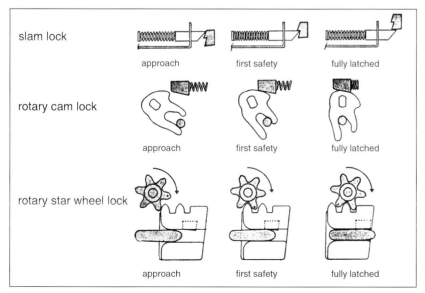

slam lock   approach   first safety   fully latched

rotary cam lock   approach   first safety   fully latched

rotary star wheel lock   approach   first safety   fully latched

solid when you turn the key and external handles which freewheel when you turn the key.

Some of these linkages operate through straight levers, some through jointed levers on which the joint pins wear and go out of alignment, and some through rods which get bent when people go inside the door to replace a window or even fit a radio speaker. With internal push-down locking buttons in the door capping, the rods get bent or the push button catches on the trim. Child safety catches sometimes don't toggle over properly, with the result that either the internal handle, and sometimes the external handle as well, jam in the latched position or the unlatched position. Then, if the car's fitted with remote locking, either by key or by electronic key fob devices, there are more linkages with solenoids or motors attached to them. If the solenoid or motor jams, it quite often prevents the lock from operating.

Only when you're satisfied that all the external linkages are operating properly should you blame the latch box itself. Unfortunately, because of the wide variety of designs, a replacement latch box for a particular model of classic car can be very difficult to find new. Also, unfortunately, the parts inside the latch box are quite often peculiar to that particular box, and not interchangeable as is the case with many other components. The only source we know of for replacement parts is from the inside of an identical less worn latch box, and if you can find one you might as well fit it and save yourself the trouble of swapping parts over.

You may be very lucky hunting round a breaker's and find an identical model car to yours with the lock for a particular door in good condition, but the chances are not very high. There's a better chance of finding a similar model, or even a different model of roughly the same age by the same maker. If so, it may well be that, though the linkage is completely different, the latch box itself is the same, and you can adapt it to fit your car by taking off the external linkages.

Quite often the latch box on the driver's door suffers most wear, and you may find a good latch box on one of the other doors. In this case, you'll be looking for either a right-hand latch or a left-hand latch, but this doesn't relate to the side of the car on which the door's fitted. Most lock makers hand their latches by the position of the latch on the door when viewed from the outside, irrespective of which side of the car the door is fitted. *Fig. 20.2* makes this clear.

As a very last resort, many latch boxes and mechanisms for British classics were made by Wilmot Breeden and, in the interests of quantity production, some of the internal cams and pawls were identical on different model latches. You may possibly be able to drill out the rivets holding the latch together, and swap the worn parts for unworn ones. You may find it easier to use bolts and nuts instead of rivets to put the latch together again.

A point which is often missed on turn-handle latches is that the handle shank binds and the lock fails to operate because the 'follow' is out of line. The 'follow' is a lock-maker's term for a specially shaped bush through which the shank of the handle operates the lock bolt inside the latch. If this is the case, you might have to enlarge the hole in the door panel slightly to line up the handle. A more brutal, but sometimes effective, method is to bend the shank of the handle slightly, but do this in the vice, not on the car, and don't try to bend it by levering on the die-cast handle itself or you'll break it off.

Even with the latches in perfect order, you might find yourself in the frustrating situation where you're stuck because you haven't got a key to fit the lock.

There could be various reasons why you're stuck without a key. If you've bought a non-runner for restoration, some of the keys may have been lost, you might have lost one of the keys or, most annoying, some yob has tried to break into the car and mangled the door lock with a screwdriver. Whatever the

Fig. 20.2. Lock 'handing' depends on whether the doors are hung left or right.

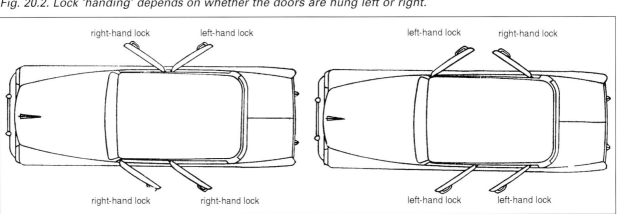

Fig. 20.3. If you can't find a key to operate a replacement lock, find one that fits in the slot.

Fig. 20.4. Most keys for classic cars run in series such as FS and FT. All keys in one series will fit into all locks of the same series.

reason, you're stuck because you can't lock the car. You could try your local friendly dealer but, though he may well be sympathetic, he probably won't be able to help because new lock barrels for most classics haven't been on his microfiche for years. However, all isn't lost because the locks on classics were made by only a few companies, Wilmot Breedon being one of the most prolific, and provided you can get a key that fits in the lock you can strip the lock out and work on the tumblers inside the barrel to make them suit the key that fits. In many cases you can swap barrels from different handles. Many breakers have boxes full of old keys that they'll let you root through, or you sometimes find them at autojumbles.

We'll deal first with the flat type of key that has serrations along the edge. Earlier keys had serrations on only one edge but later keys had serrations along both edges. All locks with this type of key work on the same principle. The keys have grooves down the sides, and each group of keys – there could be several hundred different keys in

each group – all have the same grooves, so any key from a group will fit in any lock from the same group. Though it fits, it may not turn the barrel, because the serrations along the key which line up the tumblers inside the lock barrel are different. The older keys had the group code letters, such as MRN, FS or FA, stamped on them. At one time there was also a number stamped on the key which identified the pattern of the serrations, and in more trusting days the number was also stamped on the face of the lock barrel for all to see. That really was too easy for even the dimmest thief, so later keys didn't have numbers on them and the number, if it appeared at all, was hidden somewhere inside where it couldn't be read till the lock was dismantled. With most later keys that have serrations on both edges, there is no identification letter or number, so you just have to keep trying different anonymous keys till you find one that fits.

The lock barrel may be in a door push button, it may be built into a lever handle, in a glove box lock, a boot lock or in the ignition switch.

There are far too many different types of handle and lock fittings to detail them here, so you will either have to look in the workshop manual or investigate. Usually, when you take the trim off the door, the lock mechanism off the boot lid or look behind the dash, the method of holding the handle or lock is self-evident.

Let's say you've found a key that fits in the lock but won't turn the barrel. How do you make the lock suit it? The first thing to do is to take the lock to pieces, and there are various ways in which they're held together. We'll look first at the push-button type of lock fitted to large numbers of Fords from the 1950s and 1960s. The one we took to pieces actually came from a Mk 2 Cortina in our local breakers.

Usually, when you take the handle and lock out of the door, you'll find a circlip in the inner end of the handle. Under this is a washer and the coil spring which spring-loads the button in the handle. When these are out, the button, complete with the barrel assembly, comes out of the back of the handle.

The handle in this case was badly pock-marked with the dreaded Mazak disease and, if we'd had the correct key and just wanted to swap the locking button into a handle in better condition, that's as far as we would have had to go. Typically, though, the key had long since disappeared, though the breaker was able to find us a couple of keys that fitted but wouldn't turn.

The next stage was to take the lock barrel out of the push button. In most of these push-button locks you'll find, like ours, that the barrel is held in by a wire circlip. There aren't any ears on the circlip so you have to dig it out with a small screwdriver and hope that it doesn't ping off across the garage into oblivion because replacements aren't easy to come by. The best way to avoid this is to hold a piece of rag almost covering the lock while you lever the circlip off. Even with the circlip removed, the lock barrel may not come out of the push button and, to explain why and how to overcome it, we have to look at a part of the lock you haven't yet uncovered.

The lock barrel has a series of slots going through it and in each slot is a spring loaded tumbler. Don't ask us why they're called tumblers, it probably comes from the tumblers inside the dial-type lock of a safe, but in a car lock they don't tumble, they're spring-loaded plates and, with no key in the barrel, the tumblers stick out about a sixteenth of an inch. There's a slot, or pair of slots, through the inside of the push button so the tumblers stick up into the slot to prevent the key barrel turning. Each tumbler is a small brass plate with a rectangular hole through it. The holes vary in their position up and down the plate so that, when you push the key in, the different height serrations along the key pull each tumbler down a different amount against its spring. If the key has the correct sequence of serrations, the tumblers are pulled down flush with the key barrel so it can turn.

With most push button locks, the groove inside doesn't run all the way through, so the tumblers have to be pulled down flush with the barrel before it will slide out. With the correct key, there's no problem but, with a key having the wrong serrations, some of the tumblers will still be sticking up

and have to be persuaded down flush with the barrel before it will come out. Fit the key you've got into the barrel and hope that at least some of the tumblers will go down flush, and then push the others down by pushing a thin strip of metal down into the slots from the back of the push button. Sometimes a thin screwdriver will do it but you may have to make a thin strip. It often takes quite a lot of fiddling but, eventually, the key barrel will slide out of the front of the push button.

Quite often, if the lock has been lying idle for ages and the grease has dried out, you'll find the inside of the barrel coated with a horrible white deposit mixed with hard lumps of dried-out grease. Before you start easing the tumblers down, give a good squirt of cleaner down the slot so that the tumblers are all free to move up and down. We've found that carburettor cleaner is ideal for this. Some of the tumblers may fall out when you get the barrel out, so be careful not to loose the tiny coil springs inside the barrel which will probably fall out as well.

Once the whole thing's clean, try your key in the slot to see how many tumblers are still left sticking up proud of the barrel. To make the key work, these have to be filed down flush. If any of the tumblers don't move at all when you push the key in, the lock will be less effective if you file them down because then they won't pop up at all when you pull the key out. The less you have to file off the ends of the tumblers, the more secure the lock will be. Sometimes you can rearrange the tumblers in a different order so that less has to be filed off but, just in case the key is hopelessly wrong, it's helpful to have a selection of keys to try, or even a couple of spare locks so that you can try different tumblers till you find a set where you have to file off very little. After you've filed the tumblers flush, take them out and use some rubbing down paper on a flat surface to ease off any

burrs formed by filing so there's no chance of the tumblers sticking.

With early locks from the 1950s the key very often had serrations along one edge only and the tumblers operated on one side of the barrel. With later locks, the keys had serrations along both edges in a mirror image so it didn't matter which way up the key went in. On these locks, the tumblers operate on both sides of the barrel. It made the lock a little more resistant to forcing round with a screwdriver but it means you've got tumblers on both sides to deal with.

Once you've got the offending tumblers filed down, and they all pop up a reasonable amount when you pull the key out, all that's left is to coat the whole thing with a non-hardening grease (a molybdenum-based grease is good), and put it all together again.

Turn-handle locks from classics like upright Anglias and A30s come apart in a very similar way to push-button locks, but you often find a domed cover plate over the inside end. This is held by two or four raised pips formed on the corners of the square shaft attached to the handle. These pips have to be filed off and it is sometimes awkward to raise new pips when you put the lock together. On a couple of occasions we have had to drill a 1.5mm hole through the shaft and drive in a small roll pin to hold the domed cover in place. Yes, it weakens the shaft a little but if you make sure the lock itself is clean and well greased, and that the door striker plate is properly adjusted, the shaft won't be weakened enough to break off.

Later door locks where the lock was separate from the handle are assembled slightly differently. With this type there are often push-down buttons in the door cappings linked by rods to the lock so that the door can be locked and unlocked from inside the car. When you get the lock assembly out of the door off the car you'll find a metal, or sometimes plastic, arm or lever on the end which operates

Fig. 20.5. To get some locks apart you have to file off raised pips on the shaft.

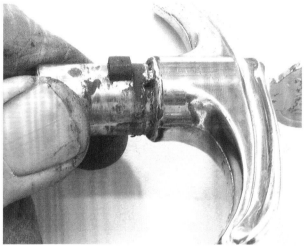

Fig. 20.6. This is the lock bolt which moves out when you turn the barrel.

Fig. 20.7. A boot lock completely dismantled.

Fig. 20.8. If it's not obvious how the barrel comes out, try looking for a small hole like this. It may house a taper pin.

Fig. 20.9. With no key in the lock, the tumblers protrude and stop the barrel from turning.

Fig. 20.10. To salvage a good condition handle, you may, as a last resort, have to sacrifice the barrel by hammering down the bolt, and then replacing it with a barrel for which you have a key.

Fig. 20.11. On key-operated switches, look for a hole in the outer casing. Pushing a pointer down it may well free the end of the switch and the barrel.

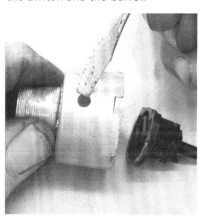

the lock itself, and this lever is spring-loaded so that you give the key up to half a turn to lock or unlock it and the key then comes back to a neutral position. The spring-loading is by a double-acting coil spring which is wound up when you turn the key. Study its operation carefully before you take the lever off because, if the spring flies off (as it often does), it isn't immediately obvious how and which way up it fits back on again, and you can spend a frustrating half-hour trying to get it right. Spring-loaded boot locks operate on a similar principle.

Broadly, for taking the key barrel out, these locks can be divided into two types. On the first type, the barrel is held by a pin. Sometimes this is a roll-pin, a hollow steel pin with a slot down it, and it's usually easy to get out because in most cases it stands quite proud and you can grip it with a pair of fine side-cutters to lever it out. Others have a solid brass pin and these can sometimes be a real pain. The pin often doubles as a stop and runs in a shallow cut-out where it can be difficult to get hold of. Quite often,

being soft brass, the end breaks off when you're trying to lever it out, so the only thing to do is chop it off flush with a very small chisel and drill it out afterwards. It means making a new pin, or using a small roll-pin, but that's a minor inconvenience compared with the awkwardness of getting the old one out.

The second type, where the key barrel is held by a chromium-plated cover cap can be even more frustrating and needs quite gentle handling. The only way we've found to get the cover plate off is to go round it with a small screwdriver, gradually levering up the crimped edge till the cap will come off. You have to be very careful not to let the screwdriver slip and mark the face of the cap. When you put it back, the crimped edge is best knocked down again with lots of light taps with a small hammer. This is more effective and far less damaging then a few heavy clouts with a big hammer or trying to squash it down with a pair of pliers. It helps, and makes damage to the cap less likely, if you rest it on a hard sandbag, or even a piece

Fig. 20.12. Choose a key that leaves the minimum to be filed off the protruding tumblers.

of hard foam from an old padded dashboard, rather then rest the face of the cap on an unyielding wooden bench.

When the cap comes off you'll find a separate small plate underneath with a spring-loaded flap covering the slot where the key goes in. It's intended to keep water and dirt out of the lock. Treat it gently, because if the spring gets distorted the flap won't open properly and the key will be difficult to get in. Once you've got this type of lock apart, the principle of making the tumblers fit the key is the same as with the push-button lock.

Chapter 21

Heaters

Most problems with classic car heaters, apart from one not being fitted as standard in the 1950s, are caused by one, or possibly a combination of, these six things: perished seals on the various air flaps; leaky joins on the convoluted pipes and trunking which take air to the heater and from the heater to inside the car and the screen; air trapped in the matrix; the motor not working; the matrix clogged with sludge or leaking; the water flow control valve stuck or corroded.

At one time, when all heaters for British cars were proprietary designs made by Smiths or Delaney, overhaul was very simple because there was a plentiful supply of spare parts, gaskets and valves in all main dealers. Later, when car makers decided to design their own heaters to fit where they wanted them, things were still relatively easy because though 'sealed for life' units were coming in, this only meant that the dealers didn't stock replacement parts, only replacement heaters, which were quite cheap.

Try asking any main dealer now for parts, let alone a complete heater, for any car more than 20 years old, and you'll get an amused smile and a shake of the head as though you're asking for a priceless antique.

However, things still aren't too bad because most heaters, unless the matrix is leaking, are repairable. Older heaters by Smiths or Delaney are very easy to take apart. With later 'sealed for life' units, the phrase meant just what it said, though the length of the life

was never mentioned. What was implied was that labour charges in garages had increased to the point where it was cheaper for the customer if a dealer fitted a complete new heater rather than spend several hours repairing an old one. The sealing for life usually meant that rivets were used to put the thing together instead of nuts and bolts. This was also cheaper and quicker in production. Sometimes, though, clips were used instead of rivets. This makes restoring them easier.

Designs of later classic car heaters, like headlamps on today's cars, varied so much from model to model that it would be impossible for us to detail them all, but they all work on the same principles. There are two types, the earlier so-called recirculating air heater, commonly called a fug-stirrer, which was just a matrix (usually circular), and a fan, mounted under the dash. It pulled air from inside the car in one side, heated it, and pushed it out the other. Sometimes, but not always, there was provision for piping off some of the air to demist the windscreen, with a flap control lever labelled 'screen' and 'car'.

Then came fresh-air heaters, the earlier designs of which were very similar to air recirculating heaters except that the incoming air was piped to the heater from somewhere at the front of the car by a long piece of convoluted paper and wire flexible trunking. It was an interim measure till makers redesigned their bodywork to put an air intake at the base of the windscreen, and worked quite well till the trunking either came off its

clips or punctured and let the heater pull in oil-fumed air from under the bonnet (not to mention lethal exhaust fumes if the exhaust manifold or downpipe gasket leaked). Also, in traffic, you pulled in exhaust fumes from the car in front, so some makers provided a control to switch between fresh air and recirculated air.

If you've got one of these heaters, make absolutely certain that the trunking from the front of the car to the heater is absolutely sealed, and either turn the motor off, or switch to recirculating, in nose-to-tail traffic jams. Later fresh-air heaters draw their air from a collection box below a grill at the base of the screen. There should be a drain flap, or flaps, at the base of this collection chamber so that in the wet the heater doesn't spray your feet with a fine hot water mist.

Temperature control on early heaters was quite crude. On the earliest, there was a simple on-off tap or valve in the cooling system, usually at the top of the cylinder head, sometimes hopefully marked 'winter' and 'summer', so that you either had hot water coming to the heater or not, and you had to stop and open the bonnet to change it. An improvement on this was the remote control valve, usually by a Bowden cable, which meant that you could turn the water flow on or off from inside the car.

It wasn't till relatively late in the classic period that air-blending heaters came in. With these, hot water is always flowing through the heater matrix, and there is a lever labelled 'hot' and 'cold', or often just with red and blue symbols, which controls a flap to blend the hot air flowing through the heater matrix with cold air from outside the car. Temperature control then became much easier, and almost instant.

Most cases of heaters trying to work, but never getting very hot, are because the heater matrix is clogged with sludge. There is one exception, or half-chance exception, and this is when someone has misguidedly taken the thermostat out of the cooling system in an attempt to cure overheating problems caused by a sludged-up radiator. When this didn't cure things, and a replacement radiator was fitted, no-one remembered to fit a new thermostat. The engine didn't overheat because the water never got hot. We're not joking, we've come across this several times. Taking out the thermostat was a favourite pub-pundit's cure for overheating about 30 years ago, and led to a whole raft of engines full of sludge because the oil never got hot enough to burn off impurities.

There was also the case of the over-cooled BMCs. In the early to late 1950s, after BMC was formed to amalgamate the old Austin and Morris companies, all their cars were fitted with 'export' radiators large enough to keep the engine cool in Africa and other hot parts of our once far-flung empire. Something like 80 per cent of production went for export, and it was cheaper to fit all cars of the same model with the same size radiator rather than make a smaller one specially for the small home market. Many accessory shops sold radiator muffs to blank off the air flow through the bottom third of the radiator in winter so that the water got hot enough for the heater to poke out a decent amount of heat. Otherwise people made do with a piece of cardboard.

This assumed that water was flowing through the heater matrix at a reasonable rate. After 25 or more years service this is not very often the case. After the car was five or six years old, very few owners bothered to drain, flush and refill the cooling system with corrosion-inhibiting anti-freeze at the end of each summer. Even if they did, the chances are the heater didn't get flushed through because in many cases, when you drained the cooling system you didn't drain the heater since the outlet pipe sloped upwards to the cylinder head, and the water in the matrix was disinclined to flow uphill to be drained. The recommended way to flush a heater of this sort, often quoted in the car handbook, was to take off the inlet and outlet pipes at the cylinder head, attach a garden hose to one of them, and another length of hose as a drain to the other, and flush water though the heater matrix for half an hour or so once a year. But again, how many owners bothered?

If your heater isn't getting very hot, and the water control valve (if fitted) is working OK, you can try this on-car method of flushing the heater matrix, but don't put too much faith in it. If, when you turn on the garden hose, the flow is still only a trickle, the matrix is badly blocked.

Cleaning a matrix which is badly blocked is a problem. You could try running the engine for a couple of days with a proprietary flushing agent in the cooling system before trying to flush it, but if the water can't get through, neither can the flushing agent. Usually you have to take the heater out and remove the matrix for treatment. Getting the matrix out of the heater case varies with different models of heater, but it's usually reasonably straightforward.

With the matrix out, try clamping a garden hose to the outlet pipe, usually the top one when the heater's in the car, and alternately flushing and shaking to get as much muck out as will come. If you manage to improve the flow, but it's still not very great, try filling the matrix with a strong solution of flushing agent, or even ordinary washing soda, in very hot water, leaving it for half-an-hour or so, flushing and filling it again. Sometimes, after half a dozen or so treatments like this, the flow improves tremendously because the flushing agent or soda has loosened the caked but still soft sludge to the point where it will flush out. If even this fails, the only recourse is to look for another

Fig. 21.1. Setting the air flap levers on a Smiths' 'box' heater.

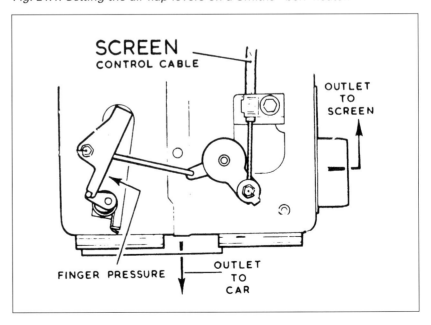

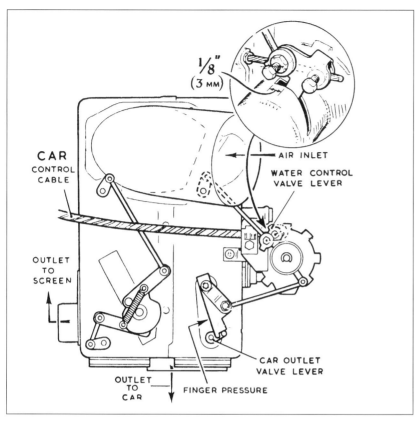

Fig. 21.2. Setting the water valve lever on a Smiths' 'box' heater.

up. If you can't find inner cable and outer casing by the metre in a car accessory shop, try a cycle or motorcycle shop. Many heater cables use a solid wire for the inner rather than a flexible stranded one, because they had to push as well as pull. In the past, we have used piano wire from our local piano tuner for this. He stocks it in a wide variety of sizes, and it solders quite easily if you let down the temper of the end you're soldering.

That leaves us with water control valves. The old on-off valves often look for all the world like household plumbing valves, and in most cases can be taken apart for cleaning and repacking the seals. The type which can be awkward are the rotary cast type operated by a cable from inside the car. They work on an internal cam pushing a diaphragm against the inlet port and, in theory, they come apart with a twisting bayonet-type action but, after putting them together on the production line, the bayonet tags were pressed down to get a good seal which made them very tight. It's still possible in some cases to get them apart without breaking anything but, even if you do, you can't get new diaphragms. If yours is stuck, and dosing with freeing agent doesn't get it working again, try one of the specialists who cater for classic Minis or MGs. The Mini and MG used this type of remote water valve till quite late, and many

matrix, or take yours to a radiator specialist such as a Serck agent, who might be able to solder a new matrix into your top and bottom tanks. They can do this on many 'box' type matrices which have tanks, but you may find they can't do anything with the round type of recirculating matrix. Look in *Yellow Pages* under radiator repairs, and find one that advertises that they handle classic and vintage work. We've always found our local Serck agents very resourceful and helpful.

Repairing springs and resealing the various air flow flaps is quite straightforward. Quite often, self-adhesive draught-proofing strip from a DIY supermarket makes excellent seals. New operating cables, if necessary, can be made

Fig. 21.3. An alternative type of combined flap and water valve setting.

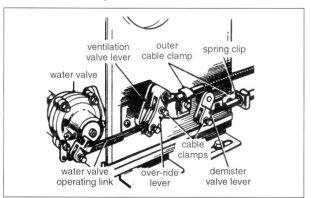

Fig. 21.4. Flow position diagram of a Smiths' water flow valve.

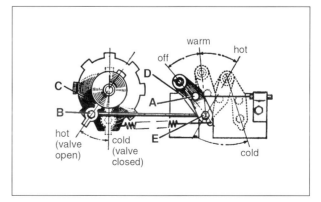

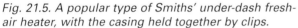

Fig. 21.5. A popular type of Smiths' under-dash fresh-air heater, with the casing held together by clips.

Fig. 21.6. With the casing separated, the matrix just pulls out, and the motor comes out after undoing two screws.

specialists have them in stock. The valve might fit straight on to your engine or heater, or you may have to use a little ingenuity to make up an adaptor.

Heater motors are very simple basic DC motors and, unless something's burnt out, they respond to a good clean of the commutator. They get relatively little use, and we've found that in most cases the brushes are hardly worn. In the very few cases where the brushes have been worn, we've replaced them with brushes from other heater or wiper motors rubbed down on emery paper, if necessary, to fit.

A very popular type of heater in the 1950s to late 1960s was the big Smiths' box-heater which sat on a ledge on the bulkhead at the back of the engine. The most difficult part of overhauling this type is setting up the control cables and links, so we've included some old Smiths' diagrams of how to go about it (see *Fig. 21.1* and *Fig. 21.2*).

Fig. 21.7. The brushes and commutator seldom show much wear on a heater motor. Most problems are caused by lack of use and discoloration of the commutator.

Chapter 22

Instruments

Instruments that don't work, or look scruffy, are a big let down for any classic, and because they are in front of you all the time they are a constant reminder. Quite apart from this, if your instruments aren't working properly you are denying yourself a lot of information, and you could find yourself with a flat battery, or running out of petrol or, much worse, some rattling big ends with no prior warning.

Looking first at plain scruffiness, it is often surprising what taking the glasses out and cleaning them, and dusting the dials off with a soft brush, does to improve the looks. It's always worth trying this before

you search for a new dial, restore the dial you've got or go hunting for a replacement instrument. Indeed, you can get away with an awful lot by cleaning and swapping about of internals, before you have to think in terms of buying a new-old-stock or second-hand matching instrument.

You can, of course, have your instruments completely rebuilt by one of the specialists, and if you have a rare car on which the instruments are in very sad condition the cost of this, though seemingly expensive, is well worth it. But for ordinary classics, autojumbles are a marvellous

source of supply for replacing instruments which no longer work, provided you get the right ones.

This 'provided' is quite a big one when it comes to looking for replacement speedometers. Except for cleaning, it's hardly worth trying to repair the movement of a non-working speedometer as even if you managed to get it working, the chances of getting the calibration right without the proper machinery is pretty slim. We deal here mainly with Smiths' instruments as these were fitted to so many British classics. Instruments made by other companies are basically very similar.

The trouble with finding a replacement complete speedometer is that though it may look the same, its calibration may be entirely different. Smiths had a whole range of similar speedometer movements with different standard calibration. This was to suit different models in a manufacturer's range where the rear axle ratio changed with different powered engines. Sometimes the difference was corrected by different gearing in the speedometer drive, but sometimes the difference was in the instrument itself.

How can you tell the difference? What you want to look for is the Turns Per Mile or TPM number. With many of Smiths' instruments this number is printed on the face of the dial and it will be somewhere in the region of 1100 to 1700. It may sometimes be followed by a code letter, but you can usually ignore

Fig. 22.1. Most classics have separate instruments, though some later classics have printed circuit boards.

this as it is probably related to some other part of the instrument. The TPM number is the important one.

If it isn't printed on the face of the dial, you might find it stamped or written on the movement itself, and you can see it when you take the movement out of its case, usually by undoing two or three screws at the back. It doesn't matter all that much if you are just a small amount out in the TPM number, Smiths used to say within 32 either way. Because of mass production you are quite likely to be able to find a second-hand speedometer with either exactly the same TPM number or one very close to it even if it came from a different similar-sized car. In this case you have to check whether or not you can swap the movement into your case. If you're really stuck, it may be possible to swap it with a little adaptation and ingenuity.

The other thing you have to watch for is the type of connection for the flexible drive. At one time, Smiths had their own connection, but later changed over to the SAE connection used by most other instrument makers. You can spot the difference quite easily. On the back of the speedometer on the original Smiths' drive, the screw thread for the knurled nut of the flexible drive is right at the end of the connector. On the SAE drive, there is a short spigot after the screw thread. A few luxury cars, Rolls-Royce and Bentley in particular, used a flexible drive that was neither Smiths nor SAE. With these, the only place to get a new drive cable is a specialist.

The flexible drive outer casings are also different. The original Smiths' casing has a smaller knurled nut, and there is a short spigot on the end of the outer casing. On the SAE casing, as well as having a larger knurled nut, there is no spigot; there is a counterbore to accept the spigot on the back of the speedometer. You will also come across two

different types of inner drive cable, not necessarily associated particularly with either the original Smiths or SAE types. On one type, the less common, there is a brass C-washer on the top end of the cable. With this type, the inner cable is removed from the gearbox end after taking off the C-washer. On the more common type, there is no C-washer and the inner cable just pulls out from the speedometer end.

There are a number of problems you may find with a speedometer. Either it doesn't work at all; it works but its reading is inaccurate; the pointer swings quite widely and often sluggishly all over the dial; the pointer wavers or flickers over a range of about 20mph all the time; it wavers or flickers intermittently or it jumps every few seconds.

If the speedometer doesn't work at all, neither the speed indication nor the odometer, or mileage recorder, it could mean a broken instrument but it's more likely to be a fault with the drive cable, either it's broken or it isn't engaging with the instrument or, possibly, with the gearbox drive. A more remote possibility is that the drive at the gearbox end has stripped a gear. If one or other of the speed indication or the odometer works but the other doesn't, the fault is probably in the instrument itself.

If the speedometer works but both the speed indication and the odometer are inaccurate, either the instrument has the wrong TPM calibration or the drive gear at the gearbox end has the wrong number of teeth. Possibly someone has changed the rear axle ratio, or has fitted a crown wheel and pinion from a similar model car with a different axle ratio or, possibly, from the van version of the car.

A pointer which flickers over a range of 5mph to 20mph all the time means either that the inner drive cable is damaged or that the cable isn't running in smooth enough bends. The minimum

radius of any bend in the cable should be 6in (150mm), and there should be a straight run of at least 2in (50mm), preferably 3in (75mm), at both the gearbox and the speedometer head. Check also that the cable is clipped so that it doesn't waver about when the car is moving, and that none of the clips is done up so tight that it squashes the outer casing.

If the pointer flickers intermittently, the knurled nut at the back of the speedometer, or at the gearbox end, may be loose so that the drive isn't engaging properly all the time, or the end of the inner cable may have become rounded off because the nut had been loose and someone had tightened it too late. If you find this, check the squared hole in the speedometer itself because this may have been damaged as well.

If the pointer is steady but gives a sudden jump every few seconds the inner cable is stretched, usually because it has been run in too tight a bend. Because it's too long, doing up the knurled nut squashes the inner cable down into the outer casing so that it rubs and winds itself up, then suddenly unwinds with a jump. An inner cable which is the correct length should project approximately 3/8in (say 10mm) from the flange at the speedometer end of the outer casing.

There are two ways you can check an inner drive cable. The first is without taking it off the car. Take the speedometer head off, put the car up on axle stands so that one of the drive wheels (or both if you have a limited-slip differential) is off the ground. Chock the remaining wheels securely, start the engine and, while you hold the end of the speedometer drive cable, engage a gear and let the clutch in gently. The inner drive cable should revolve absolutely concentric with the outer casing. If it runs eccentrically either the bends are too sharp or the cable is damaged.

The second way is with the inner cable removed from the car.

Wipe it clean, lay it down on a straight flat surface and roll it from one end. Any kinks or obvious signs of damage will show up. Then take one end in each hand and let the cable hang down in a loop with a bend of about 9in (230mm) diameter and rotate it slowly in your fingers. It should turn smoothly and evenly without any signs of snatching.

If the inner cable is stretched or damaged you may get away with just replacing it, but if the damage has been caused by a kinked or damaged outer casing, a new inner cable will have a short life. You need to replace the whole assembly.

Most instrument repair specialists stock replacement inner and outer cables to suit a wide range of popular classics. Some will even make a cable to suit. If you can't get a direct replacement, it's possible that a cable from a similar model in the car maker's range will fit, as the end fixing at the gearbox was often the same. The replacement may be a little too long, but this is preferable to getting one which is shorter, because with a shorter cable you may have difficulty getting easy bends. Stretched inner cables and damaged outer casings can't be repaired.

A pointer which swings widely and sluggishly all over the dial, or is very sluggish and seems to 'float', sometimes taking an appreciable time to return back to zero, usually means that the movement inside the speedometer head is soaked in oil because someone has over-enthusiastically lubricated the inner cable. Sometimes this has been done in an attempt to cure flickering or oscillating, and you will have both the cable and the speedometer head to attend to.

Speedometer drive cables should never be oiled because the rotation of the inner cable carries the oil up into the instrument where it clogs things up. The only lubrication the cable requires is a very light greasing of all but the top four to six inches of the inner cable. This top part, which should be a straight run, should be left dry to avoid any chance of grease being carried up into the speedometer.

Can you do anything about an oiled-up speedometer? Most books, and specialist firms, will tell you that you can't. Our answer is that you might be able to, with luck. We've had success on a few occasions, and failure on a few, so it isn't a guaranteed cure, but if it doesn't work you're no worse off, so here's what we did.

Our method was to take the movement, complete with dial, out of its case, and immerse it in a shallow bowl of white spirit, without wetting the dial, for an hour or so, followed by two or three rinses in clean white spirit with gentle agitation. After it had been left to drain and dry thoroughly, we squirted it with an aerosol can of Isoclene, an isopropanol switch cleaner which you can buy from electrical and computer repair shops. Do this in a well-ventilated place and try to avoid breathing the fumes. Don't spray it anywhere near a naked flame, and don't smoke while you're doing it. Isopropanol is highly flammable, and if you inhale the fumes through the hot end of a cigarette or pipe they can do very nasty things to your throat and lungs. Lastly we made sure the movement was completely dry by gently blowing it from about a foot away using a hair drier set on its lowest setting.

Apart from that, there isn't a lot you can do with a speedometer that doesn't work, other than to trade it in, have it repaired at an instrument specialist or find a working one from the same model car. Unless you're experienced in dealing with small delicate mechanisms, or you want to have a look inside an old one just to see how it works, we wouldn't advise trying to take the movement of a speedometer apart.

Fig. 22.2. In many cases, the bezel comes off with a twist and lift bayonet action.

Fig. 22.3. In other cases you have to bend back several cleats in the edge of the bezel.

Fig. 22.4. With bi-metallic instruments there will be a voltage stabiliser either on the speedometer or somewhere on the back of the dash panel.

Fig. 22.5. There isn't a lot you can do at home to repair a speedometer that's completely dead. If the trouble is just oil, you might be able to wash it out successfully.

Ammeters

Ammeters sometimes burn out because of a dead short, but finding a replacement is nothing like so tricky as with a speedometer. The thing you have to watch is the range. It won't affect the working if you fit, say, a 50 amp movement inside a case for a 30 amp ammeter except that the calibration will be wrong. On the other hand, if you fit a 30 amp movement in a car where the dynamo can generate 60 amps, you will burn it out. The movement from any ammeter with the same range will do, provided it fits inside your casing and the pointer spindle comes up in the right position for the hole in the dial. The movements are a moving-iron design and are pretty robust, except for the pointer, which is very delicate. Remember if you're swapping movements, that the whole movement must be insulated from the case. A 60 amp current at 12 volts can jump quite a gap, and thin plastic is no use as insulation. You need sheets of Paxolin, which you ought to find in any ammeter. The movements don't mind which way up they work.

If you have a cheap moving-iron 2in (52mm) round ammeter, and fancy having a more accurate instrument, keep an eye open for one of the moving coil type. You can recognise these because they have a small coil spring immediately under the pointer. They are much more accurate, though much more delicate, than the moving-iron type which are so basic that really all they do is to indicate charge and discharge with only an approximate indication (usually plus or minus 5 amps) of how many amps are going through.

Moving-iron fuel gauges

Fuel gauges may be one of two types. The first is the moving-iron type, similar inside to an ammeter but with a side zero. This type jumps smartly up from empty to its reading as soon as you switch on the ignition. The second is a bi-metallic resistance type which comes up very slowly, but doesn't flick about with every road bump. If you're still unsure which type you've got, check the wiring diagram for your car. Moving-iron gauges are fed directly from the battery through a wire which is live when the ignition is switched on. Bi-metallic resistance gauges are voltage sensitive and are always fed through a voltage stabiliser which reduces the voltage to between 9 volts and 10 volts and keeps it stable with varying battery voltage. Whichever type you've got, make sure you replace it, and the tank unit, with a corresponding type or you may find it doesn't work, or even burns out.

Moving-iron gauges were phased out in the mid-1960s in favour of the bi-metallic resistance type, but as there are plenty of them still about we'll deal with these first.

As well as being recognisable by the way they work, Smiths' moving-iron fuel gauges have a code number on the dial, usually just above the pointer. The code will have a prefix X or FG. The tank units which go with them are coded with a prefix F or FT. On the back of the gauge are two terminals, usually marked T and B. As you might guess, T stands for Tank and B stands for Battery. Never connect the T terminal to the battery or you'll surely burn out the gauge. Other makes of gauge may have different terminal markings but the principle is the same. You can see from the circuit diagram of your car that the B terminal connects to the battery via the ignition and the T terminal connects to the terminal on the tank unit. The body of the tank unit must be earthed to the car body or chassis, and so must the body of the gauge. Quite often the gauge is earthed through a terminal which also holds the fixing strap, and the importance of this is often overlooked where the gauge is mounted to a non-metallic panel or to a metal panel which isn't earthed to the car body. If it isn't earthed, the gauge will read 'Empty' even when you've got petrol in the tank.

The next step is to check the voltage at the B terminal on the gauge. Check it first with the cable connected, and then disconnect it and check the voltage at the end of the cable, just in case there's a high resistance inside the gauge itself.

If you're happy with the earthing and the voltage at the gauge, and still get no reading, check the earthing of the tank unit. Usually this earths via a terminal on the tank unit body, but occasionally the screws holding the unit to the tank are used as an earth. If the earthing to the tank checks out, make sure that the tank itself is making good electrical contact with the car body. Some tanks are mounted through rubber bushes, and the earthing strap may have corroded or, if there aren't any rubber bushes, the fixings themselves may have become corroded. It's always a good plan to run the tank unit earth wire straight to the car body, not to the tank.

If the earthing at the tank unit is OK and you still get no reading, reconnect the cable to the B terminal and disconnect the cable to the T terminal. Switch on the ignition and the gauge should read 'Full'. If it doesn't, the gauge is faulty. If it does, run a separate cable from the T terminal to earth. When you switch on this time, the gauge should read 'Empty'. Disconnect the T terminal from earth, and it should read 'Full'. If it does, the gauge, its voltage supply and its earthing are all OK, which leaves us with two possibles. Either the cable from the T terminal to the tank unit is shorting to earth somewhere or the tank unit is faulty.

The next step is to take the tank unit out and test it separately. Some units are mounted at the top of the tank and some are mounted on the side, so make certain that the petrol level is below the hole for the unit before you start undoing the screws, and always disconnect the battery before you start. Because of the open hole in the tank when the unit's out, it isn't a good idea to start testing electrics near it, just in case you get a spark, so make a temporary cover for the hole and take the tank unit round to the front of the car well away from the tank.

Take the original cable off the T terminal of the gauge and connect a new cable from the T terminal to the terminal on the tank unit. Take another cable from the body of the tank unit and run it to chassis earth. Reconnect the battery and switch on the ignition. When you move the float up and down you should get a corresponding reading on the gauge. If this works OK, run a new cable from the T terminal back to the tank and reconnect everything. If you get a fluctuating reading as you move the float arm slowly up and down, the resistance track on the tank unit where the slider presses may be corroded. Try squirting it with some switch cleaner or, as a last resort if it's the type which takes apart, use some very fine wet and dry rubbing paper. If this doesn't work, and the gauge reads 'Full' all the time, the tank unit is faulty.

If you've determined that either the gauge or the tank unit is faulty it's no use going to the parts department of your local dealer, he won't have stocked these items for years. You've got three choices. You can send the faulty part for repair by a specialist, like Vintage Restorations, you can search in autojumbles for a replacement in good condition or you can try to repair the unit yourself. If you're looking for a second-hand replacement and trying to match code numbers you'll come across literally hundreds of different numbers. However, any tank unit coded X or FT will work with any gauge coded X or FG. In each case, X was the older system of coding, and the FT and FG stood for Fuel Tank unit and Fuel Gauge unit. On tank units, the differences in numbers refer to the type of unit, side mounted, top mounted and so on, and to the length and shape of the arm that holds the float. You may be able to change the float arm for the one from your faulty unit. On gauges, the difference will be the shape and size. If you find one with exactly the same code numbers it will have come from a car similar to yours, so you can go ahead and fit it. If you can't find one with the same code numbers, but you can get the tank unit which goes with it, it's sometimes possible to marry and adapt, swapping movements or float arms.

Bi-metallic fuel gauges

Smiths' bi-metallic fuel gauges are coded BF which, as you might guess, stands for Bi-metallic Fuel gauge. They look the same as a moving-iron instrument but, as we said, can be identified by the pointer moving slowly up to its reading when you switch on and slowly back to zero when you switch off. Internally they are very different. The terminals at the back are usually marked I for instrument and T for tank. Never try to test these gauges by short-circuiting the cable from the T terminal to chassis earth and never connect full battery voltage to the I terminal. In either case you will probably burn out the instrument.

The gauges are voltage-sensitive, and the electrical supply for them is taken from a voltage stabiliser, which Ford labels a voltage divider in its wiring diagrams. This gives a constant voltage to the gauges, usually 10 volts, so that the gauges don't fluctuate with fluctuating battery voltage, always provided, of course, that the battery is giving at least 10 volts. When you have a bi-metallic fuel gauge, then the engine

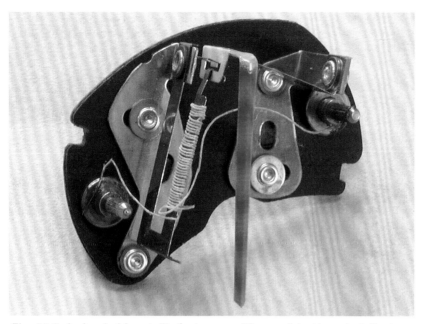

Fig. 22.6. A simple bi-metallic fuel gauge. It's possible, though delicate, to resolder a broken wire. It's better to swap the internals for those from another instrument.

temperature gauge, if one is fitted, will also be bi-metallic and will also be fed from the voltage stabiliser. The stabiliser itself is a small metal box usually with two pairs of terminals on the back, one pair labelled B and the other pair labelled I. The gauges are fed from the pair of I terminals and one of the B terminals is connected to the battery, usually via the ignition switch. The second B terminal may not be used or it may take battery voltage to something else such as instrument lighting. There is also a third terminal on the back of the stabiliser, which is marked E for Earth. This is usually connected direct to the stabiliser casing which is earthed through its fixing strap, but is provided in case the gauge is mounted in a dashboard which isn't earthed.

Voltage stabilisers are sensitive to which way up they're mounted. Most should be mounted vertically or, at the most 20° from vertical. Sometimes they are marked with the word 'Top' to guide you but, if not, mount it with the B and E terminals at the top.

If both the fuel gauge and the engine temperature gauge are not working, or giving erratic readings, the fault is probably with the stabiliser. Check, first of all, that you are getting battery voltage at the B terminals on the stabiliser and 10 volts (9 volts with some cars) from the I terminals, and that the 10 volts, or 9 volts, stays constant both at tick over and when you rev the engine up. If you don't get these readings, check that the body of the stabiliser is earthed to the chassis. If it is, and the reading at the I terminal isn't correct, the stabiliser is faulty. You can't do anything about repairing stabilisers when they go wrong, you have to replace them. It doesn't matter much what make or type of stabiliser you fit provided it gives the correct stabilised voltage, but remember to fit it upright and, if it's not a direct replacement, make sure the casing is earthed.

If the stabiliser checks out OK but you still get no reading on the fuel gauge when you switch on, switch off, take the two cables off the terminals at the back of the gauge, set your meter to ohms and check for continuity between the two terminals. If you don't get continuity, the gauge is probably burnt out and you'll have to replace it or possibly change the movement. Bi-metallic gauges can burn out for three reasons. Either someone has put full battery voltage to the B terminal instead of 10 volts, the cable from the T terminal to the tank unit has shorted to chassis earth or, just possibly, the ignition has been switched on for a long time, five or ten minutes, with no fuel in the tank. If this happens, the gauge can overheat, quite often with a smoky look to the inside of the glass, so remember this if you're restoring the car and working with no fuel in the tank and with the ignition switched on to check something else. Remove the cable from the B terminal on the stabiliser and insulate it so it doesn't short out while you're working.

A steady 10 volts at the gauge, continuity across the terminals of the gauge, but still no reading means either a fault in the cable from the gauge to the tank unit, a bad earth at the tank unit or a faulty tank unit. Remember that you mustn't short the cable from the gauge to chassis earth to test things. Disconnect it from the tank unit and check with a voltmeter when you switch the ignition on. You should get the same voltage at the end of the cable as you do at the T terminal on the gauge, or very nearly the same allowing for a few millivolts drop in the cable. If you're in any doubt, renew the cable. Then check, with your meter set at ohms, to make sure the body of the tank unit is properly connected to chassis earth. There should be zero resistance between the body and chassis earth. If everything checks out OK so far, unbolt the tank unit, take it round to the front of the car and check its operation in the same way as with the tank unit for a moving-iron gauge, but remember that you don't get an instant response with a bi-metallic gauge, you have to wait for the resistance wire inside to heat up and bend the bi-metallic strip.

Coolant temperature gauges

There are four types of coolant temperature gauges. The Bourdon tube type, which has a capillary tube running to the sender in the radiator or block, the semi-conductor type which is very similar to a moving-iron fuel gauge, the thermal type and the bi-metallic type.

With a Bourdon tube gauge, Smiths' code TD, TG or TL, you have to replace the whole lot – instrument, tube and sender bulb – because they're sealed, usually with ether inside. It's possible to renew a broken capillary tube and refill with ether but it isn't something we'd recommend doing at home. It's an involved and tricky job even if you can buy ether, which you probably can't with the much stricter controls on the sale of hazardous chemicals nowadays.

If you're really fussy about originality, take the whole lot to a specialist for repair. If you're not so fussy, replace the gauge with a semi-conductor or bi-metallic gauge and sender, remembering in the case of a bi-metallic type to feed the gauge through a voltage stabiliser.

On the semi-conductor type, as on the moving-iron fuel gauge, the pointer drops instantly to zero, or C, when you switch the ignition off. Smiths' gauges of this type are always coded with the prefix TC. There are two terminals on the back of the gauge, one marked B and one marked T. The B terminal is connected to the battery via the ignition switch. The T terminal connects to a temperature-sensitive transmitter bulb in the cooling system and the body of the gauge must be connected to chassis earth.

If you get no reading when you switch on, check that you are getting battery voltage at the B terminal on the gauge and that the body of the gauge is properly earthed. If both of these are OK, take the cable off the T terminal and use a separate cable to connect the T terminal to chassis earth. If the gauge is OK it will read H, or Hot. If it doesn't, the gauge is faulty.

Provided the gauge is OK, the fault is either in the cable from the gauge to the temperature transmitter or in the transmitter itself. The easiest way to check the cable is to run a new one. With the transmitter, all you can do is check that the body is making good earthing contact with chassis earth. Sometimes the threads on the transmitter become corroded and don't make good contact or, where the transmitter is in the radiator, the radiator itself isn't making good contact with chassis earth.

The thermal type of engine temperature gauge, Smiths' prefix code TE, is recognisable by the fact that when the ignition is switched off the pointer rises slowly to H or Hot. The two terminals on the back of the gauge, B and T, are connected to the battery via the ignition and the temperature transmitter in the cooling system. The body of the gauge doesn't have to be connected to chassis earth. If the gauge reads H all the time, check that you are getting battery voltage at the B terminal, but you mustn't earth the T terminal or you'll burn out the gauge. All you can do is check the cable from the gauge to the transmitter and that the body of the transmitter is making good contact with chassis earth. The transmitter for this type of gauge is not interchangeable with any other type of transmitter, and a Smiths' transmitter can be identified by the fact that it has a locking nut which is separate from the main body.

The bi-metallic type of engine temperature gauge, Smiths' prefix code BT, is very similar to the bi-metallic fuel gauge and is checked out in exactly the same way except that the only check you can do on the temperature transmitter is to inspect the cable from the gauge to the transmitter and make sure that the body of the transmitter is making good contact with chassis earth.

Battery condition indicators

Battery condition indicators are just voltmeters under another name, and again you may use the insides from one to swap over to another provided it fits physically. If you haven't got one, and want to fit one, there are two terminals on the back, usually marked B and E. The E terminal goes to chassis earth and the B terminal to any other terminal which is live when the ignition is switched on, except something which is connected to the I terminals on a voltage stabiliser.

Oil pressure gauges

Oil pressure gauges can be divided into two types, the mechanical Bourdon tube type which has a pipe running down to the engine, and the electrical type which has a pressure sensor on the engine. Yet again you can get away with swapping internals about, but with the mechanical Bourdon type you must be careful about the sort of connection fitted on the back of the gauge. One type has a flat end with a small raised part in the middle. This takes a flat nipple on the end of the pipe with a leather or fibre washer. Don't use a rubber washer because the oil will make it swell and go soggy. Gauges of the second type do not use washers. The connector on the gauge has a large countersink in the end, and takes either a special cone-shaped nipple or an olive on the end of the pipe. If it takes a special nipple, the central hole in the connector will be quite small. If it takes an olive, the hole will be large enough to accept the body of the pipe because the olive has to sit a short distance from the end. If you fit the wrong type of nipple to the connector you will cover your feet with oil as soon as the pressure builds up. The securing nut on the type which takes an olive is also different from that which uses either a washer or a special nipple. The nut which is used with an olive has a cone-shaped countersink inside it. The others have a plain flat-ended counterbore. If the only instrument or movement you can get should use a special nipple, and you just can't find one, it's possible to drill out the centre of the connector to accept the outside diameter of the pipe, and use an olive. Drill very slowly, don't go deeper than absolutely necessary and use grease on the end of the drill to catch the swarf.

Tachometers

Tachometers, or rev counters as they're popularly called, used to be mechanical and were often driven from the back of the dynamo, or occasionally from the distributor, sometimes via a small gearbox, by a flexible cable in the same way as a speedometer. They can suffer from the same badly routed drive cable, or excessive oil, faults as a speedometer, and the treatment is just the same.

All later tachometers are electronic, either moving-coil or impulse. Moving-coil tachometers were never supplied as an after-fitment, only as original equipment to a few car makers such as Jaguar. There are two parts, an AC generator mounted on the engine and an instrument head on the dashboard. In the case of Jaguar, the generator is driven from the back of one of the camshafts. There are a pair of cables from the generator to the instrument, and these are completely separate from the car's normal electrical system. In the case of Smiths' equipment, the instrument was always marked with an RV prefix and the generator by a TV prefix.

There's nothing you can viably do at home to repair these, just test to see which is at fault. A quite common fault is a bad connection

or a break or short in the cables, so check these and the connections first. To check, you need an AC voltmeter. Most multimeters these days have an AC Volts setting. With the engine running, an AC voltmeter connected across the generator terminals should read approximately 1 volt for every 100rpm of the generator. If it's driven off the camshaft, remember that the camshaft runs at half crankshaft speed so at, say, 3,000rpm engine speed, or 1,500rpm camshaft speed, the voltmeter should read about 15 volts.

If you don't get any voltage at all, the generator is dead. If you get a voltage at the generator, reconnect the wires to the generator, disconnect them from the instrument and check the voltage at the ends of the cables behind the dash. No voltage here means a break or short in the cables. If you get a voltage at the cables, but the instrument still doesn't record when you reconnect, the instrument is faulty. We've assumed so far that your classic is fitted with separate instruments, with auxiliaries usually 2in (52mm) in diameter, though some classics used a smaller diameter. However, the same principles apply to combined instruments, such as the A30 which has petrol gauge inset into the bottom of the speedometer dial, or the later type of instrument panel with the instruments mounted on the back of a printed circuit board. The instruments are all separate and can be changed individually.

Speaking generally, it's less trouble to replace a complete instrument. On fairly common instruments we would always recommend going for this first because there are still quite a few second-hand instruments around at autojumbles and breakers' yards, though classics in breakers' yards are becoming fewer and further between. However, you may be faced with a non-working instrument for which it is very

difficult to find a replacement. With auxiliary instruments it's worth looking at replacing the internals with those from a different instrument that doesn't match yours, provided you watch the code numbers. This is usually easiest with the 2in (52mm) round instruments popular in the classic era, but it can often be done with the segment-shaped instruments that fit in clusters inside a casing the same size as a speedometer.

Dealing with dials

A badly marked or stained dial doesn't look nice, even when the instrument itself is working properly, and until fairly recently there were only two ways of dealing with this. Either you found a skilled artist who could touch up the dial or you got someone to make a photographic copy, print it out life-size, retouch it and stick it over the damaged one.

You can still do these things, but since the advent of home computers with relatively cheap scanners and ink-jet printers, it isn't difficult to find someone who can scan your damaged dial into a computer, retouch the damage with one of the many photo-retouching software programs on the market and print out a pristine copy for you to stick over the old one. In the case of a back-lit instrument with a translucent dial you can have the copy printed on to translucent film to stick on top of the old translucent dial. You may have to clean off the old dial to stop a shadow effect. So, except in the case of a speedometer where you have the mileage recorder holes to guide you, make a mark where the zero point of the dial calibration is so that the instrument reads correctly when you put it back in the case.

There are two ways you can paste a new paper dial over the old one. One is to take the pointer and dial off and cut the holes for the pointer and, in the case of speedometers, the mileage

Fig. 22.7. A high quality Bourdon tube vacuum gauge with a small rack and pinion to operate the pointer.

Fig. 22.8. There's very little to go wrong in a moving-iron ammeter, unless it's been severely overloaded.

Fig. 22.10. Some auxiliary instruments are segment-shaped and inset in a larger dial.

recorder windows, to match the holes in the dial exactly. The other, often adopted by people who follow the current fashion for changing to white dials, is to cut the hole for the pointer slightly larger, with three fine radial cuts going from it. The paper dial is then eased over the pointer and the flaps left by the radial cuts smoothed down below the pointer boss. With care, the cuts don't show, and it's the method we would recommend if the pointer is at all tight on its spindle.

However, if you want to take the dial off, and it has a central pointer, the pointer has to come off first. In some cases you can hold the pointer by the hub in your thumb and forefinger and lift it straight up, using the fleshy part of your finger as a lever against the dial if necessary. If this fails to move a very tight pointer, use two smallish screwdrivers under the hub with a couple of pieces of cardboard under them to avoid damaging the dial further or denting it. Turn the screwdrivers so that their edge pushes up as close to the centre of the pointer boss as possible and, with luck, the pointer will come off without damage.

The exceptions are auxiliary instruments where the pointer is attached to the mechanism inside and comes out of a small slot in the dial. Here you have to free the dial first and lift it off carefully so that you don't bend the pointer.

The pointer on a speedometer is

pre-loaded against its stop pin by a little coil spring rather like a clock hairspring, so before you take the pointer off, ease the tip up over the stop pin very gently. It will come to rest some distance from the pin. Make a tiny mark on the dial, or on the inside edge of the case, where it comes to rest. When you put it

Fig. 22.10. This is the TPM (Turns Per Mile) number which you need to know if you're looking for a replacement speedometer.

Fig. 22.12. If the pointer doesn't lift off with finger pressure, use a small screwdriver right under the centre pipe and twist gently.

back again, put it back in this position, push it down and ease it back again over the stop pin. The dial itself is usually held by two very small screws, though we have come across one (not a Smiths' instrument) where the dial was held by two small wire clips at the sides.

Fig. 22.11. Before you take the pointer off a speedometer, lift it gently over the stop pin and mark where it comes to rest.

Fig. 22.13. This Bourdon tube oil pressure gauge isn't a high quality item, but it is robust and reliable.

Index